The agile Manager

"small" "a"

New ways of managing

Unlocking new ways of working

The Teal Unicorn approach to organisational agility

Rob England and Dr. Cherry Vu

Teal
Unicorn
The new way of working

Created by Two Hills Ltd (trading as Teal Unicorn™)

letterbox@twohills.co.nz

www.twohills.co.nz

PO Box 57-150, Mana

Porirua 5247

New Zealand

Acknowledgements

Our thanks go to our reviewers: Christophe De Boeck, Karen Ferris, James Gander, Suresh GP, Ben Kepes, Jayson Kurisinkal, James Macnee, Dawie Olivier, Mark O'Loughlin, Tim White, and anyone we missed.

And special thanks to all the fine writers whose books and articles taught us and enlightened us, with a special mention for Steve Denning.

Most of all, we would like to thank all the people who directly inspired us and helped us learn new ways of managing: Dean Barcham, Charles Betz, Mark Burgess, Richard Cook, Jason Cribb, John Cutler, Christophe De Boeck, Dominica DeGrandis, Troy DuMoulin, Damon Edwards, Dave Favelle, Karen Ferris, David Habershon, Mirco Hering, Michelle Holliday, Jez Humble, Dave Jarvie, Jayson Kurisinkal, Gene Kim, James Macnee, Daniel Mezick, Christian Nissen, Dawie Olivier, Harrison Owen, Niels Pflaeging, David Ratcliffe, J Paul Reed, Mark Sheffield, Steven Shorrock, Mark Smalley, Jonathan Smart, Dave Snowden, Dave van Herpen, Vũ Đức Thắng, Phil Wade, Tim White, Mark Whiting, John Willis, and many more, too many for we over-40s to remember, sorry.

What people are saying about Teal Unicorn and our New Ways of Managing

[For] the first time in our company history, we have an improvement machine which helps to remove constraint and makes the workflow much faster. People start behaving differently, they work in a co-operative and supportive way toward a common goal.

– CEO, large manufacturer

I've gained a great deal on how to explore people's talent. I change my way of working to empower people. That makes everyone happy, and, of course, we get better results.

– Vice General Director

I have changed my mind. I stop blaming people. I give my people a task with clear instructions. When something goes wrong, we all work together and find out the causes not pointing fingers at someone. That helps us to create a comfortable environment and positive thinking.

– Factory director

I see when my opinion and consciousness have changed, a lot of things changed. I can't describe it clearly, but after coming home from your training, I look at things clearer, more excited, more confident, and that inspires others. Then change happens every day. I go on making small changes and people continue to follow, I don't need to urge them.

- Company owner and CEO

Before the training, I was aware of letting my staff take the initiative, but sometimes I made mistakes. Since I learned from you, I am aware of what I do clearly when I act. Your method is easy to understand, and I could apply it immediately after the training. I got the outcomes immediately.

- CEO, midsize business

What people are saying about this book

Every organization needs to work out how to do whatever it does in a more agile way, but while many resources exist for implementing agile in technology organizations, less do so for traditional industries. This book is a useful resource for anyone wondering what agile means for them.

- Ben Kepes, professional board member, investor, commentator

When all the buzzwords become overwhelming, this is a book you can come to for a bit of clarity. Remember that dogma is the enemy of learning, and agile has a small "a"...

- Dawie Olivier, Chief Information Officer, Westpac NZ

Get this book, read it, digest it, internalize the concepts. Useful, thought provoking, informative, useful, applicable.

- Tim White, independent consultant

New ways of managing is no longer an option. Doing 'stuff' in a more agile manner is no longer an option. All you need to know to become a competent and capable agile manager is in this book.

- Karen Ferris, author of *Game On! Change is Constant*

The agile Manager is a good compendium covering many of the aspects of agile. It also comes pre-loaded with numerous recommended activities to help the reader establish the guidance provided. Readers should take note of the final call to action from the authors. 'Life is not a dress rehearsal. Do it'. Fine words to live by both in and out of work.

- Mark O'Loughlin, Managing Director, Red Circle Strategies

Dedicated to our clients,

from whom we learned all this.

Contents

The agile Manager Community

Thank-you for buying this book. You may like to be a part of the agile Manager community.

Go to www.agilemanagers.club to find links to community pages and resources for this book, or Rob and Cherry live at www.tealunicorn.com.

You can find us on Facebook: The agile Managers Club.

Rob is on Twitter @theitskeptic, and Cherry is @drcherryvu.

Drop in regularly: we will share fresh learning, and we will update parts of this book, in preparation for a Second Edition someday.

Join our mailing list: http://twohills.co.nz/subscribe.

About this book

We felt the need to compile our learning into this book to share with you. It's not a pretty book, and far from perfect. We strive for agility in publishing: this is the Minimum Viable Book, which we hope we can improve over time. We are not painting a chapel ceiling; we are sketching on a napkin. Yes, it sometimes repeats itself: we know and you know that most of you won't read it cover to cover. Right now, you have it and we hope you can run with it, deriving value. It's a personal book: our faces, family, and stories are all through it. It is conversational and irreverent in style because we roll that way - it's not a textbook. It's the New Way: passionate, authentic, and whole.

This book is Teal Unicorn's aggregation of ideas that we use in coaching and consulting in agile Management. It has some themes and flow to it, but it is also intended as a compendium of ideas, some in depth and others simply pointers for you. We focused our attention on the areas that are most important for somebody exploring the new ways of managing. We try to avoid too much theory; we point the way to it and stick to more practical advice.

This book has four sections (after an Introduction and followed by some Appendices):

1. **New Ways of Thinking**: a set of principles which you as an agile manager must get your head around in order to function in the new world.
2. **New Ways of Managing**: a set of management practices which follow from those principles.
3. **New Ways of Working**: a set of agile work practices that you need to understand and support.
4. **Getting to New Ways**: guidance on the journey through new ways of working and managing.

Introduction

The agile Manager is about how to *manage* in an agile way, not what agile *work* looks like. Plenty has been written about that. Some books about agile management don't seem able to separate the two. Managers need to know something about the agile work, but what gets overlooked or confused with that is how managers *manage* that work.

This book is for managers, and those who govern them, develop them, or consult to them. Executive managers, middle managers, line managers, governors, auditors, coaches, consultants. Business, government, not-for-profit, around the world.

It's more for horses than unicorns: "horses", the established organisations with existing management structures, need this more than the seemingly-magical ones that already work in new ways, the "unicorns".

You need this book because the world is changing too fast to continue to use the old ways of working and managing. Other books deal with new ways of working, but we think management is critical to unlock those new ways. There aren't enough books focused on agile management. We operate in this space and we want to share our ideas with you to help you.

Teal Unicorn have been working together for three years in New Zealand and Vietnam. Rob's background is Information Technology, including the Agile-related ideas of "DevOps". Cherry's background is organisational and government leadership, both teaching leaders and forming companies. Together we focus on advancing ways of management to help improve the work of organisations, through teaching, coaching, training, workshops, and consulting.

The new ways are challenging: they overturn principles on which we have based our careers. This book will confront you with those challenges, explain them, and show you how to move forward to new ways of managing.

At first sight, these ideas can seem insane, impossible, plain wrong. Stick with us while we make sense of them for you, and show how you can apply them. If you understand these ideas and embody them in your unthinking behaviour as a habit, then you are a new manager, the agile Manager.

Why

"Start with why" is the principle expounded by Simon Sinek: that only once we understand the "why" of our work can we think about the "what" and the "how" properly. He draws these as concentric circles - thinking about why is known as the Golden Circle.

Why new ways?

Change is now the permanent state, not an event. There is never any stable static state. Everything is constantly evolving, driven by a massive thinking+science+technology engine. More scientists are working now than have ever worked *in total* in the past. The internet connects us and accelerates sharing as never before. Digital, biological, and materials technologies create new possibilities daily. Often, as a result, society itself is changing; new values, new ways of thinking and acting.

This presents significant risk for all organisations:

- ❖ We can't deliver new needs quickly enough.
- ❖ What we need is constantly changing. If there is too much lag between start and end of work, then we deliver the wrong thing.
- ❖ We can't adapt what we are doing quickly enough to track changing needs.
- ❖ When we try to change too much at once, it has serious impact if we don't do it right.
- ❖ The future is opaque, it has become unpredictable.
- ❖ The uncertainty and volatility impacts staff wellbeing badly.
- ❖ Complexity is unmanageable with current practices.
- ❖ We get too slow to fix things.
- ❖ Rushing, changing, and not fixing all drive quality down.
- ❖ When we run out of time, we deploy or leave low quality in our systems.
- ❖ Security gets weakened and overlooked when we hurry.

In this ever-changing world, to address these risks, we measure the success of an organisation using four factors (p239):

- quality of work: how satisfied are customers? are we giving them value?

- speed and throughput of work: are we fast enough to value?

- sustainability of work: can we keep working like this forever?

- improvement: are we always getting better? how quickly do we adjust to changing circumstance?

How are you doing on those? Are all four tracking positively in the past few years?

If the way you work now is meeting the needs of your organisation which is thriving and leading in its sector, then you may choose to keep doing what you are doing... for now. Most industries are being disrupted by new models, so keeping an eye ahead is still wise.

If your current way of working is *not* achieving what it needs to, and your organisation is not as successful as it has to be, or is falling behind in a changing world, then doing the same thing is not going to be a winning strategy. What got you here won't get you there.

The Institute for the Future sees[1] ten essential work skills for a future which is already upon us:

- sense-making.

- social intelligence.

- novel and adaptive thinking.

- cross-cultural competency.

- computational thinking, analytical skills.

- new media literacy.

- transdisciplinarity.

- design mindset.

- cognitive load management: disseminate and filter.

- virtual collaboration.

---

[1] *Future Work Skills 2020*, Institute for the Future, 2011
http://cdn.theatlantic.com/static/front/docs/sponsored/phoenix/future_work_skills_2020.pdf

So, let's assume most of you need to do something different, and the rest of you will need to soon. Then why embrace these particular new ways of working?

Firstly, because these new ways are the emergent ways of working that logical thinking naturally arrives at when we apply all that we know. It's not someone's crazy idea: it is the answer anyone arrives at eventually when they understand the underlying principles.

Secondly, because they work. This is a global movement towards embracing Agile and resurfacing Lean and opening everything up and adopting millennial culture. The weight of evidence - both data and anecdote - is substantial, in fact incontrovertible. You should take the time to "do your research, man" and confirm this for yourself. **This book is not hypothetical.** We are not going to try to convince you.

Nothing in this world is perfect, and every human endeavour falls far short of the ideal. What's more, the path to success is through failure. Therefore, you can find plenty of negative anecdotes about these new ways thrown up by the conservative and cynical. But you can also confirm for yourself that these new ways of working result in happier people, higher productivity, and better outcomes than conventional ways of working.

Specifically, the benefits include[2]:

Satisfied and involved customers and stakeholders

The whole organisation moves faster. We get better results faster: velocity through quality. This means less wasted work, more efficiency.

Satisfied employees, better retention. We develop greater capability and confidence, excellent working relationships, better team coordination, clearer roles and responsibilities, and more celebration, acknowledgement, and enjoyment.

Reduced risk, greater safety. The organisation works sustainably, able to continue indefinitely. We see earlier problem solving.

---

[2] Most of these are from *Agile Business*, R Gower, Rally 2013

What

"New ways of managing" or "agile Management" are Teal Unicorn's terms for the aspects of the ways of working which are new (or re-emergent) in this millennium and which are specific to management.

These are the things which managers need to learn, understand, apply, and eventually grok. If you are not one of the cool kids you may be unfamiliar with the term "grok": it means to understand something viscerally, with your gut, with the very fibres of your being[3].

Teal Unicorn's realisation (p213) is that most organisations find themselves locked, unable to advance to Agile (or Teal, Beta, or Open: there are many words for future ways of working – read on), and the key to advancement *isn't* about new ways of working. **The key is new ways of *managing*.**

> "Learn to fix the system instead of fixing symptoms"
>
> - Niels Pflaeging

Change the governance, policy, KPIs, systems, products, services, and people development. The culture and work will change.

Trying to change the culture (beliefs, attitudes, behaviours) and work (procedures, rituals, roles, models, structure) directly is futile until you change the ways of managing first to unlock advancement.

It's the system, stupid. **Change the way we manage work, in order to change the system of work, which will change the way we work, which then entrenches itself in our culture.** Attempts to "make work agile" or to "change culture" on their own will fail.

Changing how we manage is another way of saying change the conditions of the system. **Changing a complex system is an organic process**, like healing a patient. You can't directly change it, you must treat it with stimuli and observe the effect.

Granted, direct change to ways of working succeeds at a team level up to a point, if you can create enough white-space for change to survive. But beyond that point, change must be systemic. Managers must change the work system.

---

[3] originally coined in the science fiction book *Stranger in a Strange Land* by Robert Heinlein in the 1960s

As well as inducing *intrinsic* change in people to change culture, we must make *extrinsic* change to the system they work in.

And, fairly soon, it must be holistic at an organisational level. Executive leadership must direct managers. More of this in section 4.

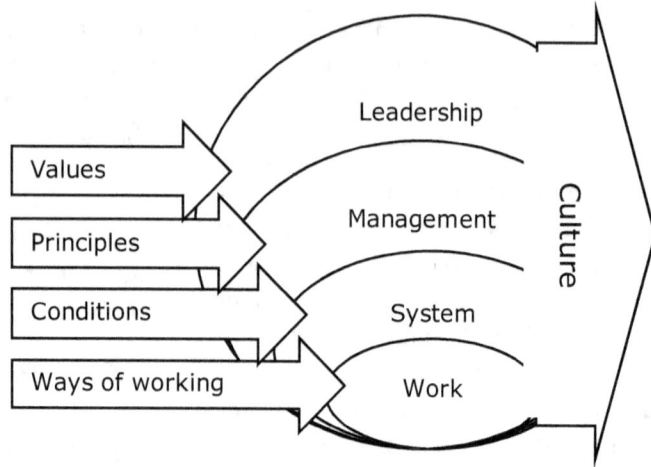

According to Accenture[4], agility comprises four capabilities:

Deliver fast and responsively (delivery agility)

Innovate and disrupt (product innovation)

Adapt organisation and culture (organisational adaptability)

Lead through complexity (leadership effectiveness)

(Note that those four capabilities are more about management of work than doing work). There are many models and methods for new ways of working, discussed in Section 3 and the Appendices, with plenty of other books going into greater detail.

This book is not about intrinsic culture change - what people think and believe and feel. That is also well covered by others.

Nor is this book about those new ways of working, it's not about what organisational agility is. There are books about leadership, and systems,

---

[4] Accenture are a major business consulting and accounting firm. This quote comes from an acquired subsidiary Solutions IQ.
https://www.solutionsiq.com/capabilities/unlock-business-agility/

and new ways of working, but we think there isn't enough attention paid to the middle bit, the managers.

This book is about the key that unlocks how to get there: management. These new ways of working struggle for acceptance amongst some managers, especially in established organisations. The primary obstacle to advancement in our experience is conservatism and risk-aversion within management: the lock is adherence to old ways of managing. This book is about unlocking new ways of managing.

Let's be clear that those conservative managers are reluctant to change for valid and intelligent reasons[5]:

> While "losing control" is one of the biggest fears in management, "having control" is one of the biggest illusions.
>
> -   Bjarte Bogsnes

- We often neglect equipping them and helping them to change (that's the reason for this book).

- They are tasked with, amongst other things, protecting the organisation and controlling risk.

- We will never get it right first time: it's the managers who will most likely see the faults.

- They are loyal and caring to "their people": they will resist anything they see as unjust.

- They need time to absorb new ideas.

- Conservative people stop at middle management.

- They have their own interest in status and power.

"Consciously or unconsciously, leaders put in place organizational structures, practices, and cultures that make sense to them, that correspond to their way of dealing with the world.

This means that an organization cannot evolve beyond its leadership's stage of development."

- Frederic Laloux

[5] Niels Pflaeging taught us this in *Organize for Complexity*

So what

In a world of constant change, these new ways of working and managing give us the agility to constantly rethink, redesign, and rebuild the ways we work, so that we constantly adapt, evolve, and thrive.

What got us here wasn't wrong for the world of the past. Hierarchy, projects, budgeting, command and control were all demonstrably successful ways of working. But what got us here won't get us there, into that fluid turbulent unpredictable world of the future.

Agility is now the essential survival skill of an organisation, to be able to quickly change how it works and what it does. These new ways of working and managing are targeted at exactly that.

It goes further. This renaissance in work is driven by higher causes than mere survival. As you will hear in this book, we want to create organisational culture that is "teal", that according to Frederic Laloux[6], makes three realisations or "breakthroughs":

> **Self-organising**. People work best in small autonomous teams with no one "in charge". Work flows to the teams and people flow to the work. Staff have skills rather than roles. The organisational system works on peer relationships not hierarchies.

> **Wholeness**. being true to ourselves, bringing our whole self to work (Maslow's "self-actualisation"). We restore the unity between truth, goodness, and beauty.

> **Emergent[7] purpose**. The organisation is organic, it grows. We are driven by a purpose and direction that emerges from the organisation.

Although we get the concept of "teal" from Laloux, the colour spectrum came originally from Ken Wilbur's Integral Model[8] which sees it slightly differently and talks about even higher levels still. Laloux stops at teal because that was the highest level he could find in practice, but teal is

---

[6] Laloux is a current philosopher, writer, and politician who wrote an influential book *Reinventing Organisations*

[7] Laloux uses the word "Evolutionary", but, as we discuss in this book, evolution is a complicated concept that often leads us astray when thinking about organisations

[8] *A Theory of Everything*, Ken Wilbur

notable as the first colour in what Clare Graves called "second-tier" human evolution. We are breaking through to new levels of enlightenment.

Does being self-organising eliminate management? Mostly, eventually. We need less managers and sometimes very few. One business Cherry, the author, owned employed hundreds (and in her father's case, thousands) of staff, with a couple of bosses, an accountant, a foreman, a delivery clerk, a few sales people, and almost no other defined roles. They make complex and exquisite carved furniture with few roles, no job descriptions, no written policy, no HR, no written procedures.

Design © Cửa Hàng Đồ Gỗ Mỹ Nghệ Đức Thắng (Duc Thang Fine Art Furniture)

Will we get there soon? No. Teal is our aspirational goal, a star we sail towards. In the meantime, this book is about better managers, not eliminating managers.

"The 21st Century is a different game with different rules... The pursuit of efficiency was once a laudable goal, but being effective in today's world is less a question of optimizing for a known (and relatively stable) set of variables than responsiveness to a constantly shifting environment. Adaptability, not efficiency, must become our central competence."

- Gen. Stanley McChrystal

New ways of working

Agile is a way of thinking about work. Agile is a <u>thing</u> now, it has become a noun as well as an adjective. Agile thinking is impacting Information Technology, organisations, government, and now society, in expanding ripples. It may have started in IT but now it is transforming work everywhere, and even how we operate as a society. It's not just the cool kids doing "digital transformation": Agile is changing conventional - even staid - organisations too. It is changing government, and social policy[9]. Its impact is far-reaching enough to talk of it as a *renaissance* in work, a refresh or step change that comes only once or twice a century.

The new ways free people to be knowledge workers (p33), to design the work and make the decisions. We treat them like they are over 18 and on the same side. We build capability and confidence. Conventional management too often treats people like clerical workers, plug-compatible wetware, "human resources"; who can't be trusted, who are evaluated numerically, who need to be shaped and standardised, who are an overhead to be minimised, who need to be told what to do and how to do it. That approach is not productive, nor conducive to satisfaction and mental health. New ways of working are a tonic for unhealthy organisations, or if you prefer a coarser analogy: a laxative.

The Agile way is iterative, incremental, experimenting, exploring complex systems. This is displacing the principles/myths of conventional organisations: big-bang projects; zero risk; certainty and accuracy; plan once execute perfectly; make it stable; failure is not an option.

It is not just Agile: there is a suite of ideas transforming work. Along the way, Agile is resurfacing (and standing on the shoulders of) the ideas of Lean (p280), the leading methodology for work flow; and Agile is drawing on the principles of complex systems theory; and on the modern understanding of human behaviour and social constructs. Most of all, it seeks to open the organisation, to restore humanity to work, to make the workplace a more natural community. They all aim for what Jonathan Smart calls "better value sooner, safer, happier".

---

[9] E.g. *The Path to "Agile" Policymaking*, Arjun Bisen,
https://www.innovations.harvard.edu/blog/path-agile-policymaking

These ideas aren't new. Some are a century old. Most are decades old. What is new is the synergy, the coalescence, the synthesis of them all. Especially, what is new is their increasing adoption and impact, the wave that is building, the renaissance. There are three key themes to the new ways of working:

Human: people, humanity, wholeness, culture, sharing, empathy, diversity, inclusiveness, egality, trust, integrity, authenticity, open, transparency, learning, mastery, pride, empowerment, freedom, authorisation, servant manager, safety, wellbeing, health. [states]

Systems: customer, value, flow, feedback, quality, lean, streams, iteration, networks, complexity, chaos, antifragile, shift left, teams, organisation, collaboration, ritual, sharing, resilience, human error, holistic, data, science. [artefacts]

Agility: ambiguous, uncertain, iterate, increment, experiment, explore, observe, adjust, fluid, improve, curious, embrace failure, fail fast, small, granular, simplify, flexible, pragmatic. [actions/adjectives]

We searched far and wide for a collective term for all these ideas of the new ways. We found no generally agreed word or term for what is happening. This renaissance in social thinking, this new age of work, this confluence of a century of work and social philosophies, has no name (yet). Isn't that bizarre? The following terms are in use but don't quite capture everything for us:

- Agile
- Adaptive Management
- Radical Management
- Creative Economy
- Cybernetics
- Fourth Age

Other suggestions we had for new terms were[10]:

- Renaissance
- Antifragile
- Management under uncertainty
- Responsive
- Progressive
- Liberated
- Humane
- Incremental
- Continuous
- Unencumbered work
- Holistic work systems
- Free flow work
- Wigsop (Whole Is Greater than the Sum Of the Parts)
- 21st Century Management
- Pragmanagement
- Woke
- INTEAM (Its Not The Eighties Any More)

[10] https://twitter.com/theitskeptic/status/1104296474966286336

None of them resonated (sorry, all those who helped). We think perhaps one day the word will be "Open", but not yet. So, we will refer to the new ways as **Human Systems Agility** (for now).

agile Management

Part of new ways of working is new ways of *managing*. **This book is about the impact of these new ideas on *management* in the modern organisation.**

We wrote it for managers, not philosophers. On theoretical topics like Agile and Lean, the book might over-simplify or be too casual for some purists' tastes, but we hope that it is useful for people in everyday organisations trying to manage the work.

Too often, managers view the advancement to new ways as something done to improve the practitioner workforce, not management. This can't be. For an organisation to change, the managers must change our own ways. This is one of the biggest issues facing organisations moving to agile ways of working. Managers must understand and focus on freedom, collaboration, agility, openness, and flow. New ways of managing is a special focus for the authors' business, Teal Unicorn, when we advance whole organisations or their IT functions.

> "Right now, your company has 21st century Internet enabled business processes, mid-20th century management processes, all built atop 19th century management principles."
>
> -   Gary Hamel

Why focus on management in agile advancement? Because we see it often neglected, and because it turns the key, as we will explain. So, we talk about New Ways of Working And Managing. Cumbersome but it makes the point.

What to label "new ways of managing" specifically? Anything with "new" in the name gets old, and always sounds like hype. We decided on "agile management". "Agile" has baggage for some people, but it is so widely adopted as the collective term that we have to go along until something better emerges. In this book, we use capital-A "Agile" to refer to the specific Agile movement, and small-a "agile" to refer to the behaviour of new ways of working and managing in general. If you were wondering why this book's title has a small "a", that's why: this book is about agility in management.

We thought about calling the new ways of managing "Teal Management". Our brand is Teal Unicorn, because the unicorn is an Agile symbol of aspirational ways of working, indistinguishable from magic, and as we know teal is Laloux's colour-code of aspirational culture. But not everyone likes Laloux's model, and - as we will see – a teal organisation isn't keen on management at all.

We could have used "Open Management", and almost wish we did, but we don't quite go so far in this book as to base everything on the Open movement (p255). That is the next generation, what comes after agile Management. We are talking here about management ideas in existing conventional organisations on the journey to higher culture.

So, **we call the new ways of managing small-a "agile Management" (aM) and the new ways of working and managing collectively "Human Systems Agility".**

Transformation and advancement

Many use the word "transformation", but it is a dangerous word: it implies a one-time big-bang step-change finite project, a "fairy godmother" change, consultants with a magic wand and a pumpkin. Sometimes they actually *mean* this, which is a Bad Thing, as we will see. Other times they use it to mean continual improvement, a never-ending journey towards our goals, which is great, but we struggle with the word. It was all through early versions of this book, but it jarred, so it had to go.

We went on another quest to find the right word: "quest" was an option. So were journey, transition, trajectory, safari and many others. It needs to imply an endless movement, and also imply improving. We already used "improvement" for more general activity in the organisation, so the word we finally settled on was **advancement**.

A challenge for you

Lots of managers tell us consultants that they "get" the new ways of working, and then they send us off to fix their staff, while they have no self-awareness of the need for their own ways to change – they are in "unconscious incompetence". Many don't "talk the talk" (understand it) and even fewer actually "walk the walk" (internalise and exhibit the principles). Meanwhile those who do absorb the concepts struggle with colleagues who don't.

Do you get it?

☐ If you behave as if change is always happening in the world, that there are few stable states any more...

☐ If you're treating your staff, suppliers, and customers as empowered adults who know more than you do about how to do the work...

☐ If you treat work as complex systems full of people: systems which need to be designed, built, and managed holistically and organically...

☐ If you don't try to change a system, only create the conditions and inputs for it to change itself...

☐ If you understand that design-then-build is a fallacy, that the result is unknown until you get there ...

☐ If you embrace experiment and failure as the normal and essential path to success...

☐ If you never have an end state, if you have standing teams, if everything is a journey of improvement...

☐ If you increase velocity and quality and granularity of work in order to decrease risk, system debt, and culture debt...

☐ If you are agile in how you *change* the way you work...

If you do these things, then good on you, you get it; we hope you will still find value in this book.

If you don't, then you *really* need to read this book for the sake of your own career, and for your staff and organisation.

Here are two bonus questions:

Can you show how your staff's work will be better in a year?
Is there any improvement programme, or any bandwidth for
improvements, or any culture based on improvement?

Can they keep working in this way indefinitely? Is the current
rate and way of working sustainable? Or is there system debt
(compromises made and shortcuts taken that will get in the way in the
future) or culture debt (damage to people and culture) being accrued?

These are two powerful challenges. Few managers in conventional
organisations can look you in the eye and say they are happy about both
these questions.

If you want some pre-reading before you embark on this book, we
recommend *The Age Of Agile* by Steve Denning. He masterfully
elucidates the expansion of Agile into the organisation.

What if I told you...?

As we said at the outset, the new ways of thinking can mess with our
heads, challenging deeply held beliefs about work:

> You don't know the end when you begin change. You don't know
> what it will be, when it will be ready, how much, or how hard.

> Most of the system of work is hidden.

> Managers are servants of their employees.

> Success is found under a pile of failure. Failure is a normal part
> of working. Welcome and reward failure.

> Managers don't know more than workers. The higher they are in
> the hierarchy, the less they know about the work.

> Management is too often an overhead, a burden on the work. Flip
> the hierarchy so management supports the work.

> If your staff are too slow, ask them to do less.

> If you have to fire someone, consider you may have failed.

> Don't run anything or anyone at 100%.

> Don't blame the individual first. Look at the system they work in.

New ways of managing

Management is about getting stuff done with the organisation's resources, through people. That doesn't change, but managers need to change the _way_ we manage. The roots of conventional management thinking go back to the start of the industrial revolution. For the past century[11], management has been seen to have the following five functions, but they aren't working for us anymore.

Forecasting and planning.

> In a state of constant change, we can see less and less of the future (as if we ever really could). It becomes more important to plan for how we will be working, how to be more agile, not what we will be doing, what the work will be. And we change how we plan, to create constantly evolving, disposable plans.

Organising.

> Amidst constant change, organisations must be fluid, organic, responsive. The good news is people are self-organising anyway: we can command but the reality is always different, something that evolved. Managers must empower this, create freedom, enable people to organise around work, and evolve their own work systems under our guidance.

Staffing.

> It has become a centralised specialty management function to recruit staff. Much of the organisational fluidity of the future will come from smaller self-organising teams, who need to trust each other and work together. Recruiting needs to be more in the hands of colleagues, with central guidance and support. Growth is more organic than planned. Employee development is still essential, but we do it in new ways: coaching, empowering, learning on the job.

Directing.

> Managers should no longer tell people how to do work, or micromanage them (with exceptions: the inexperienced, or the low-performing). Managers never really did have an advantage

---

[11] _Administration Industrielle et Générale,_ Henri Fayol (1916)

in coming up with the answers – being smartest isn't the only criterion for promotion – but that is even more so in a changing world. Management is shifting to directing policy not process: set the rules not the gameplay.

Controlling.

We still need to track the work system against goals, and act when it moves away from them, but the way we do this changes. The goals themselves are ever-shifting, the controls must promote agility not limit it, standardised repeatability can be a problem not a solution, and most of all we move from making staff meet the goals to motivating them to do so.

The world needs to rethink management, to do different things.

There isn't as crisp a generally-agreed model for the new ways of managing as there is for the conventional ways. The ideas are still forming and coalescing around the world.

Here is our model. Teal Unicorn see the functions of agile Management as being:

Attracting.

Managers act as an attractor, a magnet bringing resources and people together around a stream of work. We are inclusive, we build diversity. We throw the net wide, bringing in as much as we can to get results. We gather and orchestrate resources to help them. We recruit.

Nurturing.

A manager is a gardener: we provide the conditions and the inputs for people to flourish and a work system to grow. We encourage constant learning, and improvement in all systems.

Freeing.

Managers flip the conventional hierarchy: we act as servants of the value work. We give staff the authority, capability, space, and resources to get the job done. We define the challenge not the solution. We open the work system up, remove impediments, get out of the way, and trust people to find the answers and do their work. We deal with controls and reporting so that those doing the work don't have to.

Motivating.

> Managers give people the vision, goals, incentives and most of all the feeling of engagement to help them want to achieve our goals. We give them a reason and a desire to do the work, and we build their confidence. We restore humanity to work.

Exploring.

> The source of most work innovation is managers[12]. We have time to step outside the work and think about it. We allow freedom, we look for new ways, we understand that diversity means discovery, we stimulate curiosity. We take intelligent risks, embrace failure as the path to success, welcome the unknown, and see chaos as opportunity.

Observing.

> Managers keep close to the work. We observe, monitor, and measure how it is going. We analyse work and track trends. We provide fast feedback to everywhere where it is needed, from the people doing the work to the governors, across all parts of the value network from customers to colleagues.

Harvard Business Review has a similar model[13]:

> To help organizations meet today's challenges, managers must move from:
>
> **Directive to instructive**: helping others extend their own frontiers of knowledge, and learning through experimentation to develop new practices.
>
> **Restrictive to expansive**: Too many managers micromanage.
>
> **Exclusive to inclusive**: Too many managers believe they are smart enough to make the decisions without anyone else's aid.
>
> **Repetitive to innovative**: Managers often encourage predictability.

---

[12] *Gemba Kaizen : A Commonsense Approach to a Continuous Improvement Strategy*, Second Edition, Masaaki Imai (2012). A good read but beware it contains some outdated concepts.

[13] https://hbr.org/2018/10/the-role-of-a-manager-has-to-change-in-5-key-ways

Problem solver to challenger: Solving problems is never a substitute for growing a business.

Employer to entrepreneur: Many jobs devolve into trying to please one's supervisor

This is a huge shift in thinking, organisationally and personally. Never underestimate the impact on you: most people are not fully aware of how far they need to grow. This book will help you get there.

The management renaissance

This shift is often spoken of as a "Copernican revolution", meaning it is as significant as when science moved from an Earth-centred to a Sun-centred model of the solar system.

It is important for managers to realise that the organisation doesn't revolve around them, but we think the analogy should be even broader. This is as profound a shift in ways of working and managing as the Renaissance was to artistic, cultural and scientific thought and method.

Consider the characteristics of the Renaissance[14]:

1. A focus on humanism: personkind as the driver of all thought, not abstract entities.

2. A resurfacing of learning from classical sources.

3. A flowering of literature, a greater sharing of ideas.

4. Depicting a more natural reality, model things on how they are not how we might stylise or imagine them.

5. Reform for learning for everybody, not just elites.

6. Emphasise observation, data, and inductive reasoning.

7. Upheaval, reform, disrupting the status quo.

The new ways of managing do the same:

1. Making work human again, treating people like people not resources, adults not children, as if we are all on the same side.

---

[14] Wikipedia, so it must be true

2. Building on work that goes back a century: scientific management (1900s), statistical production (1930s), Training Within Industry TWI (1940s), Toyota Production System (1960s), Total Quality Management TQM (1980s), Lean (1990s), complex systems (2000s), Agile (2000s).

3. A flow of management ideas flourishing on the internet, coming from all directions: e-commerce, war, information technology, space travel, robotics, medicine, social policy, politics...

4. Overcoming our cognitive biases and defeating the myth of simple systems; modelling how the world really works, not how we would like it to.

5. Freeing knowledge workers to invent their own solutions instead of imposing models from gurus and consultancies.

6. Making observation and experiment the centre of our work.

7. Flipping the hierarchy, getting out of the way, bringing real work to the fore. Communications and networked ways of working breaking down hierarchies.

The Renaissance brought new ideas (Section 1), a new culture (Section 2), new ways of working (Section 3), and a fresh start (Section 4). The same is happening to management around the world, and has been for two decades – it's a management renaissance.

M: "New ways of working doesn't mean people can do anything they want".

R: "Sure it does. Why not? They're adults, working for you."

M: "What if they do the wrong thing?"

R: "Then we'll explain why it is wrong without blame or punishment, and learn better ways."

M: "I'll be held accountable for it."

R: "So we better focus energy on explaining policy clearly and often, so they make the right choices".

Target state

There isn't one.

Many frameworks and methodologies and bodies of knowledge tell you what the ideal state looks like (p289). Having some aspirations - some navigational stars - is useful and gives us a direction, but there is no state that we seriously expect to arrive at and stop.

Agile is a means of improving work. As fast as we improve towards some aspirational state, we will never reach it, because the world changes and that aspirational goal moves. The Toyota Improvement Kata[15] has always recognised this by setting short term goals that we iterate towards, but each time we reach that short-term goal we revalidate the long term vision because it is likely to have moved in the interim.

Some modern thinking goes further: *any* consideration of future state is not the best use of effort. Consider instead the optimal <u>current</u> state and work towards that. We haven't found anything more solid on this than online discussions, but it bears watching, and thinking about.

If expensive "kids in suits" consultants claim they can tell you what your operating model will look like in two years' time you should show them the door. Nobody can know that.

A big leap forward in our understanding is the realisation that in much of the real world we are dealing with complex systems: in a complex system we can never know what the future state will be at any point in time nor do we expect that state to ever be a static one. The concept that our operational state is a static stable state with brief interim periods of change is outdated and outmoded.

We must understand that change is the permanent state; that stability is a myth or at best an occasional accidental state; and that future conditions are arrived at by exploration, experiment, and iteration. We are on an endless journey of advancement.

---

[15] *Toyota Kata*, Mike Rother

The Teal Unicorn solution

We haven't got one.

Again, if some consulting firm claims that they have a solution for how your organisation should find its way, you should find someone else. Exactly what approach will change the behaviour of a group of hundreds or thousands of people can only be discovered by experiment. Every organisation uses different methods to follow a different journey. Any model named after a company is a snapshot of that company at some past point in time. Those organisations are constantly changing, or should be. Case studies are interesting sources of ideas which may or may not apply.

The solution to advancement is unpredictable; in fact, the very idea of a solution is invalid. The journey is unknown except in hindsight. The only things that are common across organisations pursuing new ways of working and managing are the principles and general theoretical models which we apply along the way. (Because so many want The Answer, we relented somewhat and provided patterns in Section 4 which we think often work in advancing a culture).

What we at Teal Unicorn can do, or any good consultant, is:

1. guide and coach an organisation to find its own solutions within itself, especially within those doing actual work.

2. build an understanding and capability within the organisation which renders the consulting services redundant.

We have to be careful not to patronise managers. Most managers will be doing at least some of these new ways already. So assume nothing. Ask questions. Listen before speaking. Find out what managers know and what they need help with.

These new ways are universally applicable, so long as you use intelligence. There are no templates, no formulas. We apply common principles to guide us in our designs and decisions, but we must think to understand their applicability in each context.

For example, some of the Agile ideas work best when you build something fungible, like software. It is cheap and easy to rebuild, to change, to improve, to copy, to throw away. Tangible physical constructions are less forgiving: you must get them right first time, they're expensive to fix.

Some Lean concepts work best when you are making the same thing repeatedly, incrementally improving quality of a stable standardised flow, like cars. Intangible work is harder to observe, and is usually different every time, so smooth repeated flow is harder to achieve – we need more buffering and other mechanisms to deal with variability.

Some systems are simple, such as... Actually, we think all real-world systems are complex, because they all have humans in them somewhere. Sometimes a simple system model or a linear flow model is a useful approximation, so long as we remember that it is – like all models – wrong.

None of these things preclude using the new ways of working and managing, and none of them mean that the new ways aren't better. Because they are. This stuff works a charm in creating the fluidity, the responsiveness we need for an organisation to be constantly reinventing or at least adjusting itself in the volatile, uncertain complex and ambiguous modern world.

To summarise:

- This is the biggest change in management thinking in a century, ever since we invented "management".

- Nearly everything you based your work and career on gets flipped upside down.

- We don't have any answers.

- You have to find your own answers, and you can't see them from here.

M (after a team in a simulation game quadrupled their throughput): "I'm in shock. It can't be that easy."

R: "Sure it can. You just saw it. What's hard is the politics, and the cultural baggage. Fixing the system is easy if you're allowed to."

M: "But what to fix? How do we know how to do this?"

R: "You don't. I don't. Experiment. Find what works and do more of that."

At this point, many of you will be perplexed or frankly incredulous. Perhaps an example will help. It is fictional, but not hypothetical: it combines many of the experiences we have seen or heard about.

Narwhal Design, a tale of agility

Simon owned a costume jewellery manufacturer, Narwhal Design. He knew something was wrong with the company. Their competition was beating them out of the market with new designs and faster delivery. Everything he tried wasn't helping. So he brought in some advisors to help who a friend had recommended.

The first thing the advisors did was to walk around. Talking to those doing the work, they soon learned his designers were frustrated because Simon had to approve all of the designs personally, and, frankly, Simon didn't understand what customers wanted. One of the first changes made was to convince Simon to believe in his designers, and free them to approve their own designs as a team. The designers would be rewarded based on the success of their designs in the market, and the higher the sales the more likely that a designer would have their future designs chosen by their team.

Building on this example, the advisors convinced the management team to rip more approvals out of the workflows. They ran workshops with teams to challenge the controls, and everybody agreed to take a lot of unnecessary governance out in many places. Plenty of managers were relieved not to have to do rubber-stamp approvals that they had never understood anyway. The advisors were careful to review and beef up the risk management process to ensure that gates weren't being left wide open. Work freed up in many areas. A lot of workload came off managers and governors.

Managers started to be uncomfortable. Simon was always keen on reducing head-counts, and some of them were feeling extraneous. The advisors put them to work re-designing the reporting structures. Everywhere that line managers - or even worse, workers - had to do reporting work, the managers were to change the process so that a manager observed the work, noted the data, and wrote the reports themselves. This got managers out of their offices and further freed up the workflows. (It also exposed that more than half the reports served no useful function, or were redundant; suddenly managers want reporting to be efficient when they have to do it themselves.).

Digging deeper into that flow of work, it was discovered that the team building the prototype jewellery to test the designs weren't really talking to the designers at all. There was a strained relationship between them because of past frustrations: the designers are the higher-prestige team, and wouldn't accept feedback from the prototyping team if a design was hard to make. The prototypers had to figure out how to build a design, and were seen as not clever enough if a design was unbuildable or had problems in production. All communication happened through their managers, often escalated up to the common boss, Simon.

The advisors sat the two teams down face to face and led them to talk through the issues. They were asked to create better feedback and iteration between the design and prototype teams, to make sure that designs were practical. This was to happen directly, not through managers, and preferably by getting up and walking over there. The team managers also organised informal activities between the teams, a curry lunch every Thursday, where they could informally talk about anything they wanted as well.

The next step in the value stream was passing the prototype to the engineering team to set up the factory to make the jewellery at large scale, and then a production run. There were many delays in manufacturing and sometimes a design would not be produced fast enough to catch the season it was designed for, or to meet the customer's delivery expectations. It turned out that production runs would need to be set up two or three times, only to be cancelled part way when something more urgent came along, or when a design fault was discovered part way through the run, or one component hadn't arrived in sufficient quantity. Then the half-completed products and materials needed to be stored somewhere (where it was sometimes cannibalised to meet another shortage). This was news to Simon, and to everybody outside of the production factory. The factory had been managing the turmoil internally, presenting a brave face. They didn't want to show how bad the problems were: Simon wasn't good with bad news.

A lot had been invested in "increasing efficiency" in the factory. Production lines ran flat out, never pausing longer than they had to for a re-fit for a new product. Staff - including managers - were exhausted. The slightest hitch (and there were always some, due to design and materials problems) caused work to pile up everywhere. With such high utilisation in the factory, the work still moved slowly.

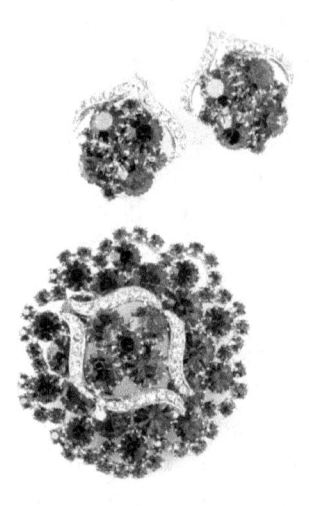

The advisors applied Lean methods to map the value streams. They analysed the flow of information, and quickly showed that production's chaos wasn't entirely of their own making, but also came from failures of communication and low-quality work elsewhere. These other areas thought the defects were trivial, but the impact of these small hiccups were catastrophic on a factory running flat out.

They analysed the flow of work of a design from initial idea all the way to delivery of product to the market, and the flow from materials to market of a single piece of jewellery. Although each department's workflow was well understood, nobody had ever tracked the timelines end to end.

This uncovered a big time-lag between prototype and production which had lain hidden to pretty much everybody except one clerk who did his job diligently managing the huge queue of work. And it showed that all the work to speed up the factory had actually only addressed a few percent of the total time of a value flow, and in fact slowed the over-all cycles down with all the chaos caused by them being flat out. It was making them worse.

The advisors coached the clerk and the factory managers to introduce a visual work management system, on the wall outside the clerk's office in a corridor where everybody could see it. Every new batch of work appeared on the wall as soon as a design was in prototyping. It flowed across the wall, with its status and problems shown in different colours. They had to expand the column for the backlog that the clerk was managing because nobody had realised quite how much there was.

A new gating technique was introduced, where work didn't start until it was 100% ready, with all materials onsite and a tested design. Materials were locked down on a palette dedicated to the job so they couldn't be cannibalised. If a job needed more material than fit on one palette, then it had to be split into smaller production runs. The job went up on the wall in a backlog of work ready to run. The senior managers agreed the priority of the runs for each day, and everybody had to agree to suspend a job part-finished. All the planning and decision making was done standing in the corridor around the planning wall. This kept meetings short.

Simon was upset that he was excluded from the advisors' whole improvement process. His advisors explained to him that it was better to let the people doing the work design the work without him in the room. He didn't like what he was hearing about reducing utilisation in the factory, and holding work until everything was ready to start. It sounded like backward steps to him. He wanted to know what was going on, but the advisors kept him at arm's length.

A crisis came six months into the changes, when Simon realised that the factory was working in new ways that he didn't understand, and the designs being produced were ones that he would never have chosen himself. The sales results were yet to be seen, and he was deeply uncomfortable about losing control of his company.

He became moody and critical of everything. He was deeply frustrated that he seemed to be losing control of his own company.

Then several things happened to change his views.

One of the largest projects which Simon's advisors had convinced him to do was to consolidate several small lunchrooms into a new larger area in an unused end of the warehouse, fitted out with a kitchen, good coffee, and nice new furniture. There was even a barbeque outside and some indoor plants! The senior managers also lost their own private lunchroom, which was a tough battle. Simon was brooding in the brand-new cafeteria one lunchtime - worried about its expense and the message it sent while the company was in trouble - when the background noise finally intruded on his thoughts. It dawned on him that all he could hear was laughter and chatter at energy levels that he had never heard in the company before. He looked around and saw tables with staff from all parts of the organisation sitting together in conversation.

Several days later, he went for a walk around the factory, as his advisors had coached him to do. He asked the foreman of the production line about a problem with a particularly complex piece of jewellery, and she said "Not to worry, we worked it all out over lunch with the design and prototype teams". Simon had resisted the new cafeteria, because he saw them as time-wasting spaces. He had kept the lunchrooms small and cramped to encourage people to get back to work, but here they were breaking down barriers, and having a good time doing it. Had he been wrong all along?

Where the factory joined the warehouse, there was another open area in the warehouse, and a new table tennis table had appeared. Nobody was using it at the time, but Simon scowled anyway. And where was all this free space in the warehouse coming from? It was a worry if buffer stocks of materials were being run down. And yet Simon knew throughput and profitability of the factory was up, with less stocks and apparently more spare time. Something didn't add up.

He was walking down the corridor outside the production clerk's office and saw several employees standing around the wall covered in work, in heated conversation, working out a production problem. Simon stopped to ask what the issue was, and made a call to help resolve the deadlock. Only after he walked away did he realise they were all low-level team leaders and – gasp – actual workers, and that it had been so easy to resolve because they were involved directly in the work and knew exactly what was going on. A similar problem had been an agenda item of his executive team meeting over and over again for weeks in the past.

When he got back to his desk, the initial sales figures had at last arrived for the latest round of designs, and it was clear from the numbers that one of the designers had a particular flair. Three of his designs were selling hot, higher than any previous design the company had produced. They were all designs that Simon would have rejected. He felt crushed. He had been holding back his own company.

Simon met with one of his advisors, Amalia, who had become something of a mentor to him. She had introduced him to the habit of walking meetings, so they set off on a stroll away from the factory. She sensed he was unhappy, and soon had him sharing his disappointment in himself.

Amalia explained that such a reaction was natural, and some of the self-criticism was valid. "But don't be hard on yourself, Simon. You built a successful company. The recent problems were a sign to you that what got you to here isn't going to work anymore. The world is changing too quickly. You can no longer keep up with design tastes as you once could. It was time to let go of that. Your customers want more variety and they want it faster. The old production methods that were so low cost can't keep up any more. The world is still scrambling to come up with these new ways of working and managing. They haven't been around long and are still evolving. You didn't cause any of that to happen. That is change in the environment. Our job is to increase your agility to deal with that new environment. You need these new ways, and you are already seeing the results, even if you still have plenty to improve. Look at it this way: you feel bad because things are getting better. That's silly. Celebrate with your staff. Throw a party."

So they did.

Terminology

There is no glossary in this book. The index entries where the number is in **boldface** point to the definition in the book.

We already defined our own terms Human Systems Agility (p12), agile Management (p14), advancement (15), new ways of managing (p17) and renaissance (p21).

We define a few more terms here:

Conventional

What do we mean by "conventional"? Conventional ways of working are characterized by some or all of:

Central power

- Hierarchy.
- Command and control.
- Status linked to seniority and power.
- Defined enforced roles.
- Demarcation of siloes.
- Big bang changes.

Constrained

- Large monolithic product systems.
- Bureaucracy.
- Formal procedures, high levels of ceremony.
- Many complicated intrusive controls.
- Slow difficult change, often unsuccessful.
- Large amounts of work waiting at multiple points.

Inhumane

(That's a harsh word, isn't it?)

- Bravado and heroism are lauded.
- Failure is unacceptable.
- Management by numbers.
- "Human resources".
- Workers are standardised to roles.

Knowledge worker[16]

As we move into a service and information economy, we are moving from industrial workers and clerical workers (who are treated as industrial workers working with information) to knowledge workers.

Knowledge workers have been around forever, but they now account for a third of workers or more in modern economies. Knowledge workers are professionals who are "empowered" and trusted to use their own expertise, methods, and tools, to solve a given problem.

"Empower" is a difficult word, because it still implies something granted by those in power, and hence something that can be taken back again. It's still an imbalance of power, so we are starting to use the word "free" instead. Perhaps "free" troubles you as implying no control at all, but we use it on the understanding that we are freeing professionals not children. Another great word is "authorise".

> "Authorization is the right to do work"
>
> - Daniel Mezick

Davenport[17] defines knowledge workers well: "Knowledge workers have high degrees of expertise, education, or experience, and the primary purpose of their jobs involves the creation, distribution, or application of knowledge."

When we talk about freeing employees, the emphasis is on freeing knowledge workers, although there are situations where we should set industrial and clerical workers free too. Everybody needs more freedom.

Knowledge workers have important characteristics[18] that we must deal with:

Knowledge workers like autonomy. Don't impinge on it.

Specifying the detailed procedures is harder and less valuable. Accept unstructured work.

They need to be observed to be understood. Be with them and review their work.

---

[16] This section comes from our book *Plus! The Standard+Case Approach*, R. England. See also p212

[17] *Thinking for a Living,* T Davenport.

[18] Davenport again

They have good reasons for what they do. They are the experts on improving their work.

Commitment matters. Don't damage it.

They value their knowledge as a personal asset and don't readily share. Gently coach them to open up.

It is not possible to learn everything about how a knowledge worker works by observation or measurement. The results of knowledge work are notoriously difficult to quantify. They work in their heads.

Nor is an external expert likely to be more expert than the person performing a knowledge-worker role. Knowledge workers know what they are doing better than anyone else and need to be allowed to do it.

Nothing is black and white between process/clerical workers and knowledge workers – it is a spectrum. There will always be repeated process present in any role, and there will be opportunities to improve it with external expertise. A balance needs to be found between interventionist external process improvement and consultative facilitated knowledge-work improvement.

Trying to impose standardised ways of execution, measurement, reporting and accountability to non-standard situations is counterproductive. Allowing people to use investigative case methods when appropriate will increase efficiency and effectiveness by getting process out of the way when it is not applicable. Experienced experts don't like to be told what to do.

Considerations such as culture, organisational structure, physical facilities, co-location, remuneration, benefits, leadership and management, are all important in getting top performance out of individually-empowered workers.

Knowledge worker is a broad categorisation. Be careful not to treat all knowledge workers the same. It is useful to have a more finely grained understanding of the people responding.

For example[19], an "eWorkforce" group at Intel created one based primarily on mobility and behaviours and attitudes toward technology. Its categories are as follows:

---

[19] Davenport again

Functionalists: Primarily manufacturing (there are some office workers here, however) workers who use information technology occasionally, but do not rely heavily on "office IT" to perform their job functions

Cube captains: Spend the majority of their time in the office, are very mainstream in their office IT needs, and are overall very happy with the tool sets they have

Nomads: Heavy users of remote access; whether while traveling or working in remote offices, they need mobility in their IT environments

Global collaborators: Interface often with people around the world; they have elements of the nomad segment, but they work across time zones and do a lot of collaboration and hence need access to collaboration tools anywhere, anytime

Tech individualists: They want and need the latest IT tools and are willing to take risks with them; are also often early adopters

Management, leaders, governance

We should define "management". We are throwing a broad net here to include the executive and governance, as well as personnel management and work management.

Our definition of a manager is one who organises the resources made available to them and the people working with them to achieve outcomes asked of them.

In this book, we avoid the word "leaders". Leadership is an intersecting set with managers. Our definition of a leader is one who influences others in a group setting, usually in a particular direction. Executives should provide leadership, and some managers should too, but non-managers will also lead, and (in a large organisation) *most* managers are not leaders. Leadership is a behaviour. Management is a role. There are lots of books about leadership. This isn't one.

Leaders / Managers

By "governors", we mean those who direct the organisation, usually a Board of Directors directing management, or a government directing civil service. We may also mean the executive layer, who in many organisations perform more of a governance function than a management one. Governors perform the three functions of governance defined by the ISO/IEC 38500 standard[20], which are direct, monitor, and evaluate.

System

We use the term "system" in this book to refer to the entity which produces value with its many interacting interconnected components, including people, roles, governance, policy, money, resources, goals, KPIs, measurement, reporting, activities, processes, procedures, events, machines, software, forms, documents, facilities, physical spaces, virtual objects, and more. No one of these on its own is the system. All our systems at work are complex (p74), if only because they include humans; and all complex systems have emergent properties - they are more than the sum of their parts.

In this book we will try to always say "work system" to refer to the way that we work and manage, the kind of system which this book wants to improve, as compared to the more general system which we work **on** or **in** to produce value for customers.

Complex systems are often talked about as if they are organic. They have properties and behaviours that are almost like living things, but we should be careful of such analogies. A system doesn't die: it can be restarted. It doesn't reproduce, and it certainly doesn't "evolve" in a Darwinian way (p80), although small parts of it might. Complex systems do have properties that show growth, health, response to their environment, healing, learning, and even moods.

---

[20] ISO/IEC 38500 *standard for corporate governance of information technology*. The "of Information Technology" is misleading: it is a useful standard for all corporate governance.

Let's go

In section 1, we will look at the new ways of thinking, the new ideas that underpin it all.

Then in section 2 we will unpack the new management ideas that embrace these concepts.

Section 3 discusses the new ways of working, but only the management aspects. We assume familiarity with the basics of the new ways of working. If you don't have that, we summarise them in the Appendices.

Finally in section 4 we look at how to grow out of the current state and advance towards these new ways of working and managing.

All through, the common threads are our realisations that:

1. management practice organically drives the system to change, allowing people to work in new ways, which becomes new culture.

2. this advancement requires a continual improvement "machine" to drive it, as a source of energy, direction, and coordination.

3. management is naturally conservative, and unlocking those managers who resist is the key to advancement in management practices.

Image CC Tyne & Wear Archives & Museums

1. New Ways of Thinking

The story of Narwhal Design in the last section might be fiction but it isn't hypothetical. These new ways work. The unicorn organisations amaze us with their cultures and results. More ordinary "horse" organisations report back on major shifts. We want what they are having.

To get there, managers must get their heads around some principles[21] in order for the organisation to work in new ways. If they don't understand these principles then improvements will seem wrong, even crazy.

As we already discussed, these principles will challenge some of the foundational beliefs of your work (and even your life). You will have to let go of some principles in order to embrace new ones. Give yourself time, and practice a lot, but push hard, because this new thinking is the future.

> Belief is like a red helium balloon. You can't bear to let go of it. But letting go is easy, and once you do, it floats away and you wonder why you ever held it.
>
> Work, politics, race, religion... try it with ever larger balloons.
>
> The world changes, beliefs don't. They deflate.
>
> - Rob England

We listed some challenging ideas right at the start of the book, which can make readers uncomfortable. You have to remind yourself that sane rational managers run their organisations based on this thinking. Let's look at these ideas more closely.

We discuss these ideas under a series of twelve broad headings:

Human: People, Customer, Culture, and Trust.

Systems: Transparency, Slack, Flow, and Science.

Agility: Complexity, Agility, Failure, and Improvement.

At the end we draw out the main principles of the new thinking.

---

[21] "Principle" is a noun. "Principal" is an adjective except when they're in charge of a school. We have seen a few "Principle Consultants" which must be challenging.

People

People first, not customer first, nor shareholders. We need a customer focus, but put your people first. If people – in our organisation, and our partners, our suppliers, our consumers - are genuinely valued, then we give them satisfaction, we respect them, we don't wear them out. All else flows from that: higher performance, quality, agility, customer satisfaction, and especially innovation. If you treat your people like crap you will get crap. People are not "resources", they're people: colleagues, comrades, friends.

The restoration of humanity to business has roots going back to the "Hawthorne Studies" of the 1930s[22], and Drucker thought it was a *fait accompli* from the 1960s. Yet here we are, decades later, still pleading to treat people like humans. The century-old Scientific Management (or "Taylorism", p42) still has us in its grip. As discussed later in this book, we prefer the term "Personnel" instead of "Human Resources" for the staff function of an organisation, but another alternative which retains the "HR" acronym is "Human Relations". An organisation needs to maintain a healthy relationship with its employees. They are comrades, we are all on the same side.

People are humans: they have good days and bad, they get tired, they have family members die, they are all imperfect in many ways. If you must treat them as "resources", at least understand how vital that knowledge work is to modern organisations, how the human resource functions, and what it needs for optimal performance. Any system must adapt to the peculiarities, the uniqueness, of each one to maximise value from them, it has to enable the optimal use for each one. It must also provide inputs other than work, such as fun, stimulation, challenge, opportunity, growth, satisfaction, and reward.

Work doesn't have to be "so bad that they have to pay you to do it[23]". If we care about people, we can make even the most unpleasant jobs more bearable. Toil[24] is unfulfilling work. This is waste that can be eliminated entirely, or it is drudge repetitive work that can be automated(p142).

---

[22] *Management and the Worker*, Fritz Roethlisberger, Harvard University Press 1939

[23] We got this from the great business philosopher, Garfield the Cat.

[24] This wonderful term is used by Google's *Site Reliability Engineering* book

Smoothly flowing work is less frustrating. A focus on value means work doesn't feel useless. And, of course, success feels good.

People are also animals. We have basic instinctual needs and mechanisms (e.g. Maslow's Hierarchy of Needs). If you don't cater to them, work will fail. See "Lizard Brain", p121. We all need:

- A sense of physical place where they belong.

- A tribe to belong to, camaraderie.

- A squad to work with, small enough to form a team.

- Emotional connection with people around us.

- A feeling of safety and security.

- A sense of control in our own lives, empowerment, freedom.

- A sense of fulfilment and value.

Protecting mental health is essential. Burnout is a serious issue in IT. So is other mental illness. It is good to see this getting more attention. Employers don't have an obligation to treat staff's problems, but they do have a responsibility *not* to break people, and to accommodate mental disability in the same way as physical. See "Mental Health", p132.

> The fear and unease that arise from mistrust and suspicion, seeing other people in terms of "us" and "them", is not easily overcome by just closing your eyes or saying a prayer. It's real concern for others that breeds trust and leads to friendship and a sense of security. Inner peace, a practical source of peace and confidence, depends on warm-heartedness and a concern for others' wellbeing.
>
> -   The Dalai Lama

Don't manipulate behaviour

Some managers and consultants are enthusiasts for psychological techniques which manipulate the behaviour of staff, sometimes overtly e.g. punishment and incentives, sometimes covertly e.g. neurolinguistic programming.

We have an ideological objection to the concept that staff are machines to be adjusted. Even when these techniques are supported by science – and many are not – they send the wrong cultural message.

Again, people are humans: diverse, irrational, unpredictable, exciting, and creative. Attempts to standardise them or shape them don't treat them that way. Embrace staff for who they are, and encourage them to behave in new ways because they want to, because they share our goals. Change the work system and help staff find their optimal role in that.

Be careful with Scientific Management

Scientific management, or Taylorism, seeks to use science and reason to analyse work logically and empirically. These are fine ideals shared with much of Lean and Agile thinking, but Taylorism is often regarded as objectifying people, taking standardisation of work to extremes that aren't palatable as we seek to restore humanity to the workplace.

Modern workplaces are much more dynamic and creative, where diversity and humanity are essential. Many of the ideas of scientific management still have a place, but in its pure form it runs counter to what we are trying to achieve with agile management. At its worst, scientific management is brutal.

You can't manage people through numbers. There are depths of human relationships and ethics that numbers never portray.

Customer

Peter Drucker said "There is only one valid definition of business purpose: to create a customer".[25] This is often misinterpreted to mean finding new customers. That is part of it, but equally, we must maintain a relationship with existing customers to retain them: new customers cost more than keeping existing ones.[26] Success flows from that.

The idea that an organisation exists to make money or deliver shareholder wealth (a) is now regarded as an unethical and destructive idea[27] and (b) was never generally applicable anyway. What does that even mean for government or not-for-profits?

Define the customer as the entity(s) paying for the value delivered by the organisation (which is not necessarily the same as those consuming the services), and make the purpose of the organisation to attract and retain those customers by creating value for them.

If we deliver satisfying value to customers, we are likely to create a healthy, sustainable business. Profitability and shareholder returns will follow - they're the result not the purpose.

Be careful of the manufacturing paradigm that says value only flows one way, to the customer, pulled (initiated) by the customer. This works for some contexts but not for others. We talk later of co-creation in a value network: we should push value when we innovate, and we should draw value from customers when they offer or provide it. In short, work together with your customers, collaborate.

That idea can be generalised to government and not-for-profits. They too need to appeal to and keep those customers who have the funds.

---

[25] *The Practice of Management*, p37. Yes, that's the correct quote, not the one you see everywhere. Or it is in the author's 1982 version. I don't have the 1955 original, or the more recent editions. He repeated the quote in *Management: Tasks, Responsibilities, Practices* (1974).
Drucker went on to say "Because it is its purpose to create a customer, any business enterprise has two - and only these two - basic functions: marketing and innovation. ... Marketing is the distinguishing, the unique function of the business." In a later book, he repeated this and added "Marketing and innovation produce results. All the rest are costs". That would seem a bit extreme to many.

[26] Somewhere along the line the Drucker quote morphed to "The purpose of business is to create and keep a customer."

[27] https://www.theguardian.com\business/2006/dec/03/economicpolicy.comment
https://www.forbes.com/sites/stevedenning/2013/06/26/the-origin-of-the-worlds-dumbest-idea-milton-friedman/

Sometimes organisations are in a monopolistic position, but not as often as they like to think. Government agencies and not-for-profit entities must satisfy[28] those who hold the purse strings.

Still, it feels strained to be talking about government agencies attracting customers. We need a broader purpose for all organisations. **The broader purpose of an organisation is to provide more efficient and effective services grouped together than we could apart** (something that organisations who are entirely deconstructing themselves into outsourced services should think twice about). That's why it is called an "organisation". It will only be more efficient and effective together if we all have a common focus: that's why it is called an "enterprise", singular.

Which brings us back to customer: we will only work together in one consistent direction if we share a customer focus.

Customer focus

The phrase "customer focus" gets used a lot, but it needs to have a practical form embedded in every system. The Voice of the Customer (VoC, a kaizen concept, p271) should be present in all discussions: somebody should be speaking up on their behalf if they aren't actually present. Everybody needs to have a line of sight to the customer: they get feedback to see the impact on the customer of what they do.

One of our customers has tried for several years to develop their domestic market. Their target customers (according to them) are middle-aged, and successful. However, most people who are "middle-aged successful" who we asked, hardly used or even knew the company's products. Looking deeper, we learned that the company only produced what it decided to, disconnected from the customer's demands. They tended to exchange information within the company, listen to each other and forget the customers who will pay for them. They didn't make what the customer wanted. They made what they thought the customer needs. Designs were selected by managers, not by the market. Our advice to them was put all their attention on their customers, then come

---

[28] At Teal Unicorn, we dislike the word "delight". Customer delight is seldom the goal of waste management, farmers, forestry, utilities, road builders, war-zone charities, machine-tools, abattoirs, prisons, armies, or police. It's a retail-centric term (it should be "user delight") which ignores the reality of many organisations: pragmatically satisfying customer needs in a sustainable way.

up with a suitable business plan accordingly. Always ask questions: If customers are sitting in this meeting now and listen to us, what will they think? Will they oppose or agree with the plans we are creating to serve them? That client now produces better designs that sell more successfully. By being market driven, they can experiment more freely to discover new possibilities and test ideas. In short, your level of success is determined by how you satisfy your customers.

Culture

Employees' behaviour is influenced by different cultures: their national, social, ethnic, occupational, or organisational culture. This book focuses on the latter. Organisational culture is the behaviours and beliefs of the staff working there. "Organisational culture is the pattern of basic assumptions that a group has invented, or discovered in learning to cope with its problems of external adaptation and internal integration, and that have worked well enough to be considered valid and, therefore, to be taught to new members as the correct way to perceive, think, and feel in relation to those problems".[29] More concisely: "corporate personality".[30]

Culture doesn't just appear; it is the residual of the experiences of an organisation. Therefore, **culture is an output not an input**. Culture is an emergent property of the work system, how we behave; and the work system emerges from history, beliefs, and external conditions.

Culture is a heuristic: it gives us a shortcut for making decisions: "What would the company do?"

Culture influences everything: culture eats strategy for breakfast[31], lunch, and dinner. Having a healthy culture does not happen naturally. A collaborative culture can help employees thrive and do as best as they can. An organisation which has a strong culture will also support their own particular values and attitudes. They are far more productive and resilient than an organisation which does not.

Working for many businesses and organisations, we found a common issue where employees are clearly aware that something is not quite right, however they do not talk or do something about it because the culture makes them silent and passive. These cultures prevent people from telling the truth or debating the problems, and this leads to serious issues.

Although we can have healthy culture or dysfunctional culture, there is no one "correct" organisational culture. Which type of culture works

---

[29] *Organizational Culture and Leadership*, E.H. Schein

[30] Flamholtz and Randle in *The Oxford Handbook of Organizational Climate and Culture*, Schneider, Benjamin; Barbera, Karen M. eds., Oxford University Press (2011)

[31] Peter Drucker didn't say "Culture eats strategy for breakfast". It's a great quote and he would like it, but it's not him.

depends on an organisation's current state: its success, vision, values, employees, history, narrative (the story it tells itself, the company "legend"), and environment (the national and industry cultures it exists within).

Humans do aspire to "better" culture, to values not value. We crave humanity at work and a higher purpose. This is called teal, Beta, Agile, open, holistic: they are all different perspectives on the same aspiration.

You can't just change culture directly. As well as intrinsic influence, you must make extrinsic change. You change the work system, which changes behaviour. Those new behaviours become accepted as normal and absorbed into the culture. They drive attitudes, and eventually the deepest beliefs. Extrinsic influence on the system makes intrinsic personal change possible. Managers are gardeners, not commanders. Grow the culture by creating fertile conditions.

Pull, don't push. Let the organisation pull the change it wants and needs. Experiment with virtual teams, and allow the teams to recognise what works and to propose what should be the formal structure - let them ask for incremental reorganisation. Doing reorganisation to staff is often destructive. Reorganise in an agile way: iterate, increment, experiment, explore.

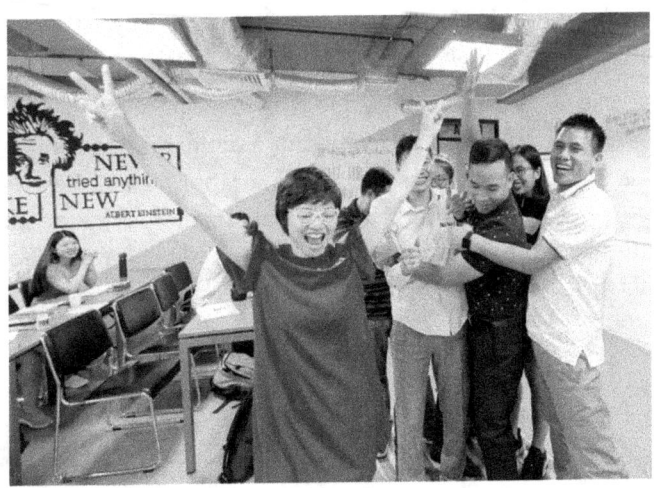

Watch the observable culture

Organisational culture is "the way we do things around here"[32]: it is the implicit attitudes and beliefs which lead people to do the things they do. If you want to know the culture of the organisation, don't listen to what they say; watch what they do, and especially how they treat their staff, suppliers, and customers.

The "climate" of an organisation is the immediately observable character: the buzz, the vibe, the mood, the feeling you get when you are there. This is driven by the underlying culture and is another observable symptom.

As culture starts to improve, climate improves even faster. No matter how bad things are, people feel better when they see improvements. Happiness is relative. This is hard to measure but easy to feel, especially for outsiders moving between multiple organisations.

Beware though the cult of compulsory happiness[33]: in some organisations you need to hang around a while to see behind the facade.

Understand your culture

There are a number of models for analysing organisational culture. We like Laloux[34] and the concept of "teal culture"(p10).

We also use corporate anthropology's concept of Alpha and Beta culture.[35] Alpha culture is conventional command and control; beta culture is sharing, openness, and collaboration. There is a feminist overtone here too: the implication of "alpha males". We have no doubt beta culture is more feminine: we could use a whole lot more feminine values at work.

---

[32] John Kotter

[33] *The cult of compulsory happiness is ruining our workplaces*, André Spicer
https://www.theguardian.com/commentisfree/2016/dec/12/cult-compulsory-happiness-ruining-workplaces-office-fun

[34] *Reinventing Organizations*, Frederic Laloux

[35] *The Fall of the Alphas*, Dana Aldi (2013)

There are many others:

- Integral[36], probably too abstract for us here.

- Spiral Dynamics[37], likewise more of a philosophical model.

- Westrum's model[38].

- Competing Values Framework[39] which gives us Organizational Culture Assessment Instrument (OCAI).

- another "competing values" model from Schneider[40].

- the older Organizational Culture Profile[41].

- the Rightshifting or Marshall model[42].

...and many more. Which one you use will probably depend on which experts you engage.

It can be enlightening to map where your culture is right now (or multiple cultures across the organisation) but don't expect to measure culture change in any timescale other than years. It is more useful to measure climate[43] (mood, morale, engagement) and results (see "Measure progress", p239).

[36] *A Theory of Everything*, Ken Wilbur

[37] *Graves: Levels of Existence*, Lee, Cowan, Todorovic (eds)

[38] *A typology of organisational cultures*, Ron Westrum

[39] *Diagnosing and changing organizational culture*, KS Cameron, RE Quinn

[40] *The Reengineering Alternative*, William Schneider

[41] *People and organizational culture: A profile comparisons approach to assessing person-organization fit*, Academy of Management Journal, 1991, C.A. O'Reilly, J. Chatman, D.F. Caldwell. Refined by others several times since.

[42] https://flowchainsensei.wordpress.com/2015/10/20/rightshifting-in-a-nutshell/

[43] We like Gallup Q12 Employee Engagement Survey, originally *from First Break All The Rules*, M Buckingham and C Coffman.

Have a vision and purpose

The "start with why" principle is important because a healthy culture depends on a common understanding of why we are together, where we came from, and where we are going. We share an organisational narrative. This shared vision results in a distinctive self-image for the organisation, which drives our mental models, names for things, style, and brand.

One purpose of any organisation is to lead people to go in the same direction. If they head in different directions, as happens in many organisations, this will lead to waste of resources. It will be hard for an organisation to develop. We have seen in many organisations that people work in a way that they oppose and restrain each other. With new ways of working and managing, we create work systems that allow them to be themselves, to collaborate, and to share a common vision. This common vision should be focused on the customer.

We support the aspirational vision with navigational/directional goals. Coaches often use the language of navigational "stars", points of reference when navigating. One does not aspire to reach these stars, only to move towards them. People call these goals Pole Star, North Star, Big Dipper, Subaru. In New Zealand, we at Teal Unicorn use Matariki, the Māori name for the Pleiades, used by them as a navigational aid for their extraordinary Pacific journeys.

Determining these matariki[44] is a useful visioning exercise. Like any stars, they move over time (and less predictably than real stars), so revise them regularly, perhaps every year, or quarterly in a volatile environment. This is important: we can become wedded to a vision as something simple and absolute, when the real world is always more fluid and uncertain. (See "Platonicity", p85).

We will show some matariki for the New Ways as we go through this book, and we give you a set of suggestions at the end.

---

[44] There is no "s" in the plural in the Māori language. Matariki is the name of a constellation so it should have a capital letter, but once we have co-opted the word to refer to our goals we then use a small "m", so our matariki are named after the Matariki.

Be holistic

It is difficult to find a single word for the culture we aspire to in agile Management, but "holistic" comes close, with several aspects:

- End-to-end understanding of flow.

- Systems view of work: people, practices, partners, and things.

- An Integral view of the individual's role in the organisation:

	Intrinsic	Extrinsic
Individual	"I" Intentions, beliefs	"It" Behaviour
Collective	"We" Culture	"Its" Organisation, society

- Restore humanity to work: unify ethics, aesthetics, and science/reason – the Good, the Beautiful, and the True. Humans aren't machines (and machines will never be human). Don't try to treat people as if they are machines: we care about all three aspects of reality, and must treat humans as an integrated whole.

If that is too philosophical or "hippy" for you, read Laloux's *Reinventing Organisations*: society is evolving – highly evolved communities aspire to be self-organising, whole, and with purpose: "teal". It is necessary to move our thinking at philosophical and emotional levels.

Trust

We must trust people. If we boil all the new ways of working and managing down to one word, it's "trust". We want to restore trust between individuals, teams, units, and organisations.

Nobody will trust you as a manager unless you trust them.

You don't always have time to earn trust by what you do. You may even have the baggage of things you have done in the past on behalf of an unreasonable work system. Managers and leaders most quickly earn trust by trusting others.

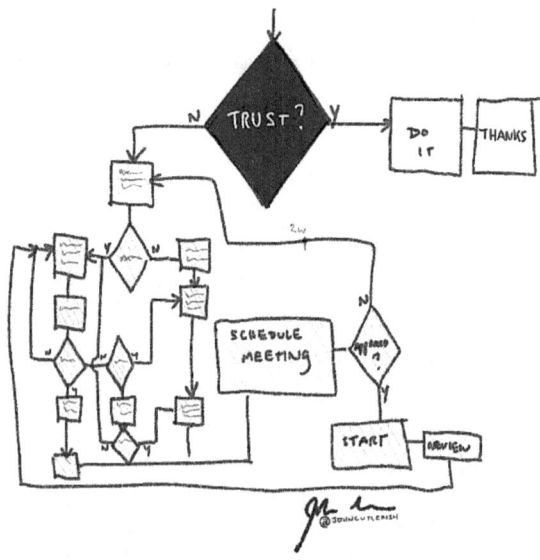

Image ©John Cutler

Assume goodness

Our staff are over 18 and on our side: we have a common cause, we are all in the same boat. Most act with good intentions. Start with an assumption of goodness, not suspicion.

Performance manage the individuals who behave badly: that's what managers get paid for. Don't punish the whole team with rules and controls just because we don't want to deal with the one or two who won't play nicely.

Promote collaboration

Collaboration is fundamental to effective agility. It comes from trust and it builds trust.

We need to all be in the same boat. We are all going to the same place, and if it sinks we all go down. People in siloed organisations are prone to say "Not my end of the boat that is sinking".

We should have each other's backs. Not just within our small teams, but across the organisation. We share a vision of where we are going and why. We help each other get there. We share everything.

"I thought I was doing all I could to move the boat faster, but my coach said it's not enough, he asked me what I was doing to get the best out of the others in the boat"

- Jessica Eddie, Olympic rower

Ensure trust between teams and managers

As well as building trust across siloes, we must build trust up and down the hierarchy. There is often culture debt to overcome. Staff need to see that the new ways are real, that managers are exhibiting the espoused behaviours towards them. They need to see that:

"I don't want to work for a company that values my output but doesn't value my input."

- Anon, via Erica Joy

- managers come to the gemba (the places where the value is actually created, see p106), listen, respond, and follow up.
- ambiguity and uncertainty are navigated. It is understood that the outcome is unknown at the beginning.
- experimentation is encouraged.
- failure is praised and rewarded, not punished.
- review is blameless.
- managers come talk in order to do something to help, not to criticise or "spy".
- time and money are committed.
- their manager trusts them.

...a meta-analysis which examined the results of 105 studies...states "Empowering leadership can motivate employees and fuel their creativity" but goes on to add it can also "create additional burdens and stress that may hurt their routine performance". When empowering employees works well and is done effectively it seems to "encourage employees to generate novel ideas and think of new ways of doing things, and to help others in the workplace"

— Paul Wilkinson, reviewing an HBR article https://hbr.org/2018/03/when-empowering-employees-works-and-when-it-doesnt

The biggest contributor to building trust with senior stakeholders higher in the hierarchy is results. It takes time to build trust: it grows as we are seen to deliver, not just promise. Therefore, early pilots and proof points are essential to create enough trust to be given the opportunity to do more. Make sure to celebrate these early successes, let everybody know.

People blossom

Unreasonable systems make unreasonable people. Many people are "victims of the system": they behave the way they do because of the unreasonable position they are put in by conflicting or impossible expectations, or accountability for that over which they have little control.

"When a flower doesn't bloom you fix the environment in which it grows, not the flower."

- Alexander Den Heijer

Never write someone off until they have a chance to change within a better work system. See how they respond to more reasonable conditions. Fix the system: make it actually help them get their job done. Give people permission. Let them know it is OK to experiment, to fail, to take initiative, to lead. See how they blossom.

Free knowledge workers

When we authorise people - when we give them the ability to make decisions over their work, and over how they work - then we show them we trust them.

> "If you tell people where to go, but not how to get there, you'll be amazed at the results"
>
> - George S. Patton

The people doing the work often know the best action. They shouldn't need to ask permission every time. Give authority.

They also usually know the best way to do the work. Stop asking managers or experts to determine how. A funny meme said "I don't know anything about your job but my book says you're doing it wrong". Let the people doing the work design the work. This doesn't mean abandon them to work it out. Give them the resources they need. Provide advice, training, and knowledge so they make good decisions. A good consultant facilitates clients finding their answers within the work, injecting relevant theory or experience at the appropriate points.

Part of allowing people to design work is letting them choose their own techniques and tools that they are most familiar and comfortable with, instead of centrally providing standardised tools. The more experienced they are, the more important (and safe) this is. There are times when the benefit of standardisation outweighs empowerment, but lean to the latter.

We said we prefer not to use "empowerment", but it is in some ways a better word because it also covers giving people the *means* to succeed: time, money, resources, skills, knowledge, mandate, permission, power. Don't set them up to fail.

There are two very different product development worlds. Some product development ("cogs") is constrained by the overall system it takes place within. Other product development ("flowers") has more freedom to grow in different directions — to "discover" the customer[45]. Set talent free.

Give clear policy guidance. When you delegate and empower, they need to know the bounds, the constraints, the rules so that they can work

---

[45] *Managing Digital*, Charles Betz

safely: safely for themselves and for the organisation. This is one of the biggest tasks for management as we advance: develop better policy.

Make sure you authorise appropriately. Some people don't have the capacity, skills, or experience to be set free in an open space. They need to be told what to do, at least initially. Give empowerment wisely, it's not open slather.

K: "We can't just do that".

R: "Sure we can. It's in your job description."

M: "What does my manager think?"

R: "I haven't asked her."

M: "Why not? She needs to know."

R: "Sure. Update her in the next stand-up. You don't need permission for everything".

Embrace diversity

Humans have a wide range of rates at which they change their behaviour. Give people time, find them space until they come around. The more impatient change is, the more human capital you lose.

'Two goldfish swimming in the water and an older goldfish comes up and says, "Morning, boys. How's the water?" They're kind of confused. He swims off. Then one says to the other, "What the hell is water?"'

- David Foster Wallace

Trust people with different backgrounds and views. Every team, panel, or meeting should look like the bar scenes from Star Wars: a wildly eclectic assembly of unlikely members[46]. Diversity of views is essential to creativity. The more you restrict collaboration (and recruitment) to those you feel comfortable with, the more potential you miss out on, as you fall

---

[46] For you academics: Ashby's Law of Requisite Variety.
Dave Snowden calls it "Finding the 17%": there is a great story behind it
https://cognitive-edge.com/blog/of-experts-and-expertise

victim to groupthink. Practitioners get focused and miss some wider perspective or left-field ideas. Bring in opposing views, outsiders, and those who will be affected. Bring in the critics, the naysayers, the rabble-rousers (judiciously).

Get collective answers[47]. By freeing those doing the work to come up with answers, and assembling a diverse range of voices, we get group answers which help correct for cognitive biases, and harness the collective wisdom. Run Community Collaborations (p155).

Honour the past

Unreasonable work systems lead to unreasonable decisions. Just because mistakes have been made in the past does not mean that they were not acting intelligently, in good faith. There may be system debt but there is value in there too.

People are not stupid: there is a reason why the existing systems are built the way they are. They represent a legacy of past recognition of what was valuable and possible. There is a lot of reasoning embedded in the existing systems: don't throw the baby out with the bathwater, don't use new ways of working to indiscriminately bulldoze away the old.

[47] An interesting exercise is to get a large number of people to estimate the number of jellybeans in a jar. The more estimates you get the closer the average answer usually converges on the correct one (especially if they get no forewarning).

Transparency

A major contributor to building trust is transparency: across siloes, up and down layers, and outside the organisation with customers and partners. One of the strongest indictors of a healthy culture is free flow of information. Some tools to help you achieve this are:

> "The aim of kanban is to make troubles come to the surface"
>
> - Taiichi Ohno

Visible work. When teams show their work plans, e.g. on kanban (p292), it creates empathy for their situation and holds them accountable. Likewise, managers should make strategy, planning, and programme work highly visible too, e.g. in obeya rooms[48], for the same reasons. In a computer is never visible. Put it on a wall.

Shared performance data. Everybody should know how we are doing, good or bad. KPIs should be published often, so everybody has situational awareness. Hiding bad news benefits nobody.

Open management. For example, publishing staff pay. Why shouldn't colleagues know what you make? Any secrecy in an organisation is damaging to culture.

Fair Process. This is a methodology[49] to ensure that even if stakeholders don't agree with a decision, they are more likely to regard the outcome as reasonable.

For a manager, personal transparency is important too:

Be **honest**. Most managers aren't as good a liar as they think they are. People see through it.

Be **consultative**. Make sure everyone is heard, is seen to be heard, and feels they were heard.

Be **authentic**, be your real self. People sense when you are saying or doing things you are not comfortable with. Large organisations are notorious for making managers fake their behaviour or beliefs: they are expected to be a machine of the executive. It creates

---

[48] Obeya rooms are visualisation of strategy and planning on the walls of a room. See "kanban", p102.

[49] From W. Chan Kim and Renée Mauborgne of Blue Ocean
https://www.blueoceanstrategy.com/

cynicism and destroys trust, and makes a manager look weak and uncaring. Don't agree to do it and don't make your managers do it.

Be **vulnerable**. There is no need for bluffing: tell the team how you feel. This is the hardest thing for most of us. It takes more courage to admit you don't know or you are afraid than to pretend otherwise. It is also the greatest builder of trust with your team.

> "Most...instinctively see vulnerability as a condition to be hidden. Science shows that when it comes to creating cooperation, vulnerability is not a risk but a psychological requirement"
>
> - Dan Coyle

Related to transparency is encouraging a behaviour of openness, where everyone feels safe and free to talk about the "elephant in the room", the taboo topic; to call bullshit, to challenge ceremony and theatre; to give honest feedback and have the hard conversations with people; and of course to admit mistakes.

Sharing

Build a culture of sharing.

- Managers need to collaborate. Teams need to collaborate. Work and information and resources must flow freely.

- Knowledge must be shared (nothing builds empathy between two groups more than for them to train each other).

- Build communities. Encourage guilds of staff with the same skills or roles, including guilds of managers.

- Encourage dialogue[50]. Rediscover the art of conversing. Create circles in a room, not squares around a table. Teach people to listen more than they talk (two ears, one mouth), to hear, to relate, to find group consensus.

Note: *Communication* is the sharing of information. *Collaboration* is the sharing of more: effort, resources, value.

The success of any organisation depends on this most basic factor - the sharing among employees. Sayings like "knowledge is power" or

[50] See *Dialogue: the Art of Thinking Together*, William Isaacs

"sharing is caring" all speak to it. Sharing in any form will lead to creating a stronger knowledge base. Shared knowledge can be used and reused to create new and valuable information.

In many organisations, especially in organisations with fierce competition among members, employees seem to share little with each other because they view capability and knowledge as a competitive advantage. To build a culture of sharing, everyone in the community needs to have the same awareness that knowledge is a flame: if we share it with each other, we will all shine.

Slack

Now we have made the work transparent, let's see how much there is. The work system requires slack[51] in it. All systems do, in order to function optimally. Build slack into all your systems.

Slack in utilisation

Throughput matters, not utilisation. Maximum throughput comes at less than 100% utilisation of people and most resources (often about 80%[52]). At higher levels of utilisation, you must have buffers of work, which increases wait times. This is because:

a) Work is variable. There needs to be slack to absorb the variations, otherwise work piles up in buffers and throughput slows. (Some buffering is a good thing in highly variable systems, e.g. building software, to smooth the flow).

b) The world is unpredictable. We need a slack capacity to deal with the unexpected.

The worst thing a manager can do is to try to drive people or equipment to 100% utilisation. And yet, this is often how they are measured. Actually, there is an even worse option for people: driving them beyond 100% utilisation, into overtime and personal time. That should be an exception when everybody is engaged and willing to get an urgent result, never the norm.

Allowing slack in the system is not easy. In order to make it happen, the manager needs to understand this principle very well.

We use the term "sharpening screwdrivers" from a story we heard from a client. When a group of workers in a factory were resting in mid-shift, they saw their manager approaching. Everyone grabbed a screwdriver immediately and started sharpening them. When the only thing that the manager cares about is how busy their staff are, the subordinates will somehow find a way to look busy.

---

[51] This useful word comes from the book of the same name, *Slack*, from Tom DeMarco

[52] For more on queuing theory, see
https://less.works/less/principles/queueing_theory.html

Give people room to improve

It is more important to improve work than to do work, otherwise nothing will change.

Change only happens when the work system has enough slack capacity to invent, to innovate, to develop new ways, to test and implement them, to improve them.

One rule of thumb is to limit the amount of new features in the work stream to about 80% of capacity (sound familiar?), and also paying down system debt. (If system debt isn't included in the 80% then we never get penalised for taking shortcuts – it's not debt, it's theft[53]). Retain the 20% as headroom for improvements, housework, the unexpected, and tinkering. The benefits of such slack capacity are:

- headroom to prioritise improvement (obviously).

- deal with unexpected fluctuations in workflow.

- deal with emergencies.

- a "tax" on project work. Conventional project management only wants to pay for new features. With this rule the project also funds the rest.

Limit work in progress

Do less to do more. Limit Work In Progress (WIP).

Humans can't work on too many things at once - often no more than three. If you are doing thirty things you are doing nothing. Nobody can multi-task, there is always a switching cost.

If work is going too slowly, take work out of the system. Stop starting and start finishing.

Manage the demand for work, so that we don't overburden the work system. Only let in as much work as is optimum for throughput. The faster we get high-quality work done, the faster we can move on to the next thing. Work already in the system gets done faster. If work really is

---

[53] One of many great ideas Dawie Olivier gave us.

that important that we have to take it on, then something else has to go back into waiting (the "backlog" of work).

This is a simple and seemingly obvious point, but unconstrained demand is a common problem we see. Don't let work into the system until (a) it can handle it and (b) the work is ready to go all the way through. The place for work to pile up is generally before the system, not partway through (some buffering of work inside the system is often required too).

The flow can only be optimised when the flow of the entire system is freed up. When helping a factory to apply Lean in production, we found that up to 30% of production plans were revised monthly. The rework of the plan leads to poor performance, causing a lot of waste, greatly affecting the morale of workers. The reason was that orders were put it in the production plan and even started production, even when they did not have everything in place for completing the orders. So they often had to stop working on an order and change the production plan. The problem here is functional departments which are involved in preparing inputs for production, not the production line itself. We[54] advised them to create a "gated" production plan, which only opens when all the requirements for producing any particular order are in place. Once work enters the flow, it flows to completion.

Create slack in management too

Slack applies to management too. If we free employees, then we delegate decisions, and we don't micromanage. This frees up a lot of time for higher value work, and thinking.

A crude indicator we use for how agile a manager is, is how busy their schedule is, how hard it is to get to see them. Line managers are liable to be busy, but the higher up the hierarchy the more think time a manager should have. We are only half jesting when we say that good managers play golf, or their preferred relaxation. (Of course, they may be working hard for good reasons – there are other reasons managers are busy besides micro-management and lack of delegation.)

---

[54] Our friend and colleague James Macnee

Flow

Once we have some slack in the system, we have some headroom to improve flow. We have some basic principles to help us manage flow.

In complex systems, the work flows through value networks, not linear flows. This can be hard to understand and model. The linear stream model is useful if we are careful to keep in mind that it is a simplification.

In this section 1 of the book, we look at a few of the new principles related to flow. Later, we will look more at flow of work (p144).

Optimise the whole flow

Create flow by optimising the entire value stream, not just functional departments or individual activities.

A common "anti-pattern" (behaviour we don't want) is to tell someone to optimise their local work area, their domain of control. We even measure their success on their ability to do so. We expect their piece of the machine to be more *efficient* and *effective*, and they will also naturally optimise it to make it *easier*. Unfortunately, the result is often a "local optimum" which actually degrades the overall system, by impeding the flow of value from end to end. It's like telling one cog in a gearbox to improve how it works. If I'm measured on how my silo performs, I increase my performance by making it harder to give me work, by transferring work to others, by demanding extra work by others to reduce the amount I have to do, by making others come to me instead of me to them, by allowing defects to flow downstream for someone else (even defects I introduced), by doing it my way not their way etc. These are successful strategies for local optima.

Not only does local thinking lead to local optima, but we are tightly constrained in how much we can improve when only changing one piece of the system. The analogy of a gearbox is a good one here: it's hard to change how one cog works.

Improving the delivery of value means improving the whole work system, collaboratively.

Improve flow

Lean is the leading methodology for improving system flow. See "Lean", p271. By applying Lean, we focus better on the value of what we produce; we smooth the flow; we reduce utilisation so that more can get done; and we eliminate wasteful work.

Another technique, the Theory of Constraints (p281), focuses our attention on the limiting factors, the blockages. All of these models are only partly useful, (see "Value Networks" p146), but they help us get the work moving.

If you get all the constraints out of a system, then the constraint is the entrance to the system, and we limit WIP (p62).

Minimise handoffs

Transfers between groups, departments, or organisations are common causes of work delays as well as communication problems. To overcome this, build teams that are a complete multi-functional team that can perform all tasks in their value stream from end-to-end, minimising participation of other teams.

There is no template answer to how an organisation should structure its teams, but there is a principle: organise to minimise dependencies and handoffs between teams. Draw an organisational workflow graph and then draw circles to cut the minimum number of lines.

India-Pakistan border ceremony, the most excessive of ceremonies.

Image Guilhem Vellut CC BY 2.0 Wikimedia

Get out of the way

There are those who do value work, moving value downstream. And there are those who do non-value supporting work (e.g. managers). Those doing non-value work need to get out of the way of the work. Subjugate everything to the value work – it is our purpose. We go into more detail in section 4, but in general, for managers:

- Don't add an overhead to work; make it easier and faster.

- Don't let process overhead exceed the value of the work.

- Challenge the levels of ceremony. Do we need this much ritual and detail?

- Eliminate theatre (where everyone knows it is not real, but all agree to go along with the illusion).

- Challenge controls. Do we need the control at all?

- Make the governance come to watch and measure and approve the work: don't make the workers request and report to governance. Don't make people doing value-work produce non-value control artefacts, or stop their work to go to governance.

Shift quality left

"Quality" means fit for purpose, free of defects, compliant with requirements. (It's a myth that quality means endlessly better). "Shift Left" means do it earlier in the flow, and bake it into the flow.

Quality should not be something that is done at the end of the flow by some third party. We should do it earlier, in the work, as part of the flow. Bake it into the work system: everybody is concerned with quality at every step of the work. Ideally, we don't need to check for quality at the end because we know it is there. The function of those responsible for quality is then not to test it at the end, but instead to:

- build awareness of quality considerations.
- teach and coach quality.
- build tools and automation to allow others to ensure quality.
- monitor and sample the workflow to detect quality.
- identify improvements to quality.

Science

New ways of working are evidence-based. "In God we trust. All others bring data." Increasingly, organisations have large amounts of data available about the work. Use it when we improve our work systems.

Visualise it. Seeing information in new ways bring new insights. This is our favourite example (Vietnam, Thailand, New Zealand, USA):

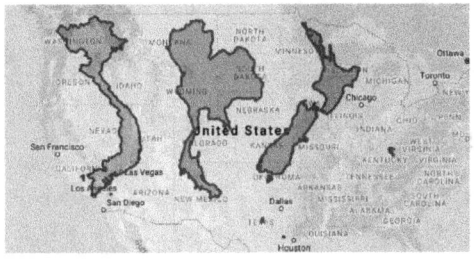

thetruesize.com

Measure what matters

"In spite of the fact that almost all orgs have a data-lake and Big Data stacks, decision-making is still largely driven by loud voices and opinion."

- Dan Creswell

At work, we are too often seduced by measurement for its own sake, measuring metrics that prove nothing. Identifying the correct key performance indicators (KPIs) is an art, to truly indicate what we care about, not just what is easy to measure. Gather data that helps us get better at delivering value to customers.

Don't consider a KPI as "too hard to measure". Anything can be measured: the question is only how well we can measure it, whether that is sufficient, and how we can improve the measurement over time.[55]

Remember a KPI ceases to be a useful measure as soon as you use it to assess people's performance: they will always game it, if only subconsciously. We discuss this more on p238.

---

[55] To learn more, read *How to Measure Anything*, Douglas Hubbard.

Beware of common sense

Even some of the smartest thought leaders have been known to recommend using common sense, instinct, your gut, heuristics.... These are shortcuts that should only be used in chaos when time is short. Using them neglects all of our cognitive biases and embraces our prejudices. Science is the set of methods for overcoming our biases through observation. The new ways of managing help us in multiple ways:

- Empowered workers come up with a collective view instead of the individualistic decisions of hierarchical command and control.

- Networked management compares and validates decisions instead of the autonomy of siloes.

- Manager communities review each other's ideas and share data and discoveries.

Experiment

We are prone to ask experts how we should do something, what is the best way of working. They don't know. It's a complex system. They're guessing based on experience. Or worse still, they are pontificating based on what their preferred methodology or framework says.

Don't take an expert's word for anything. Use it as the hypothesis to design an experiment to validate their opinion as quickly and cheaply as possible. The real world has a nasty habit of not being the way we think it is, or not doing what we think it will. There is no substitute for testing, trying, probing, doing. You don't know until you do.

If you're really scientific, you'll have a control instance where nothing has changed, in order to compare to an experimental instance where it has.

When we are probing forward in a complex system, we may do A/B testing, where we do two new versions - as small and quick as possible - for two competing hypotheses (or the control and the improvement hypothesis), and put them out there to compare the result. If you are truly scientific, you will always have a control where nothing has changed, which you could call A/B-C testing.

Even more broadly, have a diversity of options and let them compete. Pick the best and iterate again. A/B means you are limiting your guess to 2 options. Having a range of them increases the odds of finding a winner.

There is more on experimentation all over section 4 of this book.

Feedback

Measurement, observation, and historical data are of no value unless we do something with them. We must learn from them. We can say the same thing a different way: create systems of continual improvement. Or we can say it a third way: we must create feedback loops, get the information to the people who need it as quickly as possible. They're different lenses on the same reality: knowledge is an action not an object.

This is an essential function of management: to create and operate feedback loops, so that those doing the work don't have to, and so that the organisation benefits from what we learn in the work. Sometimes management impedes and filters feedback, in cultures where bad news is unwelcome (p110).

Examine all systems to ensure that observations from further down the workflow are fed back to those who need to hear them earlier in the process. For example, issues with the design of a product may show up during its manufacture and it is essential that the designers know this.

The longest feedback loop is from the customer of a value stream back to its inputs: ensure we understand the experience of the customer when assessing the success of change and designing future change.

There are three purposes of feedback: stability, failure, and improvement.

Those who have studied simple system theory will know that feedback stabilises a system. In particular, we need negative feedback. We don't mean criticism of people. The term "negative feedback" has a specific systems meaning: when a variable increases, the negative feedback applies an input to decrease it again. It is "negative" because it acts in the opposite direction to that it is measuring at the output. This means the output will always tend towards some middle value: if it gets too high the negative feedback brings it down and if it gets too low the feedback brings it back up. (There is also positive feedback which acts in the same direction as the measurement: if it increases, the feedback increases it some more. You can see this would be great in some situations where we want to reinforce an effect, but dangerous in others where it runs amok.) One place where negative feedback is particularly useful is in fast-moving systems, where humans can't respond quickly enough. Some supersonic jets stay in one piece solely because they aren't being flown by a person. The human tells the computers what to do but the computers fly the plane because only they can respond fast enough to keep everything stable: the machine is operating right at the boundaries of stability. Similarly, the faster we drive our value stream, the more feedback we will need to keep things stable.

The second purpose of feedback is to realise we are failing as quickly as possible, to minimise the impact and "blast radius" of failure. Those tight feedback loops allow us to adjust what we are doing, or even pull the plug, before the cost gets too high.

Finally, feedback is the food of improvement. The information we learn leads to the adjustments we want to make, which we feed into our improvement machine, so that we can continually and incrementally get better.

> "A bad system will beat a good person every time."
>
> "It is a mistake to assume that if everybody does his job, it will be all right. The whole system may be in trouble."
>
> "Management's job is to improve the system."
>
> "Every system is perfectly designed to get the result that it does."
>
> - W. Edwards Deming

Complexity

"Complex system" means a specific concept in the new ways of working (p273). Complex doesn't just mean complicated: it means unknown. A complex system is one in which the outputs are unpredictable from the inputs, as compared to a simple system where we have a set of rules, an equation, to describe exactly what you will get from a given input.

All real-world work systems are complex, except at a narrow scope with tightly constrained freedom and deep familiarity that makes them simple (or seem simple – generally they're not). They have humans in them, they're always going to be unpredictable.

> "The search for quick, guaranteed and certain results will almost always undermine the creativity you're after."
>
> - Seth Godin

Image CC dertomtom, Wikimedia

Avoid the simple system myth

The myth of a simple system permeates too much of our thinking about building any kind of system. We have to let go of the idea that we can define what we are going to do and then do it, and then judge how well we did against what we said.

> "What is the value of adhering to a plan that was made at the beginning of a project, when uncertainty was greatest?"
>
> - Mark Schwartz

The real world is not like that, for just about any system we build:

- It has humans in it.

- We can't see all the moving parts. Some parts of the system are opaque, some are beyond the boundary of what we can see/control, some information is out of date as fast as we capture it.

- New information emerges as we act.

- What we think is true can be invalidated when we do it.

- We can't see all the options we will have at each step.

- We can't predict changing conditions.

- A system can develop emergent behaviours that nobody predicted.

- A changing world and emerging information mean our desired end state may change.

- Therefore, we can't see the end when we begin.

All of this reality defeats the Simple System Myth. If we act as if we can plan and design everything before we start and then do what we said we would, we are setting ourselves up to fail.

Navigate uncertainty

We must navigate uncertainty and ambiguity. The strategy is to iterate, increment, experiment, and explore.

We don't know where we will be at any given time, or when we will arrive at any given state. The sequence of states is unknown before we get to them. We don't know where we are going until we get there.

> "Life can only be understood backwards; but it must be lived forwards."
>
> - Søren Kierkegaard

We don't even know we can get there. Some problems are unsolvable. Some present us with a dilemma, where we must accommodate two incompatible conditions at once – that's the real world. Whatever decision-making and planning approaches we have must handle that.

Several cultures (including the Māori) consider the past to be in front of you and the future behind you. You can see the past, and learn from it, and see your progress, but the future comes at you from behind and flows over you. This is an insightful way to see reality.

If your paradigm is to see the future ahead of you, then accept that in the modern world it is like driving in a fog. You must peer ahead to discern what is fast approaching. "Radar" sees only so far ahead. The idea of planning for 5, 10, or even 15 years is now laughable in many contexts (p117).

We have no choice but to operate on imperfect information, even deal with situations that can't be understood rationally. We mustn't wait for perfect clarity. We mustn't get caught up in analysis paralysis. In a complex system, the best way to get more information is to do something. (See "JFDI", p192).

Levels of uncertainty vary across industries and organisations. This impacts our level of planning (p117). The higher the uncertainty, the more wasteful that planning is.

> "You need to plan the way a fire department plans. It cannot anticipate where the next fire will be, so it has to shape an energetic and efficient team that is capable of responding to the unanticipated as well as to any ordinary event."
>
> - Andy Grove

Understanding complex systems

The way forward is to probe and experiment in small time iterations and small state increments. Cynefin calls this "Probe, sense, act" (p273). Deming[56] calls it "Plan, do, check, act". Or John Seddon[57] had the simpler "Check-Plan-Act". Or we say "iterate, increment, experiment, explore" (there is no order to that last list, it is not a cycle like the others).

Understand the complex system:

1. Delineate clearly what the boundary is.

2. Know what its value is, according to the customer – value must flow out over the boundary.

3. Know who all the players are.

4. Map the flows and the components, as far as is visible. Measure: get data.

5. Poke it and see how it responds; figure out how changes in one part affect others. Watch errors to see what knock-on effects they have.

6. Identify the constraints, and the waste.

7. Understand what the capacity of the system is - what resources it has, and needs.

8. Understand where demand comes from, how it is managed, and where the system is overburdened.

9. Find out what goes wrong: where the errors are, where they come from, how much variance can the system handle before it breaks.

10. Complex systems behave as if they are organic, alive. Get to know the system as an entity.

---

[56] J.Edwards Deming, one of the most noted early thinkers on new ways of working and managing. He worked before and after the Second World War, most notably helping Toyota; and wrote a number of seminal books.

[57] An influential late 20th Century writer and consultant on work systems.

Understand the people:

1. Go to the gemba often: see the work, talk to the practitioners, find the expertise.

2. Learn about ordinary everyday work.

3. Understand the perspective of those doing the work – people behave the way they do for good local reasons.

4. Make work visible: what they are working on, what is waiting, what gets done.

5. Find out what really matters to get the work done.

6. Embrace diversity: get as wide a range of views as possible.

7. Absorb the thinking and language of the gemba. Be fluent.

8. Be part of communities, turn up, be present, shut up, listen and learn.

Chaos

Systems all live on the edge of chaos. Whether we are in simple or complex states, we can tumble into chaos, into a state where all hell is breaking loose; where the state is unknowable; where all we can do is take action and see what we get, trying to get back into a more manageable state.

> "Chaos is a precursor to order."
>
> - Ron Quartel

We generally take a negative view of chaos, but it is not always so. A chaotic system cools into some form of order. Chaos throws everything up into the air, and when it settles we get novelty, innovation, disruption. We are then in a complex state where we have to learn and explore anew. Chaos demands lateral thinking, fresh ideas.

So never let a perfectly good crisis go to waste. It is an opportunity for change, a motivator to everyone, and a disruptor of the status quo. At times we even deliberately throw a system into chaos to see what we get.

Embrace chaos[58].

---

[58] *Embracing Chaos*, Ron Quartel, https://medium.com/@rquartel/embracing-chaos-34223ad75c1e

Sense making

The ways of understanding complexity fit within a broader category of thinking called sense-making. Sense-making digs below understanding decision-making to look at how and why we work the way we do, and to create diagrams/maps and narratives to explain it. Sense-making produces lines of inquiry, not answers. By understanding where we are, and the meaning to why we do things, sense-making helps us to be more action-oriented, and to deal with ambiguity and dilemmas.

There are many such approaches, useful in different ways, and with a range of cultural perspectives and biases, which means some will fit your organisation better than others. A few of them include:

- Cynefin (p273), one of the most popular right now.
- Similar models to Cynefin, such as Simplicity[59], and Agreement and Certainty Matrix. And all the others that map reality on some form of quadrant. Or the Hexagon Sensemaking Canvas[60], a *six*-sided descendant of Cynefin.
- Another one is the "Medicine Wheel" quadrant, which is more associated with the hippy 1970s than actual Native American ideology, e.g. Leadership/courage, Vision/truth, Community/love, Work (and management)/wisdom.
- Wardley Mapping (p274), and all the others that map your organisation on some sort of landscape.
- Context-space mapping[61], an enterprise architecture view.
- Many forms of "canvas". A canvas is a template format for laying out a page (also called A3 Thinking) to describe what we know, forcing us to be concise and to think about the prescribed sections. Examples include Lean Canvas, Social Lean Canvas, and Business Model Canvas.
- Confluence Sense-making Framework[62].
- Our own Standard+Case (p278).

---

[59] http://noop.nl/2010/09/simplicity-a-new-model.html

[60] https://storyconnect.nl/hexagon-sensemaking-canvas-2/?lang=en

[61] *Everyday Enterprise-Architecture*, Tom Graves

[62] http://www.storycoloredglasses.com/p/confluence-sensemaking-framework.html

Change organically

In complex systems, growth and change appear to be organic. Because we change in small increments, exploring and re-planning as we go, the organisation is emergent, unpredictable, and always replacing itself.

People want solutions. They prefer them as a formula, a set of rules, a template to apply. The world isn't that simple. Every organisation must find their way to their own version of these new ways which works in their unique case. That model must be constantly examined and challenged, and evolve over time to meet the changing needs.

It is important to have a permanent active team tasked with the definition, promotion, education, and evolution of the organisation's own new way of working and managing (p226).

Don't stop.

"you are often most successful in achieving something when you are trying to do something else. I think of it as the principle of 'obliquity'."

- Sir James Black

"In complex social situations, objectives are often best accomplished obliquely, not directly. Central planning is not the most effective way to run an economy. Frontal assault is rarely the best military strategy. The best way to become prime minister or president isn't necessarily to declare that intent. The direct pursuit of happiness is not the best way to achieve happiness. And in business, the single-minded direct pursuit of profit isn't necessarily the best way to make a profit."

- Steve Denning

Agility

The vision for all advancement in the modern age is to be more agile: to be faster and better, and to be able to change quickly. Efficiency is no longer the goal: we don't have long enough in one state to optimise. Driving down costs is counter-productive: efficiency is a by-product of agility, and agility is a by-product of quality – pursue that.

"Because Agile teams are self-organising, the only way to avoid chaos is to have a culture of collaboration, self-discipline, safety, and respect, and it's the main job of the people up the pyramid to make that happen."

- Allen Holub

Be flexible

Agility is primarily about being able to change direction quickly, and to do that we must be able to quickly change how we work. Speed and quality are requisites to being agile, but change is the goal.

"Be stubborn on the vision, but flexible on the details."

- Jeff Bezos

To allow rapid change in ways of working and managing, we must have a culture of flexibility. Be willing to change. People develop affection for places, tools, machines, ceremonies and rituals, and even processes. All of these must be expendable when change demands it. Refresh them regularly, especially when bureaucracy starts to form.

Faster than the need.

The customer wants us to deliver value faster than it is needed: don't be the bottleneck, don't cause unwanted waits. That doesn't necessarily mean fast if that is not required. Let the customer pull, let the work system set the cadence, then monitor and adjust how fast each area of work needs to be.

Velocity through quality

It is easy to go fast by taking shortcuts, by compromising quality, but that is not sustainable. It loses customers. Even if it doesn't immediately drive them away, all that low quality leads to future drag, to "system debt" (p90) which eventually must be paid. In fact, it is a vicious circle or a death spiral where the decreasing quality means increasing unplanned work, which further forces us to compromise the quality of our future work.

> "Sooner not faster"
>
> - Tim Ottinger

The only way to go faster sustainably is to increase quality, which reduces future rework and unplanned work, freeing up future time to improve quality even further.

It is true that pressure of timelines means we sometimes compromise quality to get a result quickly - we no longer prioritise defects over new - but everybody must be clear about what we just did. We borrowed from the future, we accrued system debt which must be paid. That quality needs to be fixed sooner or later or we will pay.

Every system failure is a foreclosure on system debt, and every emergency repair is an unplanned payment.

Velocitas per qualitatem

Quality through velocity

The reverse is also true: the faster we get, the higher the quality we can produce, and the higher the quality the faster we go - it's that virtuous circle.

We learn quicker, we fix quicker. We explore new changes with lower impact and risk, and get to better solutions. We build assurance into the work. Everyone owns quality.

Agility is being faster to change

> "Cheetahs are faster than gazelles but less agile, so have a hard time actually catching them."
>
> - Charles Lambdin

Agility is not just about delivering faster; it is even more about being faster to *change* how we deliver. There is a dilemma, almost a paradox: the more efficient we get at delivering, the less quickly we can change how we deliver. Manufacturers know not to over-automate, as they lose flexibility unless we are going to produce the same product for a long time – we seldom do in the modern world. We must maximise agility, not speed or efficiency.

There is a tension between the higher levels of velocity which are achieved by extreme standardization pursuing the manufacturing perfection; versus the agility and improvement - the ability to learn, experiment, and change - which comes from retaining flexibility and variance. We want to free knowledge workers to experiment and adopt new ways of working in order to create opportunities for innovation, whereas the manufacturing model wants to enforce strict standardisation and minimise variance in ways of working as well as output.

Just as with "faster than the need" not necessarily meaning fast, likewise "faster to change" doesn't have to mean fast either. Darwin <u>never</u> said "It is not the strongest that survives; but the one that is able to adapt to the changing environment in which it finds itself". Because it isn't true. Change is not essential, and it certainly isn't always a good thing.

Stromatolites do not adapt at all but they still exist. The algae that form them are one of the oldest unchanged species of life on earth. They've fit their niche for 3.5 billion years. What's more, the principle of "change or die" applies to species not individuals. An individual organism doesn't go extinct, it just dies.

Avoid evolution as a business model, it's not a good analogy (even if the word "evolve" still slips into our language to mean "change"), and forget speed of change as essential for survival. Like everything in the real world, it depends. Evolutionary models are great for experimental iteration, where we let ideas mutate, live, and die in each round. For an individual organisation, think about models that see it as a collective network, a community, not a single organism.

Give people freedom

If you want flexibility, you also need to give people room. Create white space around new ways of working, so they don't clash and grind with the old. Free them to innovate. Give them their own piece of the territory, and ask what they can make of it. Authorise them to change as they see fit within that area.

Enable people to succeed by removing impediments, and providing resources and capabilities to get *stuff* done ("GSD"). Allow curiosity. We want people to wonder, to explore, to try stuff.

Agility requires discipline

There is a misconception that greater freedom, empowerment, and flow, with less controls, documentation, and reporting, will lead to ill-discipline - we let the cowboys loose on the open range. Nothing could be further from the truth.

In order to achieve higher quality and velocity, we need higher levels of discipline[63]. Simple work needs to be standardised and repeatable, so that we can ensure consistency of quality, and so that we can automate. Dependencies need to be well managed. All work needs to be done professionally to retain the trust of stakeholders.

If you treat people like children, you will get childish behaviour. If you treat them like responsible professional adults, you will (mostly) get disciplined performance. Managers need to deal with the exceptions. Bad habits and dysfunctional culture are the worst kind of cultural debt – they are hard to unwind. Strong leadership and firm performance management are required. Again, be careful not to punish the many for the failings of the few. Don't patronise people: treat them like adults and confront cultural issues together. Peer pressure is perhaps the strongest force of all for improving discipline.

---

[63] For some reason, the Japanese term for self-discipline, *shitsuke*, hasn't caught on.

Simplify

Less is more. Do the minimum necessary. Agile is "intelligent laziness".

> "Don't build faster, build less"
>
> - Jeff Patton

- Make less so you can make higher quality. Focus on the work which has value. Cut off the "long tail" of low value features: drop the bells and whistles.

- Make just enough for minimum viable product: copper not gold.

- Don't make anything until the last possible moment, otherwise work may go stale: it may need to be changed or not be needed after all.

- Good managers take the complication out of the system, not add more in.

- Measure what matters. Embrace imperfection and uncertainty. You only need indicative information for human processes. E.g. Our pet hate is time recording systems. Look at what you are capturing this data for. There is no need to capture 100% of transactional operational data when statistical sampling will give just as useful metrics.

- When managers do the controls, reporting, and other paperwork themselves, it seems to get simpler naturally.

Our retreat. No power, no road, no phone, mobile, or internet.

Failure

Another key element of agility is a different attitude to failure. Not only is failure acceptable, we must welcome and reward it. Failure is how we get to success. Success is found under a pile of failure.

Under the influence of the Simple System Myth ("plan once, execute perfectly"), failure is considered unacceptable. There will be some resistance to introducing the idea of failure as a natural way of working and the primary source of learning. It takes time to accept and internalise failure as normal. Failure is normal for three reasons:

- Success is always achieved through failure. If we must experiment to explore our way forward, then we will fail sometimes. That's what an experiment is: potential failure.

- Every change to how we work goes backwards before it goes forward (see the "J-curve", p86).

- Success and failure happen in approximately the same way. The difference can be down to statistical variation or a coincidence of factors, i.e. luck.

Therefore, we redefine failure. We move forward in small increments, usually iteratively, expecting failure as we go. Fail fast, fail early, fail small, fail often- fail well. "Noble failure" is failure with good intentions: (1) failure because someone was willing to try, to experiment, to learn; or (2) failure because an intelligent risk had to be taken, the way to find out was to do. Fail well. Be immaculate[64]: make sure you did all the right things.

And we welcome it. Failure is only waste when we don't learn from it. The correct responses to failures are learning and improvement, not checks and penalties: "curiosity not controls". Blaming people and punishing failure only drives failure into hiding where we derive no benefit from it. Hidden failure is a cost. Embraced failure is an asset whose value we extract by learning.

---

[64] We can't recall who taught us this phrase, but it was at a DevOps Enterprise Summit.

Embrace antifragility

To capture value from failure, we create systems that are *antifragile*. Antifragile is a concept that requires a whole book, (of the same name from Nicholas Taleb), but our summation is that when an antifragile system is stressed, when something "bends" or breaks, it comes back stronger. There are two opposites to fragile: robust and antifragile, which are also opposites of each other. There are two different ways to be not-fragile.

Robust ⟷ **Antifragile**

Fragile

This one statement by Taleb blows conventional thinking wide open: "Robust systems are fragile under [sufficient] stress". Building robust systems doesn't make them less fragile. It just lifts the level at which they fail, ensuring the failure is even worse when it comes: they are *more* fragile.

Put another way, when we are antifragile, failure makes us better. We create a learning culture so that failure is a positive thing, we learn and grow from it. If it hurts, do it more until it doesn't hurt.

When we have a conventional "robust" mentality instead, we typically respond to failure with more controls, more lockdown, more fear of risk. If it hurts, forbid ever trying it again.

Much of nature is antifragile, and much built by humans is robust.

- When disease sweeps through an animal population, the ones who survive are resistant, so they repopulate stronger.
- When we build a wall to resist wind, we make it strong but eventually the wind is stronger and the wall collapses.
- When a tree lives in a windy spot, it grows stronger as it flexes, and it shapes itself to the wind. Yes, eventually the tree will break, but it will break only a limb first, reducing its wind resistance. Once the trunk fails, that is because the wind exceeded the tree's ability to be antifragile.
- Building skyscrapers to sway in an earthquake or wind is not the same thing: they don't become better/stronger from the experience of swaying.
- When a defect passes testing, we add a new test.
- When an operator does something wrong, we add protection or automation.

Beware of platonicity

Platonicity is another concept from Taleb which we summarise as the danger of becoming too attached to our mental models and out of touch with the reality they are supposed to represent.

This is the Simple System Myth again in another guise: the belief that we can design a model and build that model and it will work in reality. Every electrical circuit designer or software programmer or other type of engineer knows this one: "it worked in my head". Intellectual models are easy in the abstract. Making them work in the real world is much harder. In complex systems, we can never anticipate everything.

The same idea was expressed the opposite way in the saying "This may work in practice but it will never work in theory".

Accept risk

Why is it that so many managers and governors expect zero incidents? Stuff happens. But when it does, they introduce more controls to stop a recurrence. This is the wrong attitude and wrong response. Attempting to reduce risk through controls will also reduce agility and velocity. After a while, such organisations are so constipated by controls that nothing gets done. Many of the controls are trying to prevent a circumstance which is unlikely to recur; often it was  long ago, the risk may not even exist anymore.

As we already discussed, controls are not the correct response to mistakes. Don't bring in a control: fix the quality, the predictability and reliability, through *learning and improvement*[65]. That's the correct response to failure: maximise the return from it. Don't stop people doing things that they don't do well. If it hurts do it more. If we suck, do it until we suck less. Learn. Kata. Practice reduces risk.

---

[65] See the work of Sidney Dekker on *Safety Differently* http://www.safetydifferently.com

We must find an acceptable level of risk, which isn't zero otherwise nothing would get done. If we ran motorways by the same principle that "any accident must never happen again", the speed limit would be 3 kph, and all cars would have a man walking in front ringing a bell and swinging a lantern. To drive on a motorway, you put your trust in hundreds of strangers who could kill you. We accept not just hypothetical risk but actual graphically-demonstrated consequences in order to maximise the benefit of driving.

Ironically, by adding controls managers slow down work, which reduces responsiveness and increases defects because of time pressures.

Agility <u>reduces</u> risk: we build closer to requirements, we break it less, and we fix it faster.

Something bad will happen again. All complex systems have broken elements, all the time[66]. When the brokenness overwhelms the operators, the system eventually fails. Be fast, competent, and relaxed about fixing it.

> "Agile is a series of controlled errors in the sense that walking is a series of controlled falls."
>
> - George Dinwiddie

Allow for the J-curve

Every change to a working system will have an initial negative impact on performance until we can identify issues, fix problems, learn new processes, and start to optimise performance of the new system. New teams need to "form, storm, and norm" before they can perform. This is called the "J-curve" (for more on this, see p190).

Expect the downturn: allow for it and manage through it.

Make many small changes, not a few big ones. A very big downturn might be unrecoverable. For big changes, we need to consider scenarios and weigh up opportunity and risk. If the worst happens how much damage could there be? Can the system cope?

---

[66] *How Complex Systems Fail*, Dr R Cook, 1998
   http://web.mit.edu/2.75/resources/random/How%20Complex%20Systems%20Fail.pdf

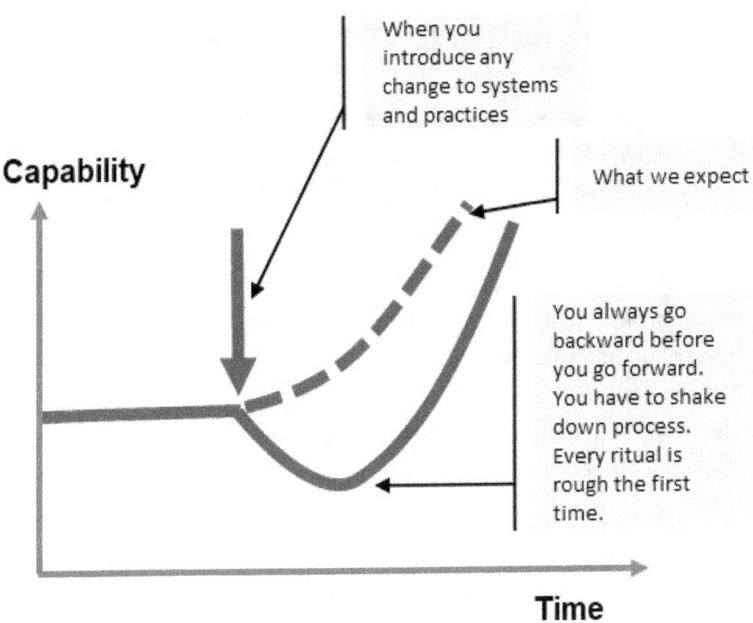

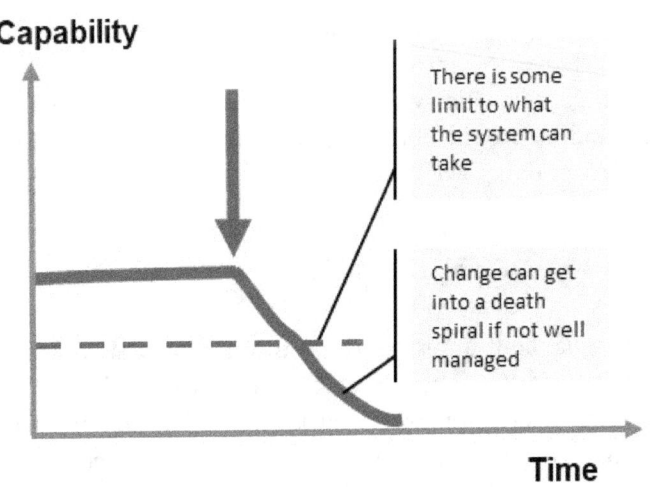

Improvement

Continual improvement should be the foundation of the work culture and the initiator of all work. We should continually improve our product and our ways of working, together, in one work stream. This is the best practice, the "pole star" aspiration.

If we create a culture of continual improvement, if it is the basis of the way we do things around here[67], then we will pursue quality all the time. Equally importantly, we will be able to adjust *how* we work all the time (see "Improvement Kata", p271). Agile organisations with a continual improvement way of working seldom need step-change transformations, they incrementally adjust to changing conditions all the time.

We are often asked: Tell us how much time it takes to complete the business improvement? Answer: This is a continuous improvement process so there will be no end.

"But we are very busy, we have a lot of work to do, not just focus on improvement." Answer: it is more important to improve work than to do work. Otherwise, when will you ever not be too busy to improve?

Try to work on that which is important and not (yet) urgent. This is where we can achieve the most at the best quality. Deal with the important and urgent as quickly as possible, get rid of the urgent and not important, and ignore the not urgent and not important. Prioritise improving work over doing work.

Be a learning organisation

Another way to talk about improvement is through the lens of being a learning organisation. If we have a culture of learning, then we are driven by data and observation; we are curious, especially about failure; we create strong feedback loops to tell people what they need to know as quickly as possible; and we act on what we learn all the time in many small increments.

---

[67] "The way we do things around here" is John Kotter's great definition of organisational culture

Work sustainably

Work rate must be sustainable indefinitely. We measure this in two areas, cultural and system "debt" (see below). When we say debt, we mean under-investment short-cuts: that which was not done that should have been done, for the people or for the systems.

If this debt is increasing, we are eating the future: we are building a debt that will have to be paid one day. This debt is a burden which decreases productivity and velocity. Sooner or later the organisation will hit the wall: the drag of this debt will exceed our capacity to move forward.

Reduce culture debt

Culture debt is the degradation of the culture of the organisation over time.

Culture debt includes falling morale, broken promises, cynicism, change fatigue, overwork, burnout, toxic culture, badly executed change, negative beliefs, mindset of obstacles, and other damage to the culture of the organisation.

A significant contributor to culture debt is badly managed organisational change (whether it was successful or not). How we manage the change is what matters: if we do it to people, if they feel unheard, if they aren't respected and treated like adults on the same side, this generates significant cynicism and resistance in the future.

Indeed, nothing can compensate for a culture that is broken. It must be addressed by changing behaviours. A broken culture is the result of a series of decisions and policies that were not carefully considered. Understand culture debt to find ways to face and gradually remove it instead of being trapped by it.

Therefore, an important aspect in agile Management will be to identify and pay down this culture debt to ensure that the organisation can fully develop its capacity and operate in the best possible way.

Reduce system debt

Low quality is system debt. When we make compromises on the quality of any of our organisation's systems, that generates future additional work (often unplanned and urgent) to deal with the defects and deficiencies. Which in turn forces future compromises, escalating the debt.

Usually we get to a point where we have to seek significant funds to literally pay the debt down, by investing in fixing systems that shouldn't have needed fixing, before they put us out of business.

This kind of lurch in quality often causes more problems as it solves others, with no visible value. It is much more sustainable to incrementally drive quality improvement all the time.

Accept imperfection

From all of the discussion so far, it should be apparent that new ways of managing allow for imperfection.

We navigate ambiguity, we accept incompleteness, we move forward in uncertainty. This seems to be contradictory to the principle of "velocity through quality" but it is not. It is essential to improve the quality of our work product and it is essential to be always improving the ways in which we work, but we accept that nothing is perfect.

> "Human beings by our very nature are fallible. When perfection is your goal, you're always left with a nagging sense of failure."
>
> - David Lewis

In particular, technology requires high levels of perfection but human systems do not. Technology generally only has a small number of working states and all other states fail, often catastrophically. (You only have to get one tiny option wrong in your WiFi router and it stops working completely, it doesn't just get 10% slower. You miss one bit of punctuation in a software program and it may crash, or all hell breaks loose).

But human work systems *are* able to function well in all sorts of imperfect states. People work around imperfect parts of the system:

they bridge gaps, they fill in uncertainty, they resolve ambiguity. They get the job done. Fastidiousness is a desirable attribute when putting together technology, whereas it is a weakness when designing human systems. For one the authors, the day his multinational employer issued standardised guidelines for fonts and spelling in documents his creativity died.

A useful phrase is "copper not gold". Copper has almost all the properties of gold whilst being much cheaper and easier to obtain. We should focus on building work systems that are as simple and expedient as possible while meeting our needs to a satisfactory but not perfectionist level. Don't gild the lily, don't seek the gold-plated result, when copper is perfectly adequate.

If we work for a large organisation, it is unlikely to turn into a unicorn overnight. As we discuss elsewhere, measure progress by how far you have come, not how close you are to perfection. The organisation may be more like a water buffalo than a unicorn. If you can pester it to lumber one mile further along, that's a win sometimes.

Wabi-sabi is the Japanese principle of accepting imperfection and impermanence, and appreciating it, finding beauty in the roughness. It can be seen as more real, more authentic. It is in contrast to the Western classical aesthetic of beauty in perfection.

Some managers need to learn to lighten up and let go. We use the word "relaxed" which scares them, but we make it clear we mean accepting uncertainty and imperfection. Stuff happens. Accept imperfection where it doesn't matter. "Be like water", follow where reality leads. Near enough is not good enough, but good enough is near enough. Focus on that which is truly important and not the pedantic details. Do our best, have the right intentions, cope with complexity, fail well, be resilient, recover fast, always improve.

Abstract principles

We have discussed twelve topics in this Section, which fall into three groups:

> **Human**: People, Customer, Culture, and Trust.

> **Systems**: Transparency, Slack, Flow, and Science.

> **Agility**: Complexity, Agility, Failure, and Improvement.

From the discussions, we can extract many principles to guide us in moving to new ways of working and managing. Every organisation makes a different journey (see section 4). The thing they all have in common is the set of principles they apply to get them there.

Here is a list of the high-level abstract principles we use to guide us. You might think of more, or reject some. We tried to group them under the three main headings above, although some cross over multiple areas.

Google's Eight Pillars of Innovation

Have a mission that matters.

Think big but start small.

Strive for continual innovation, not instant perfection.

Look for ideas everywhere.

Share everything.

Spark with imagination, fuel with data.

Be a platform.

Never fail to fail.

Human

1. Restoring humanity to work means wholeness: reuniting truth, beauty, and goodness.
2. The purpose of an organisation is to produce better services together than we could apart.
3. Believe in the goodness of people. Assume we are on the same side.
4. People first. They are not resources. They are fellow humans.
5. New ways are all about restoration of trust.
6. People trust people who trust them.
7. Have stable standing teams. Let them grow together.
8. Everybody is different: exploit uniqueness, don't try to standardise staff, or manage by numbers.
9. Embrace diversity for better results.
10. Managers are the servants of those working for them.
11. A manager is a gardener not a commander.
12. The most efficient and effective method of conveying information to and within a team is face-to-face conversation.
13. You can't change a culture directly.
14. Culture is an output of behaviour.
15. Incremental change is less damaging.
16. The best work is done when motivated people self-organise.
17. Policy is essential: set the rules not the game-play.
18. Let the people doing the work design the work.
19. Managers don't know the answers (nor do consultants).
20. Managers and governors should go to the gemba.
21. Pull change to ways of working, don't push it.
22. Manage dysfunctional staff, don't restrict everyone.
23. Free knowledge workers.
24. With authorisation/freedom comes accountability.
25. Network across siloes; organisations grow by sharing.

Systems

26. Be holistic. See and improve the whole.
27. Focus on satisfying the customer through early and continuous delivery of value.
28. The customer defines the value. Let the customer prioritise the work.
29. Quality is more important than speed or cost.
30. We iterate faster and change faster through higher quality.
31. The faster we go, the higher the quality, agility, and efficiency, so the lower the risk.
32. Good quality is difficult unless those who deliver (deploy/run/support) a product are those who build it.
33. Honour the past. It's there for a reason.
34. It's more important to improve work than to do work.
35. Get out of the way of the flow of value.
36. Bring the work to the teams not the team to the work.
37. Do less to do more. Take work out of a slow system.
38. Make work smaller to flow better.
39. Focus on removing constraints, not trying to be faster everywhere.
40. Work flows in multi-directional networks of co-creation.
41. Maximise the work not done. Copper not gold. Only do work that increases customer value.
42. Limit work to get more done. Stop starting and start finishing.
43. Manage demand at the input to the flow.
44. Merge a team's work into a single prioritised backlog.
45. Systems work better when they are not fully utilised – they need slack.
46. No known defects. Prioritise defects over new.
47. All complex systems are broken: design and build for it.
48. Human error is normal: design and build for it.
49. Build for reality, not for mental models.
50. Work sustainably.

Agility

51. Change is a permanent condition, not a passing event.
52. We build complex systems (including our work systems).
53. You can't change a complex system, you can only change the conditions for it to respond organically.
54. Complex systems have emergent properties and inexplicable behaviours.
55. Set the challenge not the solution.
56. Navigate ambiguity.
57. The future is not foreseeable.
58. Move forward by exploring: probe, sense, and respond.
59. Agility means being faster to change.
60. Success is achieved through failure.
61. All work is an experiment. Failure is normal.
62. Every change of work goes backwards before it goes forwards.
63. Punishing failure destroys its value.
64. The correct response to failure is curiosity not controls.
65. If it hurts do it more. Practice until it doesn't hurt, and then until you can do it without thinking.
66. Act on data and observation, not opinions.
67. Move in small steps (time iterations, work increments). Fail fast.
68. Planning is essential, plans are expendable.
69. Plan how we will work, not what we will do.
70. Build small teams with no leader and no roles.
71. Don't do work too soon, it goes stale.
72. Iterating faster reduces risk.
73. Take intelligent risks.
74. Zero risk is impossible – bad things *will* happen.
75. Be a learning organisation: create feedback, act on information.
76. Be flexible. Welcome and accommodate change.

Review 1

Come to www.agilemanagers.club for answers, discussion, and more questions.

Revision

1. What is agility?

2. What is Taylorism?

3. Why don't we get maximum throughput when everything is at 100% utilisation?

4. What is the value of our past systems and long-term people?

5. What does diversity give us?

6. What are some ways to improve flow of work?

7. How can we rely less on guess and opinion?

8. How does agility increase discipline?

9. How to deal with complexity?

10. How does feedback help?

11. What's so good about failure?

12. What are some different ways to think about improvement?

13. How can we eliminate risk?

14. What does "shift left" mean?

15. What is the problem with common sense thinking?

16. What are cultural and system debt?

Contemplation

1. What are your favourite aspects of agility? What resonates for you?

2. Which principle do you find hardest to accept or get your head around?

3. Do you understand antifragile?

4. Do you feel like this kind of thinking is for you?

5. Is your organisation already agile?

Action

1. Which principle do you most want to find out more about?

2. How can you connect with others in your organisation thinking about new ways?

.

2. New Ways of Managing

The ideas in Section 1 led to a set of principles that all organisations apply – to varying degrees – the get them to new ways of working and managing. Some of them may blow your mind when first encountering them, but they make sense once you unpack and absorb them.

> "As a manager, the things I need to do to create the conditions for agile teamwork are counterintuitive to the dominant narratives of heroic leadership and metaphors of mechanistic cause and effect"
>
> - Matt Edgar

These principles lead us to new concepts of managing. Again, none of these are new in time, just new to most organisations. There are a number of models for new ways of working and managing that have been derived from these principles. No one of these is best. You draw from them as needed to synthesise a new model of management for your organisation.

Recall that Teal Unicorn see the functions of agile Management as being attracting, nurturing, freeing, motivating, exploring, and observing. This section looks at what new ideas we need in order to achieve these functional capabilities.

First, we look at high-level concepts which are specific to management (carrying on from the broader concepts in Section 1).

Then, we look at how Agile thinking impacts various management practices, such as finance and planning.

Finally, we look in greater detail at one particular function: people (personnel) management.

These new ways of managing can be challenging to many managers. They need to:

- understand and embrace the concepts of complexity, Agile, Lean, and servant manager.
- achieve personal change to adopt and demonstrate the principles of servant manager.
- promote and foster advancement in the organisation and its staff.

Continual improvement

Building a product is a lot like a combat mission. A team of skilled people operate in conditions of high uncertainty; a commander sets clear outcomes with some guiding principles, but we expect the unexpected; and, we're trained to take the best action, responding to new information as the situation unfolds. All of that takes discipline. And practice.

In military operations, it's called *disciplined initiative*, and soldiers train so they can practice the movements of combat. In Mike Rother's Improvement Kata, it's called *deliberate practice*, and it's how we practice the movements of scientific thinking. This is how product teams can align with purpose, explore uncertainty, and learn their way to achieving desired outcomes.

- Jonny Schneider

The most important concept of all in the new ways of managing is to create a culture of continual improvement. This is foundational, not an afterthought or housekeeping. We live in a world of constant change, so the entire organisation must be built around constant adjustment. We increase our agility by increasing our quality, so we must get better over time. It is more important to improve work than to do work.

We often get clients saying they are too busy to do advancement activities, but when will you ever not be busy? If you don't improve now you will never improve. We must prioritise improvement over work. A simple litmus test for this is to see how readily staff get pulled from training because of something "more important". Another simple test is to see if the time recording software has a code for "Improving work".

There are many models for improvement, some discussed in this book:

- Improvement Kata
- Plan Do Check Adjust, PDCA
- Observe Orient Decide Act, OODA
- Kaizen
- Lean pursue perfection
- Agile reflect on every iteration
- our Unicorn Management Model "Improvement Machine"

They are all different lenses on the same reality. This concept of continual improvement has been promoted as foundational for a century, but it is still rarely seen as the heart of an organisational culture.

Networked

When we reduce centralised control, hierarchy, and bureaucracy, we encourage teams to create their own dynamic connections, to work in networked ways. The price is a certain level of messiness and inefficiency, but the benefits are agility, fluidity, freedom, and creativity.

We need a strong central vision and purpose, and we may also need some standardisation, especially policy. In the Roman Empire[68], subjugate nations were allowed to run most of their affairs in their own way but certain things were centrally standardised such as roads.

In a networked world, the concept of value streams can be misleading. It's not linear or unidirectional: value flows in all directions, we co-create value (see p146).

> "Those who talk most about leadership have the most difficulty forming meaningfully gelled teams. The reason is that gelled teams aren't really led. They are networks not hierarchies. All members are virtual peers. The leadership function is distributed. That is, different members take control at different times."
>
> - Tom DeMarco

---

[68] This analogy comes from Troy DuMoulin of Pink Elephant (no relation to Teal Unicorn)

Servant manager

Managers, governors, and leaders must serve those who create value.

The phrase widely usually used is "servant leader" but we prefer "servant manager". Not all managers are leaders and not all leaders are managers (p35). "Servant leader" talks about how to manage.

Managers are mostly overhead to daily work: managers don't do work, don't make many decisions. Managers don't know the answers and shouldn't be expected to. Every level of hierarchy further removed from the actual work reduces the probability that a manager will know the solutions or add value.

"Leaders eat last."

- Simon Sinek

(Alluding to the tradition that military officers made sure the men and horses were camped and fed before they relaxed.)

Servant managers know this - they don't try. They let the people doing the work design the work, in their own way with their own tools; and the management provides them with the resources, knowledge and skills they need to succeed. They provide the conditions for staff to flourish. Servant managers are gardeners not commanders. A manager needs to take control occasionally, but they should use a light touch.

"All use of the rudder increases drag and thus holds the vessel back"

- Tom DeMarco

Another way of understanding servant manager is "flip the pyramid". Instead of drawing a conventional hierarchal org-chart going up to the CEO, we like to draw the flow of work with a tree going *down* to the CEO as a supporting structure *under* the value-work. Management is not a weight on top of the work, it is a foundation below it.

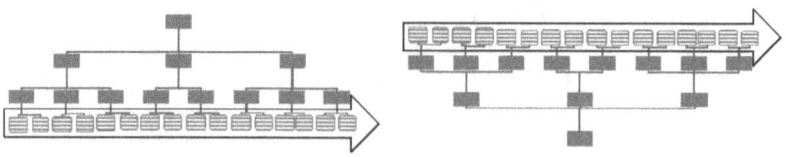

So, if they don't make decisions and come up with the answers, what do managers do? As we said at the beginning of the book, managers in the new world are attracting, developing, freeing, motivating exploring, and observing (p18). Along those lines, the behaviours of a servant manager are:

- attract and retain team members. People join jobs but they leave managers.
- inspire team members. The team is innovative and motivated.
- improve team members. Team performance improves.
- free the team members. The team is self-organising/managing/directing.
- grow team members. People move up to new work.
- improve the work system. Get it out of the way.
- support and encourage experimentation and failure.
- provide resources, remove impediments, deal with non-value work.

This is true at any level of the hierarchy: every manager has a team of staff reporting to them (even if they often don't behave as a team at higher levels of the hierarchy – that's something we try to fix, p109).

Robert Greenleaf initiated the idea of "servant leader". His Center for Servant Leadership[69] lists ten characteristics of a servant "leader":

- Listening (What do you think?).
- Empathy (How do you feel?).
- Healing (How can I help?).
- Awareness (I notice that you look happy/sad).
- Persuasion (Sell, don't tell).
- Conceptualization (In a perfect world, how could it be done?)
- Foresight (Have a Plan B and Plan C).
- Stewardship (How can I make things better?).
- Commitment to the growth of 0395
- (Let others lead).
- Building community (We are all in this together).

[69] https://www.greenleaf.org

The blacksmith's hammer

Let the people doing the work design the work, or as the Vietnamese say, "Don't teach the blacksmith how to use the hammer". Managers must resist telling people how to do their work. Managers often make this mistake, it is a common "anti-pattern". If employees are always told how to do their job, they will become passive, not self-reliant, not independent, and less creative. They develop "learned helplessness".

An author, Cherry, went to a fashion tailor shop and asked them to help fixing a dress. When the tailor was holding a ruler, a senior manager, standing next to him, constantly instructed the tailor on how to measure. The skilled tailor felt so embarrassed because he could not freely do the work he is very proficient with.

As a manager, you should remember that even if you were a good worker in the past, and you were promoted to a higher position because you had good skills, you have long left that job. Instead of teaching the blacksmith how to use the hammer, create conditions for them to do their best.

The exception here is when the manager is the master, where of course it is OK to coach and teach. This is not ideal, for several reasons:

> If a person is no longer working, they soon are no longer the master. In the modern world, techniques and technologies change fast.

> Management is seldom the best use of a master's skills.

> A manager may not have time to also be an effective teacher.

This is not to say that people don't need training and coaching in how to do their work. When they are inexperienced, naturally they do. But the "blacksmith" is a craftsperson, already a master of the art (see "Shu-Ha-Ri", p127).

Even for a junior, it is usually unhealthy for a manager to interfere – the trainers and coaches should generally not be managers. The power imbalance gets in the way of effective teaching.

Situational Leadership®

Of course, as always, it depends. Not all staff are used to being set free, empowered, self-organising. Not all managers are practiced at doing it. We must grow together to new ways of managing and being managed. A useful tool to understand that journey is Situational Leadership[70] . This is a leadership style developed by Kenneth Blanchard and Paul Hersey in the 1970s. It uses "leader" in this book's sense of "manager", so for this section we will stick to their wording, but mentally substitute "manager".

Situational Leadership theory shows that the effectiveness of leadership style depends on the situation. But what is the decision for the situation? Both employee maturity and their attitudes determine it. Hersey and Blanchard distinguish four levels of maturity in the Situational Leadership model (the fifth zone to the left, "yelling", is our little joke):

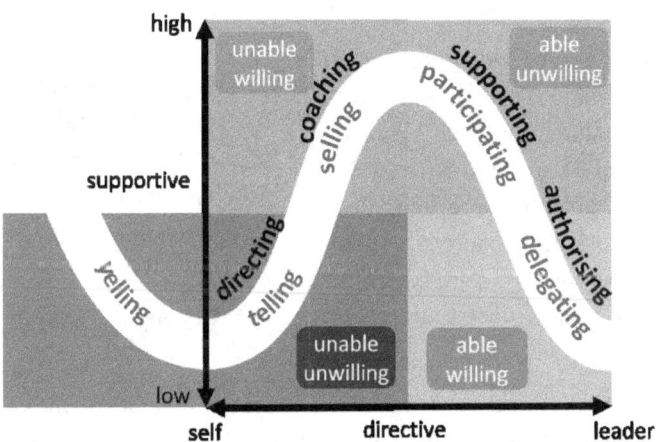

S1. Direction: Leadership that is mainly directing while providing little support leads to weak and less motivated staff. This leadership style is micro-management: from top to bottom, workers simply do exactly what they are asked.

S2. Coaching: Leadership is direct, and more supportive; staff are low in capacity but highly motivated. This style often works well with inexperienced staff who are still learning how to do it.

---

[70] Situational Leadership is a registered trade mark of The Center for Leadership Studies
https://www.situational.com

S3. Support: Leadership is less direct and more supportive. Those who work well under this style of leadership have the necessary skills but lack the confidence or motivation to achieve them.

S4. Authorisation: This leadership style, although leadership can still participate in orientation or feedback, is at a much lower level than other leadership styles. With this leadership style, employees know their role and implement it with little supervision.

It is important for leaders to be aware of their leadership style in different situations. The maturity level of employees determines the leadership style of the leader. For those with less experience, they need a directive style. For those with high competence, authorising style will be appropriate.

Gemba

A powerful phrase from Lean is "go to the gemba". This means go to where the value is created. Managers should often be closely involved with the gemba: get out from your desk. Go to the work and observe it. Talk to the people doing the work to understand what they experience and what they need. Let them come up with the answers.

> "Management exists to help the gemba do a better job by reducing constraints as much as possible"
>
> - Masaaki Imai

Go to the gemba and measure work yourself, instead of making staff doing value work also do non-value reporting. This will also have the interesting result of producing the Hawthorne Effect, where people behave differently because they are being observed. Do all the non-value work for them: controls, bureaucracy, reports.

If you are senior in the hierarchy and you want to be a servant manager, go talk to the "coalface" workers and *listen* to their problems. Then come back again with a solution to one. You're not at the gemba to sneak up on people, to catch them out. "Catch them doing it right"[71]: have a positive attitude, be encouraging, recognise performance.

---

[71] *The One Minute Manager*, Kenneth Blanchard

New management models

For agile managers, the key concept behind networks is the move away from conventional command-and-control hierarchy. Those doing the work don't all report to the one hierarchy, and they don't stay in one place in a hierarchy. That structure breaks down.

Other management models are better. For example, the concept of "wirearchy"[72] (as compared to hierarchy) is defined as "a dynamic two-way flow of power and authority, based on knowledge, trust, credibility and a focus on results, enabled by interconnected people and technology". Wirearchy says "purposeful human activities and the structures in which they are contained [are] evolving from top-down direction and supervision (hierarchy's command-and-control) to champion-and-channel ... championing ideas and innovation, and channelling time, energy, authority and resources to testing those ideas and the possibilities for innovation carried in those ideas."[73]

This is only one example of new ways of thinking that are emerging. There are other useful models for new ways of work and management:

- BetaCodex[74] is the set of principles behind OpenSpace Beta.

- The Viable System Model[75] is not about new ways of managing, more a different cybernetic way of thinking about any management system.

- Work Systems Model[76], which considers three dimensions: time horizons, five aspects of management, and three kinds of information.

- At the opposite end of the ideological spectrum is another approach: the Tipu Ake ki te Ora Lifecycle[77], a Māori management model that iteratively grows an organisation as an organic entity not a machine.

---

[72] *Wirearchy: sketches for the future of work*, Jon Husband

[73] http://wirearchy.com/what-is-wirearchy/

[74] https://www.betacodex.org

[75] *Brain of the Firm*, Stafford Beer, 1972

[76] *Making Work Systems Better: A Practitioner's Reflections*, Luc Hoebeke, 1994

[77] http://www.tipuake.org.nz

Agile management practices

The ways we do management, the management practices, all need to change in order to enable new ways of working.

Agile teams

Agile is described on p283. Here are a few considerations for managers:

Ideally, an Agile team works to a single stream of work, a single backlog, which includes all new features (functional and non-functional), defects, maintenance, system debt, housekeeping, improvements to how they work, and curiosity experiments. This backlog is prioritised for them by those who are accountable for the value produced.

Also ideally, an Agile team should be co-located. There is no equally-good substitute for face-to-face communication. Remote working will always be a challenge. Even being in different parts of the same building can encourage the wrong behaviours. Sit together. If you can't co-locate, then come together often (and share food, p121).

Interesting new research[78] suggests best results come from teams who intermittently work together. Constant collaboration suppresses innovation, whereas no collaboration results in lower overall quality. There is a sweet spot of intermittent collaboration which results in the best of both: higher innovation and higher quality.

Ideally, a team has a finite amount of work to do at any one time, and they are never over-burdened by others trying to jam more in. In return, the team commits to improve the velocity and quality of their work over time.

There is a tension between the concept of stable teams who can form-storm-norm-perform, and the ideal of teams flowing to the work – a dilemma between stability and fluidity, between bringing the work to the team and the team to the work. In practice, this usually resolves itself in the hurly burly of real-world constant change: teams reinvent themselves, sometimes reorganise, take on new products, drop old

---

[78] *How intermittent breaks in interaction improve collective intelligence*, E. Bernstein, J. Shore, and D. Lazer, PNAS August 28, 2018
https://www.pnas.org/content/115/35/8734.short?rss=1

ones; people move around with the workload; some continuity remains, and familiarity grows.

Resist the temptation to re-badge project managers as scrum masters. And the scrum master is emphatically not a team manager or boss: the team is self-organising. The best analogy we know for a scrum master is Yoda from Star Wars. The scrum master sits on the team's shoulder coaching them in the ways of Agile. And occasionally they get down, get out their light-sabre, and go sort something out to help the team.

Hourglass

Beware the hourglass model: "everybody in the team must go through one person - the Product Owner - to talk to customers, and all customers must come through that person". This is obviously a bottleneck, plus it disempowers the team, ruins communication, and becomes a different form of hierarchical control. Sure, somebody needs to be primary contact, primary representative, owner. But the relationship must be more flexible, open, and nuanced. Teams will be professional enough to know when the Product Owner should be involved and when it is appropriate to discuss things directly with others.

Agile management teams

When work is performed in new ways by teams, the managers must manage in new ways to support them, especially as the scope of new ways of working grows to many teams.

You can't continue to have management be hierarchal and command driven when the teams aren't. As managers become servant managers, they must see the work groups as customers of management: the teams they serve will be diverse, with different challenges, needs, success, and maturity. Management should function as a self-organising team (or networked teams), nimble in its ability to adapt to conditions, fast and responsive, and focused on value to the customer - exactly what it expects of the workers. Managers work closely with their staff, at the coalface, diving in to help where needed, removing obstacles.

A side benefit of managers changing the way they work together is that they are on the same journey as their staff, creating understanding and patience.

Agile governance

The ways of working and managing cannot change until the ways they are governed change, to make the new ways acceptable, directed, and valued. Define vision, goals, strategy, and policy; not what or how. Free your managers as much as they should free their staff. In the same way as managers should get out of the way of work, governance should get out of the way of management. Go to the gemba to monitor the organisation, don't make them come to governors. Use the teams' data and format to measure the work.: ask what and how they can report, don't demand particular formats. It is important that governors understand the work, so that the new ways make sense. Have intelligent conversations. Always be learning.

The strongest direction that governors can give is written policy (p147). When you set somebody free, the best thing you can do is define the bounds of that freedom, for their safety and for the organisation's. Policy is essential to define what employees may and may not do so that they are free to make their own decisions dynamically. Elsewhere in this book we talk about the Plan-Do-Check-Act (PDCA) cycle, but the military have a similar cycle called Observe-Orient-Decide-Act (OODA) where the second step, Orient, involves understanding the policy and guidelines under which a field commander operates, in order to guide the third step, making a decision. This frees distributed command. Policy is made at headquarters, but decisions are made in the field.

Governors should inspect the reporting received. If all the news is good news, you are not getting the news. Go to the gemba. Observe and gather data directly, not filtered through layers of management. In a command-and-control culture that punishes failure, the reporting up the hierarchy gets filtered to only report good news, and bad news will be buried as long as possible. This creates a "thermocline of truth: a line drawn across the organizational chart that represents a barrier to accurate information... Those below this level tend to know how well the project is actually going; those above it tend to have a more optimistic (if unrealistic) view."[79] Even after a culture of empowerment and reward of failure starts to be adopted, the instinct will still be to filter out bad news. People need to see messengers being rewarded not punished.

---

[79] *The Wetware Crisis: the Thermocline of Truth*, Bruce Webster,
http://brucefwebster.com/2008/04/15/the-wetware-crisis-the-themocline-of-truth/

Agile risk management

Governance processes sometimes operate on a principle of pursing zero risk, that all risk reduction is good. As organisations pursue agility, every part of the organisation has to understand that there is no such thing as zero risk. Driving towards lower risk is like driving towards lower cost - both are equally destructive. The correct strategy is to drive towards higher quality and velocity, the incidental consequences of which are lower risk and lower cost without ever being the targets. With agility, we are always reducing risk (compared to conventional ways of working) in multiple ways:

- working closer with those who need the change, including customers, to build the right thing.
- accepting change at any time, constantly adjusting to changing circumstances.
- making smaller-impact changes, at minimum blast radius.
- exploring our way forward, with strong feedback to track direction and progress.
- improving staff wellbeing, and retention.
- meeting the need more quickly.
- driving up quality.
- making systems more secure.
- fixing things more quickly.
- taking out system debt and culture debt.

Just as important as reducing risk, with agile Management we are mature about accepting the residual risk (p85). Things break, stuff happens, the outcome is always unpredictable. Nobody is ever certain, there are too many confounding variables. Therefore, we must become adept at accepting residual risk and determining minimum acceptable risk. And fixing fast.

There is a cognitive bias in people that somehow translates "likelihood is estimated at less than 5% probability" into "it won't happen". When it does, there are recriminations with those who estimated the risk, as if they had somehow promised that the laws of probability would be suspended. The probability of something happening once is unknown:

in a sense all outcomes are equally possible. Probability only tells us about trends, averages, and variances over time.

Remember, the correct response to failure is not more controls. Most of the excessive process and ceremony around governance – especially finance and procurement - arises because of single events that happened in the past, so now everybody is punished because of the crime or mistake of one person years ago. As the controls accrete like barnacles on a ship, staff learn to game or subvert the rules in order to get things done, which defeats the purpose of having the controls in the first place.

On the other hand, the removal or reduction of controls does of course present risk. We may not get it right. It is important to review and improve risk management processes, and associated audit and monitoring processes, to protect from inadvertent risk. Both "zero acceptable risk" and "it's not a risk" are dysfunctional extremes. We must find a balanced approach.

When assessing risk, we should listen to those building, not those managing. The imperatives are technical, not commercial. The Challenger shuttle disaster and the 737-Max disasters should have taught us this. The other thing all those deaths taught us is that conservative institutional knowledge saves lives. The laws of physics - of O-ring chemistry, aeronautics, or control systems stability - don't get suspended for business priorities. We (should) retain those people who are at the Conservative end of the bell-curve (p185) for a reason: they're an essential balancing voice in a diverse community.

Agile finance

As agile ways of working expand in the organisation, the operating model changes, and that impacts how we fund work. Agile ways of working need buffering (p166) from the conventional parts of the organisation. One of these gaps or interfaces is the flow of money, which conventionally is often released in large lump sums for projects, but we want continual streams of funding for standing teams. A mechanism is needed to "mince" the large sums up into smaller continuous flows, and to "underwrite" times when there are gaps in project funding so that we can provide continuity to teams (see "Project Management", p159).

In a larger organisation we want longer commitments of the stream of money so that a team can function, e.g. annually. In smaller or more fluid organisations, teams compete for funding on each released increment of work, delivering value to justify another increment of money.

Beyond Budgeting

Beyond Budgeting is a philosophy for freeing up finance, i.e. making it agile. It is based on twelve principles[80] which sound very like the Agile Manifesto (p286). By abandoning conventional annual budgeting process in favour of a more iterative "rolling" approach, an organisation decentralises decision-making and frees managers. Like all agile decentralisation, Beyond Budgeting depends on strong policy, transparency, team structure, and customer focus. (Zero Based Budgeting is an entirely different idea that does nothing to reduce the impact of annual budgeting.)

Internal market

If we are truly committed to empowering employees, give them the money to spend. Create an internal market. Hand the funds to those deciding and designing the work, and allow them to spend it as they see fit. Likewise let them negotiate to take money from others for collaboration, as they value it. There is an advanced body of knowledge on how to do this[81].

---

[80] https://bbrt.org/the-beyond-budgeting-principles
[81] *Internal Market Economics*, N. Dean Meyers

Agile procurement

Agility of procurement is a major issue for many organisations. As we try to increase our agility in working, it is often the procurement department that we run into like a brick wall. E.g. from personal experience it can take months to hire a consultant or contractor, which makes it impossible to be agile.

RFPs (requests for proposal) are a great example of the problem. RFP process is CYA (cover your arse): due diligence theatre to justify a decision that is often already made. It is a bloated control, the perfect example of excessive levels of ceremony. RFPs are easy to mock as a procurement tool. They are an inefficient and ineffective way to buy anything.

- RFPs eliminate the lightweight providers who do not have the infrastructure or resources for written responses.

- The RFP response process is an expensive one which is often not worth the prize. The responses to RFPs are legally binding, so they need to be carefully prepared and reviewed by multiple parties. Costs can easily be in tens or hundreds of thousands of dollars, sometimes millions. The purchaser ends up paying this.

- They are equally expensive for the purchaser to prepare and process.

- It is not always clear what was intended by a question. From a cynical viewpoint, there is usually enough ambiguity that any answer can be defended, if they want to answer yes.

- Because RFPs are legally binding, you won't get much frank discussion in them.

- They can easily make the selection process takes 6 months instead of the 6 days that it should take for many purchases.

- Most RFPs end up with responses scoring within a few percentage points of each other, with the difference depending on interpreting ambiguous text and subjectively scoring, so it is all theatre anyway.

There are better ways to qualify prospects, which are lighter, and win-win. Agile Procurement is a thing. This isn't going to turn into a detailed discussion about all the better ways to procure but, simply to make a point, here are some suggestions:

Nothing is perfect and nothing is ever an exact fit, so fit-for-purpose should not be your primary criteria; the most important criteria is the supplier:

- Do they have a local presence?
- Do you already have a relationship with them?
- Do they have a good reputation for products and especially for support?
- Are they going to be around for a long time to come? This is especially important for a service where the moment they go out of business so do you.

What does good look like? Go and see products in action, preferably not at places picked by the vendor.

Get the vendor's product people in a room and eyeball them to workshop your requirements. If you can't get them in a room with you, then perhaps you shouldn't be buying off them anyway (for any deal big enough that it needs an RFP).

Build trust. This is the foundation of successful procurement: as much mutual trust as you can create. Without trust, suppliers will build in risk margins and protections which increase costs and slow processes.

Fitness for purpose can be formally evaluated by identifying a small number of key criteria that you know (a) are a differentiator in the market and (b) are essential for you in the near future.

Often, we don't even need a specific requirement in order to procure. We can forecast how many laptops or vehicles or software licences we need based on past trends, and buy accordingly in incremental fashion.

Take a risk. It's what all improving organisations do. Create a procurement environment where intelligent noble risk is acceptable.

Agile outsourcing

The current buzz-word for managing the relationships with service providers is SIAM (service integration and management[82]). As we increasingly outsource activities to third parties, there is a need for a management methodology to "manage, integrate, govern, and coordinate the delivery of services from multiple service providers"[83] to ensure quality and continuity of service.

The relationship with outsource service providers ranges from provision of all of the value stream to simply being an off-the-shelf provider of one component of the build, and everything in between. Therefore, we can only talk about general principles here: each individual relationship has to be dealt with on a case-by-case basis. But in general:

It is difficult to achieve quality when the people who build a system are not the people who run the system. In cases where it is one and not the other, we want over time to increase the service provider's responsibility, so they are accountable for building and operating the system, or we want to reduce their responsibility to be components.

Nor can you easily achieve agility if you outsource strategic capabilities. Outsource commodities, and keep everything that matters. Wardley mapping helps here (p274).

We need to help our service providers understand our ways of working and how it fits into our strategy, and encourage them to be supportive of our advancement.

The challenges are a lack of co-creation (bi-directional flow of value) and lack of close collaboration. Any time you have an outsource service provider, the relationship is contractual not collegial. Part of the solution is to explain to them how things will be changing the next time the contract is renewed, and that now is the time to start building a different relationship: working more closely and beginning to experiment with working in new ways in preparation for contract renewal.

It is important to have sufficient level of sophistication internally before we talk to our service providers so that we can look prepared and

---

[82] *SIAM Body of Knowledge* https://www.scopism.com/free-downloads/
[83] *VeriSM*, https://verism.global/.

knowledgeable. It is not about putting demands on a service provider; it is about enabling them to deliver what we need.

Equally we need to understand how *they* are changing: all of the service providers are under market pressure from their customers to demonstrate new ways of working. We provide opportunities.

Existing contracts sometimes do not give service providers incentive to reduce consumption of their services, so the conversation has to be about preparing them for changing the mix of their revenue on next contract renewal: showing them that their existing revenue streams are going to decrease, and they need to build new capabilities to make it up. For example, they are going to be processing fewer manual changes in future, but they could provide more cloud services.

Fundamentally we need to build a higher trust relationship with our suppliers so that they trust us to go outside the contract and we trust them to deliver outside the contract, so that we enable each other to experiment until the contract can change. We should find early experiments to create proof points, to be showcases of what is possible working in new ways with that supplier. They ought to be eager to help us do that.

Agile planning

Planning is essential but all plans are expendable. Plans are constantly invalidated as we move forward so planning is a continual process. A military saying is "No plan survives the first contact with the enemy"[84].

> "I have never had a plan of operations."
>
> - Napoleon Bonaparte

Plan no more than you are willing to throw away. Plan enough to perform the next experiment. Over-planning is one of the largest forms of waste in conventional management. It stems from a lack of trust and freedom, and an unreasonable expectation of zero risk.

---

[84] "The tactical result of an engagement forms the base for new strategic decisions because victory or defeat in a battle changes the situation to such a degree that no human acumen is able to see beyond the first battle... No plan of operations extends with any certainty beyond the first contact with the main hostile force"
- Field Marshal Helmuth Karl Bernhard Graf von Moltke

We explore our way forward in increments, re-planning as we need to[85], based on what we discover (see Case Management, p277).

Agile attempts to do everything at the last "responsible" moment – a concept that comes from Lean thinking. Work goes stale if you do it too soon: things can change before we get any value from it.

The finance industry uses Real Options, a complex mathematical method to determine the value of available options. Using the maths in general business is seen by many as overkill, but the basic principles present us with a different way of thinking about decisions.

Real Options says:

- identify all the options.

- we don't have to choose between making a right decision or a wrong one – we have the third option to make no decision... yet.

- determine the date by which we have to make a decision, if possible.

- delay the decision as long as is responsible.

- push the date back whenever possible.

- sometimes we hedge our bets and pursue multiple options.

- collaboration allows us to keep each other's options open.

- act quickly once we decide.

By delaying – and this is key – we retain flexibility. It's not uncertainty or indecision if we are simply leaving our options open as long as possible.

> "The aim of strategic planning is action now"
>
> - Peter Drucker

People are uncomfortable with uncertainty, and want to make the decisions. We must embrace uncertainty as freedom. Once we make a decision, we tend to become emotionally committed to it, making it hard to change our minds. If we don't make the decision, we don't lock in to it.

Longer term strategy is still required to give us direction. We set a vision (see "Vision and purpose", p50), give ourselves some goals or matariki,

---

[85] An early version of this thinking was *Discovery Driven Planning*, McGrath and MacMillan, Harvard Business Review, 1995

create policies to steer us, and devise strategies to get there. But business plans of 5-year or even 15-year(!) durations are increasingly ridiculous in the modern world, especially in industries highly impacted by technology. Long-term planning is usually theatre to make everybody feel better. We must embrace ambiguity (p73) and accept that agility is more important than long-term visibility.

By all means, know where you are going, but plan, design, and build on the assumption that it will change. Architect and engineer your organisation to change direction quickly: to be agile. Some sectors of society have more stability than others, but all of us increasing must deal with VUCA: volatility, uncertainty, complexity, and ambiguity.

Agility is not only the way an organisation operates but is also reflected in its strategy. An agile organisation requires teams and units to create agile strategies. Agile strategies will stimulate creativity to create new markets, and bring competitive advantages for the business.

We liked this planning model from a client, which brings together customer value, principles, strategy, roadmap, the improvement kata, and matariki:

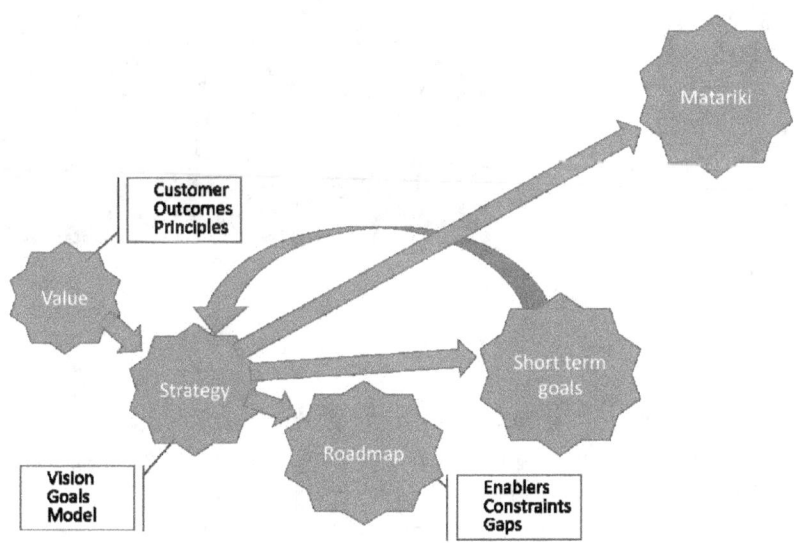

Image: Jason Cribb

We at Teal Unicorn sometimes make roadmaps to show what we are working on now; what we intend to work on later; and what the sequence and major dependencies may be. But we never put a timeline on it, which some find disturbing. Be suspicious of timebound milestones and targets: we have made it clear that you are guessing. The negative impact of failing to meet them, and the costs of misleading others, and the effort of predicting and constantly revising them, all outweigh the small benefits of having them.

> "Everyone has a fight plan until they get punched in the mouth."
>
> - Mike Tyson

A useful tool at all levels from organisation to team is a future radar, showing things we can see incoming from the future. Put this chart up on a wall and encourage everyone to post things they see, showing how far out they are from having an impact. Choose the range circles for time periods that make sense in your context, and choose relevant quadrants.

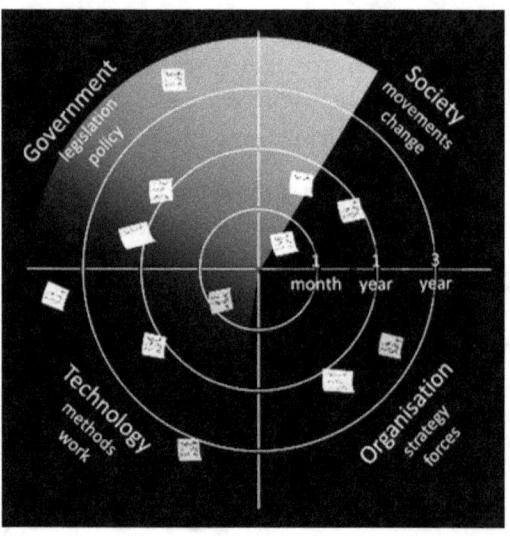

> "Agile planning is the future of planning. First, replacing the traditional obsessions on hard data and playing the numbers-game with a more balanced co-existence of hard and soft data where judgment also plays an important role. Second, introducing new mechanisms and routines to ensure alignment between the hundreds of self-organizing autonomous local teams and the overarching goals and directions of the company."
>
> - Alessandro Di Fiore

Agile people management

We dislike the term "human resources" although we do use the acronym HR sometimes to refer to the existing conventional organisational function. "Human resources" sound like something plug compatible, ordered in batches, moved around on plans, measured in spreadsheets, and scrapped.

"People" is too vague. We like the words "personnel", "employees[86]", or "staff". It was good enough for Dad. It embodies the idea of a function without being too dehumanising.

Because we must get back to humanity. Staff are individuals: irrational, imperfect, fragile, creative, and precious. Each one is unique, with differing value and potential.

The new ways are a bit hippy, as Rob likes to remind us with his hair. Peace and love, man.

Lizard brain

Humans, like all animals, have an instinctual primitive brain function as well as our higher cognitive functions. This is colloquially known as the Lizard Brain: the stuff you have in common with anything as advanced as a reptile or higher.

It is essential that we take account of the instinctual animal needs of people, and not treat them as cognitive machines.

---

[86] The word "employee" is on the way out too. In the Forbes "Workplace 2025" survey, the preferred term was "contributor", which encompasses the wider range of modern work arrangements.

- We go tribal. No group of more than about 40-250 (opinions vary) is a tribe. This is known as Dunbar's Number[87]. Any larger group naturally splits into two or more tribes.

- Tribes bond through ritual[88]: repeated familiar patterns of behaviour.

- No group of more than about 5-10 people is a real team: sharing, collaborating, self-organising, working as peers. Humans can't form sufficiently complex relationships with more. (Even rugby teams have forwards and backs).

- Every group of people at any size needs to form, storm, norm, and perform. Only after they get to know each other and establish territory and relationships can we even begin to improve performance. They need time to share experiences and adventures which build bonding. So, groups (especially teams) should be long-lived and stable. Re-forming and re-organising always has a negative impact on performance (see "J-curve", p86).

- It's not a team until they have eaten food together.

- Humans are playful. Play stimulates creativity and refreshes energy.

- The sense of place is essential. Dehumanising facility ideas like hot-desking, clean desk policy, nothing on walls, no personal items, banning pot-plants, open-plan office, bland sterile decors, or endless cubes are all barbaric. We should be militant in resisting them[89]. Create human spaces that are personalised, colourful, playful, stimulating, dynamic, configurable, productive, and owned.

- There is no substitute for face-to-face communication, not even video. We need to see subtle emotional cues. In fact, we need to subliminally smell each other.

---

[87] Dunbar hypothesised based on primate research, so be as sceptical as you like. But you've probably seen this. We experienced it strongly as a company approached 100 staff, who had a natural split geographically between Australia and New Zealand.

[88] *Rational Ritual*, Michael S-Y Chwe, 2013

[89] Our experience is that these purist directives get diluted and subverted after a year or two, but that is a lot of lost productivity.

Psychological safety

The most important instinctual need is psychological safety.

Safety is dependent on the contextual level. People feel safe anytime when speaking about stereotypes or typical contexts. They usually feel safe speaking about those present as a collective group. They less often feel safe speaking about "us here now" when at work, and even less often feel safe talking about our personal lives. When inviting people to say something, or when offering comments, be sensitive to which of these contexts you are using, and generally avoid the last two at work[90].

If people don't feel safe, they can't function. Management by fear destroys safety and hence productivity: staff will be constantly in high-stress fight-or-flight mode. A simple test of safety is how easily and willingly staff can deliver bad news.

In some organisations we have worked for, especially in a command-and-control culture that punishes failure, employees seem reluctant to speak up in a group and especially in the presence of senior managers. Even when it was a principle of the organisation to "Dare to speak", we have seen them not speak. We have had feedback that this is the case throughout the organisation. Reward outspokenness, don't punish it. Let the one who dares to speak be an exemplar for everyone.

Consider having an "employee ombudsman" that employees can appeal to anonymously for help on their behalf if they feel unsafe.

Make allowances for people who don't function well in front of others. Don't force them to participate. Find alternate mechanisms to get their input, usually written. Some people can't deal with even being in a high energy room – don't make them stay. Many activities should be by invitation.

Time and again, we are told that psychological safety is the biggest predictor of a high performing team[91], but somehow it is still lost on many managers. Be nice.

---

[90] Our colleague Dan Randow taught us this, we are not sure of the origins.

[91] Stephen Covey's *Seven Habits* said it.
Harvard said it https://www.hbs.edu/faculty/Pages/item.aspx?num=2959
Google said it https://rework.withgoogle.com/blog/five-keys-to-a-successful-google-team/

Personnel function

The conventional Human Resources function is being transformed by the requirements of new ways of working and managing. Personnel staff have to go to the gemba, to work with departments and teams to understand what they do and what they need.

Changes in personnel management should be introduced in an agile manner, incrementing and experimenting, ensuring the models actually work in reality, and allowing the people doing the work to design the work.

In particular, we must move away from changes, especially structural reorganisations, being done _to_ staff, in a "big bang" manner. Such "reorgs" are almost always dysfunctional. They damage productivity and morale: they accrue culture debt.

Instead, reorganisation should be pulled by the teams doing the work, not pushed by management. Let employees experiment with new ways of working through temporary virtual teams and other collaborative networked ways of working. If it is better, they can ask for it to be formalised. Change to the organisational structure should be a process of continual incremental improvement, driven by those affected.

Some conventional HR is actively toxic. Don't assess people by numbers alone. Stop trying to beat people into defined standardised shapes. Stop using psychometric voodoo which has no scientific basis (or even worse, lie detectors). Stop trying to manipulate people with equally voodoo mind tricks (p42). Drop the inhumanity of sterile environments, open plan (or cubes), clean desks, and hotdesking. And don't lie.

Other big changes are in recruiting:

- Recruit for attitude[92] and aptitude, teach skills.
- Don't create positions and then look for the best fit. Recruit good people, then find teams for them where they add to the capability and fit the culture.
- Let teams determine who they need.

---

[92] We used to say "recruit for culture" but Dawie Olivier explained that this becomes a filter for group-think, reducing diversity.

Flourishing programme

Agile organisations are looking to the Personnel staff to make a more positive contribution to organisational culture: to foster "happiness", staff satisfaction and retention. "Chief Happiness Officer" is a thing. We encourage organisations to have what we call a Flourishing[93] Programme, to ensure staff are thriving. It promotes:

- physical and mental wellbeing in the workplace.

- sense of community and belonging.

- collaboration and teamwork.

- shared values and purpose.

- satisfaction with recognition and reward.

- communication and celebration of success.

- a sense of fun and play.

Skills not Roles

Agile thinking presents a challenge to conventional HR because it looks at the mix of skills in a team, rather than defining specific roles for staff with standardised job descriptions. Work can no longer be described by job descriptions. It requires greater fluidity for teams to self-organise. It is more important to understand the skills profiles of teams, and help them to develop and recruit to meet their needs for capability.

We look at the aggregate skills of the team to meet all the needs for capability of the team, not the skills of any individual, because we don't assign any individual to one particular role. The team between them need to cover the capabilities. If we still call them roles it's a different concept of "role". If there is a gap for a particular skill, one team member may train another to increase the coverage, or several team members may go get training, or the team may recruit a new member.

In a conventional organisation, managers can assign an individual to play a role and do a certain task. But in an agile organisation, teams will

---

[93] We got the word "flourishing" from Jacqui Maguire, Clinical Psychologist, in her keynote at the ITx conference in Wellington in 2018. It is a better word than "happiness".

determine how they assign the work to individuals. This does not mean that the manager has no effect on the allocation of work: the manager provides policy, and they can give advice about the group's decision.

In an organisation accustomed to command-and-control culture, we must work hard to establish the first self-organising team, and train them to work in new ways, focused on skills not positions. Then protect them and give them space to succeed.

KPIs

Another important factor that helps changing culture is to change the way to measure employees, their Key Performance Indicators (KPIs).

> "Tell me how you measure me, and I will tell you how I will behave"
>
> - Elivahu Goldratt

Every KPI distorts behaviour: people work to maximise a metric they are judged on, either consciously or unconsciously. And no KPI ever perfectly reflects what you are trying to achieve.

A similar mechanism is OKRs, Objectives and Key Results, which uses a simple statement to tie an objective to a set of KPIs. This has the same distorting problem, although at least it is a set of metrics, and it is usually implemented to more frequently review the metrics than traditional KPIs are.

So, make sure you evaluate employees on a portfolio of metrics, e.g. a balanced scorecard (see "Measure progress", p238). Better still, don't manage by numbers; manage by knowing what is going on. You can drive a car without a dashboard.

Shu-Ha-Ri

In the Japanese martial art of aikido, there is the concept of *shu-ha-ri*, a form of learning progression.

Shu: The student follows the rules of a given method precisely, without addition or alteration. Follow tradition. Apply known solutions.

Ha: The student learns theory and principles of the technique. Become free from tradition. Think for yourself, apply theories to create new solutions.

Ri: The student creates their own approaches and adapts technique to circumstance. Transcend tradition. Create new theories.[94]

This can be loosely mapped to other concepts such as the four levels of learning, Tom Graves[95] model of learning, and the Cynefin model[96]:

	Learning levels	Graves		Cynefin
Shu	Unconsciously incompetent	Trainee 10-100 hours	"follow the instructions ..."	Simple
	Consciously incompetent	Apprentice 100-1000 hours	"learn the theory"	Simple and Complicated
Ha	Consciously competent	Journeyman 1000-10,000 hours	"it depends..."	
Ri	Unconsciously competent	Expert 10,000+ hours	"nothing is certain..."	Simple to Chaotic

[94] *The Digital Practitioner Body of Knowledge*™ https://publications.opengroup.org/s185

[95] http://weblog.tetradian.com/2013/01/28/over-certainties-of-certification/

[96] Graves would be unhappy about me doing that, as he strongly differentiates his own SCAN model from Cynefin.

Graves suggests the following capability for each level:

Trainee	Work instructions; application of work-instructions in live practice; how to identify when to escalate to someone with greater experience.
Apprentice	Shared terminology; theory behind work-instructions (various levels of theory); links between theory and practice; reasoning from the particular to the general.
Journeyman	Complexity, ambiguity, uncertainty, probability, possibility; adaptation from the general to the particular (context-specific).
Master	Practical application in unique contexts, in multiple and often interleaving (recursive) timescales.

Beware of the Dunning-Kruger[97] effect: self-confidence peaks when people learn something new. The little knowledge they have acquired makes them not know what they don't know: they're unconsciously incompetent. They don't know how subtle and complex it is, to implement agile management or organisational advancement.

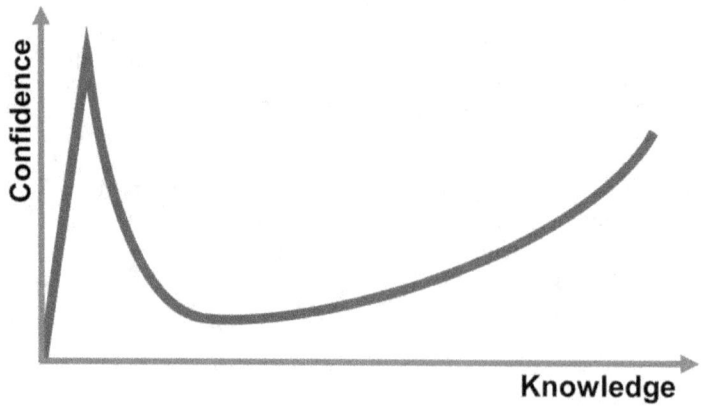

[97] *Unskilled and Unaware of It: How Difficulties in Recognizing One's Own Incompetence Lead to Inflated Self-Assessments,* Journal of Personality and Social Psychology, 1999

Seniority and salary bands

Job Descriptions no longer work. Work shouldn't be categorised into bands or levels to determine pay. People need to be rewarded for the value they create or enable.

Conventional management bestows authority and respect based on seniority of age, tenure, and hierarchy. In agile organisations, respect is earned based on behaviour and capability. Respect isn't demanded, it is given. Pay and promotion should be based on performance and value delivered, and/or mastery of craft, not length of service or "rank". Career paths aren't about climbing the "slippery pole' hierarchy any more; they're about a series of experiences which grow the individual.

If managers talk one set of values and reward another, good behaviour is discouraged.

The HR department needs to establish effective reward policies. That is, incentives and rewards need to be tied to personal worth, and those who receive them need to see it as fair treatment. If the calculation is inexplicable for individuals, or the result is beyond their control, it means they do not have any motivational impact. Money is not the only motivation, but it is a powerful demotivator.

Performance reviews

Evaluate performance regularly throughout the year to ensure employees understand clearly how they perform their work to achieve the desired goals under specified standards.

When consulting for a client which has more than ten thousand employees working in more than ten locations, we were surprised that every year, they have nearly 50% of employees rated as "outstanding". However, the average labour productivity is quite low. Digging deeper, we found that every year this organisation rewards workers according to their skills, following of rules, and commitment to the organisation. They rewarded skilled workers who are not good, just finished the job at an average level, yet during the year they did not violate the rules, did not get sick, and did enough work.

Having said that, performance is as much about behaviour and values as it is about productivity: the end does not justify the means – it's not 1980 anymore. Rewarding the wrong things is not only ineffective in encouraging workers but also makes good employees feel unfairly treated. An organisation should have performance feedback and targeted criteria that both managers and employees understand.

Make sure employees know their work is appreciated when they perform well, and discuss how they continue to develop their skills. Linking performance evaluations with pay is of course useful, but employees are also motivated by job satisfaction, empowerment, and especially a feeling of being respected and valued. You can't substitute money for those.

Annual performance reviews are not the same thing. There is a place in some contexts for these rituals, but accept that they are an odd way for two adults to communicate, they encode command-and-control, and they don't work for everyone. Some organisations are abandoning the practice of individual annual performance reviews entirely, realising that they are often theatre, and do more harm than good. They prefer real-time feedback; or even to review the team not the individual. If somebody is not performing, the team will take steps to resolve that themselves or will escalate to management. Dealing with unproductive individuals should not require putting everybody through an unproductive ritual.

Performance management

The performance management process for individuals is not only essential for business activities but also important in developing relationships between employees. Equally it can be damaging, creating culture debt; if you don't do it well, don't do it at all.

Having a clear performance management plan creates a strong message to employees that the organisation invests in their professional development and career development - an important factor that reinforces motivation and compassion, and builds loyalty of employees.

On the other hand, performance management of under-performing staff is just as important, perhaps even more so in an agile organisation. Too often when individuals are not performing or their behaviour is bad, managers lock down the whole team with controls and constraints, punishing everybody for the behaviour of a few.

Performance management is not the same as "managing out". Firing people is a blunt instrument - violence which traumatises those who remain. It's a last resort not a positive cultural tool. You better be sure that everybody who you want to stay agrees with the firing decision.

Firing is expensive. As well as the cost of the exit process, you lose institutional knowledge, relationships, and acquired skills. Then recruiting is expensive, a massive cost in time and money, and you still never really know what you've got until long after they start. You think you will get somebody better, more ideal, but it is hard to actually know that until it is too late.

It is usually better to work with who you've got. Build the staff you have instead of seeking some elusive idealised employee. Agile is inclusive of diversity and plays to the strengths of the individual. Love them and be loyal. Nobody is a perfect "fit". People have a diversity of views. Don't sit in judgement of who's got your culture and who hasn't.

> "Value human effort not dispense with it"
>
> - Tim O'Reilly

The need to fire someone is as often a sign of bad management as it is a sign of a bad person. That's what this whole book is about: fix the system to change the behaviour. People come around.

One of our clients used to have too many checks and monitoring on processes, including financial and accounting procedures and approval processes. These controls emerge over time, growing more and more because of the mistakes people have made before. Eventually they become so much that it makes work nearly impossible. The work system becomes clogged by controls: they are stopping the flow.

We convinced them to simplify approvals. They took large numbers of sign-offs out of the work system, especially limiting how high in the hierarchy they had to go to sign off on trivial things. They can show direct benefit from time savings and accelerated rate of work.

This control culture comes from not believing in goodness of individuals. Just because one person had bad behaviour or mistakes in the past, everyone must be punished forever. Good managers should set their team free and then performance-manage the problem individuals. This is what people-managers get paid for.

This can be a challenge in environments of modern labour legislation or heavy unionisation. The protections tend to favour the employee even when their performance is poor. In such situations, managers need to rely more on peer pressure and transparency to modify behaviour. In the worst case, we have to get so good that we can carry them.

Mental health

Good mental health is valuable to an organisation. Those where they care for workers' mental health are more effective, reducing absenteeism and increasing productivity. When mental health improves, morale is better and job satisfaction is higher.

Patrick
@PatJD

Follow

EVERY COMPANY: We'd like to promote mental health in the workplace.

EMPLOYEES: How about hiring more people so we feel less pressured & increase our pay so we can keep up with the spiraling cost of living so we're not so stressed out.

EVERY COMPANY: No not like that. Try Yoga.

8:43 PM - 20 Mar 2019

There are two aspects to mental health in the workplace. One is ensuring the general well-being of everybody and not creating an unhealthy environment that damages them. The other is allowing for the fact that a large proportion of personnel have mental health issues and disabilities that we should cater for, just as much as physical ones.

Embrace diversity. Mental variations that are considered psychological disorders by some are considered difference by others, often including the "sufferers" themselves. For example, some consider their autism to be a more advanced evolutionary level. Others see their disorder as not all bad, a mixed blessing. Some schizophrenics embrace the creativity it brings. Some manic depressives enjoy the bursts of energy. Some sociopaths use their detachment to get results and make hard decisions that have to be made. Nobody is truly normal, on the zero point. Value everybody's contribution to the creative energy and adaptability of your organisation.

Many of us can experience psychological issues - stress or anxiety, even depression, disturbed episodes, disorders, or breakdown - at some point in our lives, reportedly about a third of us.

There are several things that the workplace can do to support and help staff deal with permanent or passing psychological problems, and thereby gain advantages and opportunities, in the same way we do when we accommodate physical illnesses or disabilities.

Consider whether the organisation's culture, policy, and practice are doing these things well[98]:

Does your organisation have a culture of respect for good deeds in both formal and informal ways?

Are staff encouraged and conditioned to exercise at work?

Do people have the opportunity to learn new skills?

In working groups, do members respect each other?

Do managers have a good relationship with their subordinates?

Are personal conflicts handled well in the workplace?

Is there a policy and measures to prevent bullying, harassment, and discrimination? Is action taken to deal with incidents and support victims?

Is psychological illness talked about openly, without stigma?

Are mental disabilities accommodated in the same way as physical ones?

Resilience

Not only must we design systems to be resilient (and antifragile), but managers should build a resilient culture. Failure is a normal part of progress, and sometimes the failure isn't small.

Our organisation must survive failure, our employees must be able to bounce back. Mental resilience is as important as systems resilience. We need to build change resilience in our staff so that they cope with the constant state of change of the current world.

An extreme example of building resilience is *kobayashi maru*, an exercise to test the resilience of a team: a no-win scenario, a test of one's character or a solution that involves redefining the problem and managing an insurmountable scenario gracefully.[99]

---

[98] *The Five Ways to Wellbeing at Work Toolkit* https://www.mentalhealth.org.nz
[99] Wikipedia

Burnout

Don't run systems at 100% of capacity and don't do it to people either. They need rest and recreation. It's great when everyone pulls together to work long hours or weekends to achieve some special goal that they are committed to. It's not great when it happens often or becomes the norm.

If a team completes work *ahead* of schedule what should we do? Instead of pulling more work, how about celebration, team building, or a planning session at the pub?

Exhausted people are not productive people. Morale goes down and error rates go up. In the worst case, they literally work themselves to death, which the Japanese call *karoshi*. It should be obvious that this is completely unacceptable in any workplace and yet it seems it bears reminding ourselves that the impact of work on the well-being of the employees is the responsibility of the employer.

Good managers understand that everyone has limits and there are different limits for each person. Good managers understand their employees, and show respect for them by keeping an eye on whether they are stressed or exhausted. Don't take high performers for granted: they're the most likely to burn themselves out. Encourage employees to take care of each other and make them feel comfortable telling their managers if one of their colleagues needs help.

Review 2

Come to www.agilemanagers.club for answers, discussion, and more questions.

Revision

1. How is servant manager style different from conventional management?

2. How important is continual improvement?

3. Who leads an Agile team?

4. What is gemba?

5. How does conventional HR need to change?

6. How do we make finance and procurement agile?

7. Can we be agile if we have outsourced?

8. What are some instinctual "lizard brain" aspects of managing people?

9. Why is mental health so important?

Contemplation

1. Do agile easy of working really reduce risk? What's risky for your organisation?

2. What's wrong with flipping the hierarchy? Can you imagine yourself as a gardener?

3. Do your personnel systems allow for fluid job descriptions and self-organising teams?

4. How supportive of mental health is your organisation?

Action

1. What are the biggest threats to the wellbeing of your staff?

2. Which teams are already agile? Which team could try it?

3. What management behaviour are you going to work on changing in yourself first?

3. New Ways of Working

In the new ways of working, we use many methods - a bag of tools - which fall under our broad umbrella of "new ways". We at Teal Unicorn stay out of ideological wars as to which is better. All tools are useful in some context. All organisations should mix, match, and adapt to best suit the requirements of the situation, their culture, and the context.

A warning: don't let any method (of managing or working) become dogma. The Agile philosophers passionately oppose codification (or certification) for this reason. As soon as somebody reads the nine "immutable" principles of SAFe[100] out to a meeting (actual story), you're in trouble. It's not scripture.

To resist dogma:

- mix methods, don't make one "the one" above others, pick and choose useful bits.

- don't use a method as a label, don't define yourselves by it, don't say "we are a Lean organisation, or "we are transforming with Agile", use your own labels.

- experts should provide advice, not leadership or control.

- de-program zealots after training (see Dunning-Kruger).

We group these ways of working into three categories:

Improvement

  o   Kaizen
  o   Improvement Kata, PDCA, OODA, 5 Whys
  o   Complex systems theory (Cynefin, Cook, Wardley)
  o   Human error, and Checklists
  o   Case Management
  o   Standard+Case (our own model)

System flow

  o   Lean, and Value Stream Mapping
  o   Theory of Constraints
  o   DevOps

---

[100] Scaled Agile Framework, p120

Agility

- o Design Thinking
- o Agile
- o Backlogs and User Stories
- o Agile models (Modern Agile, Heart of Agile, Agile Fluency, AgileSHIFT)
- o Kanban
- o Scrum

It's not the purpose of this book to go into these new ways of working in any depth, but in this Section 3 we have reflections and advice specifically for managers. Before reading, if you are not familiar with the above ideas and methods, you can find a brief description in the Appendix.

In Teal Unicorn's *Diggers* simulation workshop, attendees learn new ways of working through making little toy excavators/diggers.

www.twohills.co.nz/diggers

Improvement

Continual improvement is foundational to advancement of the organisation in all ways, not just getting to new ways of working and management. It is the basis of any healthy culture. It is another way of saying we are a learning organisation, that we change incrementally, that we are agile. learn the basics of Continual Improvement, Kaizen, Toyota Kata, PDCA, Lean, safety, and other improvement ideas elsewhere. Here we discuss some of the management considerations.

Root cause

Teal Unicorn are not fans of the "Five Whys" method of understanding a problem. The idea of the Five Whys technique is to keep asking "why?" to dig deeper to root cause, and the premise is that at least five iterations are required. It implies several fallacies which are worth examining.

One fallacy is that there is a single root cause to anything. This is not true in complex systems, which are always broken: it is a combination of causes that results in any condition, a combination which may be unlikely to ever occur again.

Another fallacy is that, even if we recursively dig down multiple paths to find multiple causes, there is any bottom to that enquiry. In the real world you can dig forever until you reach profound philosophical questions. Ultimately the things you designate as causes are chosen for political reasons not logical ones. We advise that you just identify as many contributing causes as seems practical, add them to your improvement backlog, and move on. Techniques of Safety Culture (p275) break this down in more sophisticated ways.

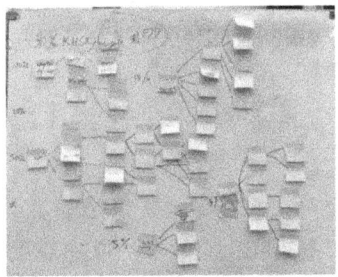

Dealing with complexity

John Hagel pulls seven principles[101] out of Taleb's book *AntiFragile* that could serve as a manifesto for dealing with complexity:

1. Stick to Simple Rules – don't attempt to model complexity, but rather let humans fill the gap with real intelligence.

2. Decentralise. See "Social networks", below.

3. Develop layered systems. e.g. In a service desk, we use the Level 0 to 3 layered support model, plus the Standard+Case (p278) layers as another dimension across those.

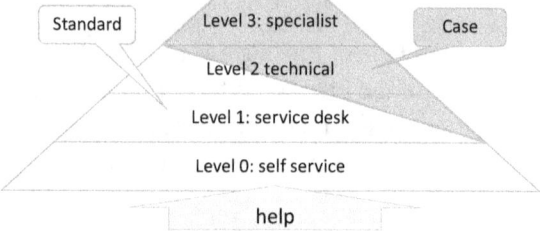

4. Build in redundancy. Avoid the temptation to reduce action to the minimum necessary to do the job, in a misguided attempt to reduce costs. Firemen clean fire engines and run practice drills. Lean is not case-work's friend.

5. Resist urge to suppress randomness – uniformity is not the goal. Diversity produces the best ideas for future standardisation.

6. Ensure everyone has skin in the game – it is about shared responsibility, not elimination of any need to know who is responsible.

7. Give higher status to practitioners rather than theoreticians – the theories are mostly wrong, but the practitioners are the ones who know it. Experienced case workers know better than just about anyone else.

---

[101] https://edgeperspectives.typepad.com/edge_perspectives/2013/04/getting-stronger-through-stress-making-black-swans-work-for-you.html
Keith Swenson brought this to our attention https://social-biz.org/2013/04/15/pull-systems-are-antifragile/

Social networks

We can see[102] the Cynefin model (p273) in a fresh way, from the perspective of the social networks within each situation type.

We tend to find decentralised networks in all states except Simple/Obvious. The Simple situation tends to suit a hierarchal "star" network: central management of workers working on assigned tasks, i.e. the standardised approach.

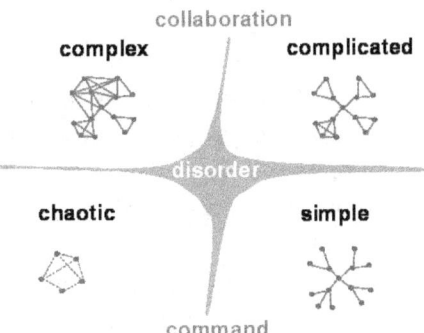

The Complicated situations tend to have central orchestration as well as local networks, whereas the Complex is typified by multiple networks of workers coming together to explore and develop ideas.

In the Chaotic situation such as an emergency, networks are loosely coupled trying to gain control and move it into another state.

So, in situations that are unfamiliar or unknown we need to reduce the central command and control, and allow workers to decentralise and collaborate locally. In situations that are known we can take central control and use standard responses. In chaotic situations we try to find control.

Automation

We too often leap to technological solutions to difficult work problems, but automation does have a role in the new ways of working.

If we want to improve "velocity through quality", people need to work faster and better. They need to be both more efficient and more effective. Manual processes can only achieve this up to a point, then humans hit their capability limit: efficiency and effectiveness start to get traded off one for the other. Automation can break that impasse.

---

[102] Managing Structured and Unstructured Processes Under the Same Umbrella, A.Manuel, in How Knowledge Workers Get Things Done, p88

Standardised

Standard+Case (p278) is Teal Unicorn's contribution to the field of complex systems and simplifying work, conceived by Rob in 2010[103]. It can be thought of as a simpler model than Cynefin (p273). Standard+Case is a method for categorising and resolving any sort of repeated or transactional work. You can only industrialise that which you can standardise, i.e. make known: described, predictable, and repeatable. Only some of the world can be standardised. Some situations will always be unfamiliar due to change, or unpredictable due to complexity. Standard+Case is a synthesis of conventional "standard[104]" process-centric approaches to responding, with Case Management (p277), a discipline well-known in industry sectors such as health, social work, law, and policing.

If we then overlay Standard+Case with the Cynefin model, we get this:

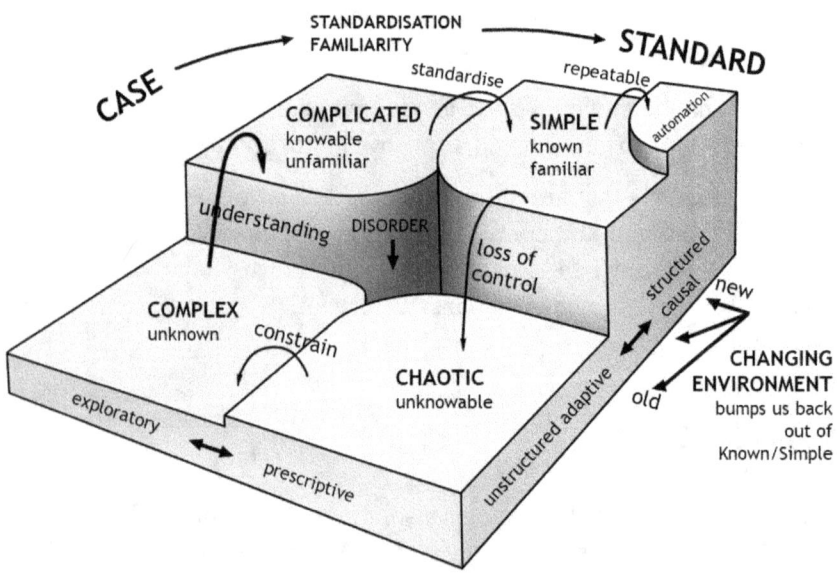

Note[105] the tiny "automation" slice in the top right corner of the above diagram. We can (currently) only automate that which is defined and

---

[103] http://www.basicsm.com/standard-case

[104] The IT framework called ITIL refers to simple known work which has been described and documented, as "standard" because there are standard ways of responding.

[105] Also note the step down from chaotic to complex, which many people find counter-intuitive. The vertical axis is "negentropy": energy, order. It takes energy to make a system chaotic, it settles into complex. Dave Snowden himself made this improvement to the picture. He approved of this 3D view of Cynefin.

repeatable. We must standardise to automate. Automation only removes the boring stuff, toil and drudgery, not other work; so that people can focus on the novel complicated new situations, which is a more interesting and valuable use of their time.

Newer forms of automation involve machine learning (mis-named "AI, artificial intelligence, robots") and access to big data. Which means automation not only does drudge work but it starts to extend the capability of the human - it makes us super-human[106].

Self-service

The real value of automation kicks in not when a task is automated so that the same person can do it, but when that automation is made available to others so that they don't need to ask that person to do the work, they can self-serve instead. This takes all of the wait times out of workflow. Those who are given access to the automation may then build on it with higher-level automation of their own.

Risks

Beware though, there are risks to automation.

First, people forget – or never learn – how to do the work manually. We lose the ability to function in emergency, when automation fails us. And we forget what the automation is doing so we are unable to change the automation.

Second, automation can reduce agility. Automation technology is less flexible than humans. Agility is not about how fast we can work: it's about how fast we can change how we work. Automation can slow that change down. We sacrifice agility on the altar of velocity. Over-automation is a risk: there is some optimal level of automation where the gains do not outweigh the costs, as Tesla found in 2017 when they over-automated their car factories. "...the world's best carmakers, the Japanese, try to limit automation because it is expensive and is statistically inversely correlated to quality. Their approach is to get the process right first, then bring in the robots – the opposite of Musk's."[107]

---

[106] Please don't waste our time with the idea that these new technologies will supplant humans: see http://www.itskeptic.org/content/automation-best

[107] Max Warburton, Bernstein https://www.businessinsider.com.au/tesla-robots-are-killing-it-2018-3

System flow

The heart of system thinking for managers is to understand flow of work. Here are some considerations for managers, not a comprehensive review of flow theory.

Value streams

It's a complex mess of flow in the real world, not a nice clean stream (except in production-line factories). But modelling it as a stream is often useful, to simplify the situation. it is important to do value stream mapping (p280) early, to get the big picture.

Here are some initial issues you want to look for when mapping any value stream:

- A delay slows the flow.

- An obstacle limits the flow.

- There is excess inventory at one point.

Track a piece of work through the flow. Graph the time spent adding value in each step, and all the other time as waiting idle (a form of waste). The resulting square-wave timeline is always enlightening. The ratio of this value time to the total time is the efficiency of the flow. People are often horrified at how low it is, how much time work spends lying around.

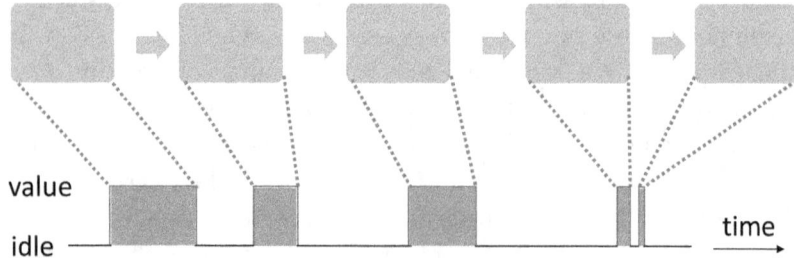

Although value stream maps were originally applied in factories' processes, these principles can be applied anywhere.

Blocked

One CIO had the policy "Blocked is not an acceptable state". Whilst that is a bit harsh, the point is good: waiting on somebody else is not an excuse to do nothing. Especially, we shouldn't hide work in a wait state, off our reporting.

The person blocked should collaborate with the blocker to move it along; or break the work up into smaller pieces until something is complete; or remove the dependency; or find a way to flow around; or escalate it as an impediment to work.

Keep momentum going.

Cadence

Having a cadence to our work, a beat, a "takt", is useful to help achieve smooth flow of work. A cadence:

- makes work predictable, more manageable.

- helps coordinate teams. ("Harmonic" cadence means teams may not all work at the same beat, but they work at multiples of it).

- encourages us to break work down into smaller, similar-sized units that all work within the same cycle time.

- makes it more visible if we are trying to do too much in a cycle.

- makes work time-bound, which keeps people on schedule.

Try to stick to cadence: keep the time fixed, vary other things.

A cadence can also feel remorseless, a hamster-wheel of work. Break cadence occasionally (planned and predictably), to give people relief from the machine, e.g. a quarterly pattern of six 2-week sprints plus a week doing planning, improvement, and fun.

Teams should have as much freedom as possible to set and plan their own cadence.

Value T

"Value T" is our own term for the important concept that a value stream within the organisation can have as its "customer" a broader value stream in the same organisation, into which it delivers one step or component.

We draw these at right angles to each other, a "T".

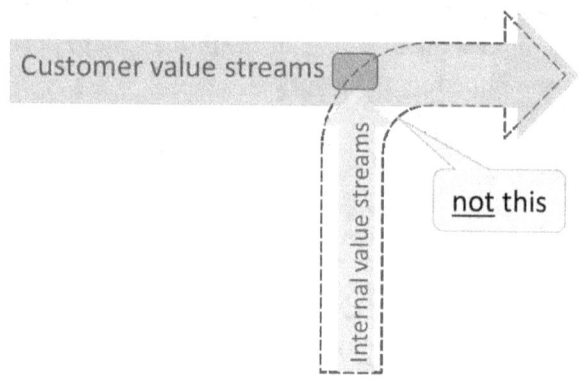

This concept helps clear up confusion where internal teams try to define their value all the way to the external customer, which results in a complicated and confusing value stream map that "goes round the corner" on this diagram. The same idea is depicted differently in the diagram in "Service and Product Management", p 294.

Having an external customer focus, and understanding that your local value stream goes to an internal customer as part of a broader value network, are not mutually exclusive.

Value Networks

Much of the world's work does not flow in linear streams, unless you zoom in close. Step back and most organisations are value *networks* of interconnected streams, a little like a braided river.[108]

---

[108] Thanks to our fellow Kiwi, Mark Whiting, for this analogy.

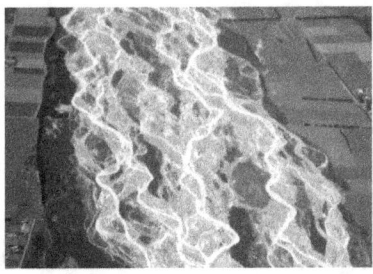

It is a useful analogy. There is a flow direction from mountain to sea, but the exact pattern of streams can never be mapped, and it is constantly changing. Even the bounds are vague, or vary depending on how you define them. If you zoom in close enough, you get a single linear stream. If there is a constraint, the flow usually finds its way around it - it takes a huge obstruction to actually dam the river.

What the river analogy lacks is flatness: value networks are multi-directional, it doesn't all flow one way. Customers participate, suppliers consume as well as supply, feedback loops constantly modify flow. Value does not flow in one direction – we *co-create* value.

Hoshin Kanri

Hoshin kanri, also known as *catchball*, is a way of flowing the central vision and strategy down through the organisation, and ensuring feedback flows back up.

At Teal Unicorn we expand the concept to also flow policy down through the organisation. Policy is a product of our vision equally as important as the strategy. It is essential when you free employees that you also equip them with clear policy guidelines along with a shared vision and strategy. (see "Policy governance framework", p271).

If you set people free, for their safety and your organisation's, you must let them know what the clear boundaries are and what they are authorised to do.

This is an Alpha-management (p48) concept. As we move to Beta, people will collaborate to establish their own policies.

Agility

As we have discussed, agility is the ability to quickly change how we work in response to changing conditions and demands (see the appendix on Agile, p283). To summarise, we:

- do smaller units of work, usually in cadenced iterations.

- do them faster.

- experiment and explore because work is unknown until we do.

- learn from every unit we do, with observation and feedback.

- reflect and improve how we work on every iteration.

- do less, simplify.

- work on the right things to maximise value.

There are some important Agile considerations for managers: visualisation, prioritisation, velocity, estimation, scale, and large events.

Visualisation

One of the first things to do in advancement is to visualise work, if it is not already visualised:

- **map the flow**, with Value Stream Mapping (p280) and other workflow methods.

- **graph the work,** with kanban (p292) and other graphical methods.

Current generally accepted practice is to visualise physically, on vertical surfaces, i.e. put it on the walls. Digital tools are useful, but there is no substitute for being able to see and touch the work. And everybody can see it. A common collective term for all sorts of work on vertical surfaces is wall-boarding, but we say "work murals". You may also like "wallwork", "information radiator", or "drywall spreadsheets".

Photograph the visualisation regularly in case anything happens (the Great Cleaner Disaster of '18). Some teams keep work both on a physical wall and in a digital tool. They manually synchronise the information because they see the benefits of both a physical wall version and a digital version. It's not redundant when each adds different value. Software is available to do the synchronisation for you[109].

Remote workers present a challenge. Teams overcome this:

- send photos.

- maintain a wall at each location.

- point a remote-controlled, zoomable webcam at the work.

- webconference in to stand-ups, and ask locals to move cards for them.

- use a digital tool as well as the physical.

You may have to deal with the building-facilities barbarians who want to make you work in a sterile environment with pristine walls (p121). Wear them down, be subversive, reclaim the walls for work:

- use low-stick adhesives: "Command" brand hooks" or "white-tac" (the blue stuff stains). We had success with one Command hook under a foamboard to take the weight, and white-tac across the top to hold it.

- use low-stick tape to make lines or labels.

- use "SuperSticky" Post-It notes (the normal ones fall off).

- sneak drawing pins in up high where the hole can't be seen, or hook paperclips over ceiling structure, then hang foamboards, posters, or decorations on fishing line.

- use old cube partitions as free-standing vertical surfaces.

- build three-sided pillars out of foam-board about 2 metres high and half a metre on each side; tape bottles of water inside the bottom for stability; and use them free-standing as work surfaces.

Another variant of work murals is an *obeya room*: a space where strategy and programmes of work are made visible. An obeya room is the macro view, the "bridge of the ship"; a kanban board is the local view.

---

[109] Three synchronisation tools we have heard of are Truffler, WallSync, and Agile Cards Scanner. We haven't tried any of them.

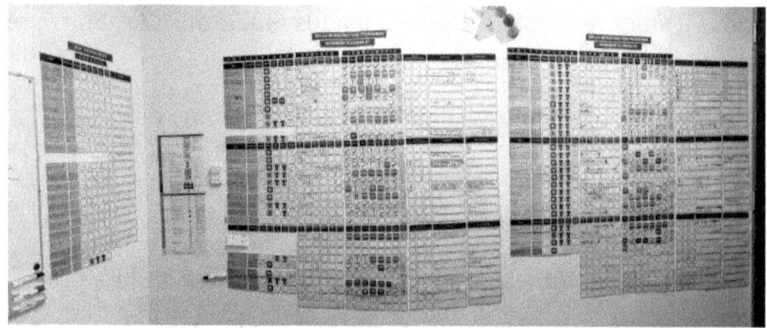

Strategy of an organisation or a business unit can be visualised in many ways. One way is Goldratt's Strategy and Tactics Tree. Most organisations have their own ideas.

Wall murals can also include many other ideas such as radar of incoming opportunities and threats (p117), or celebration of success:

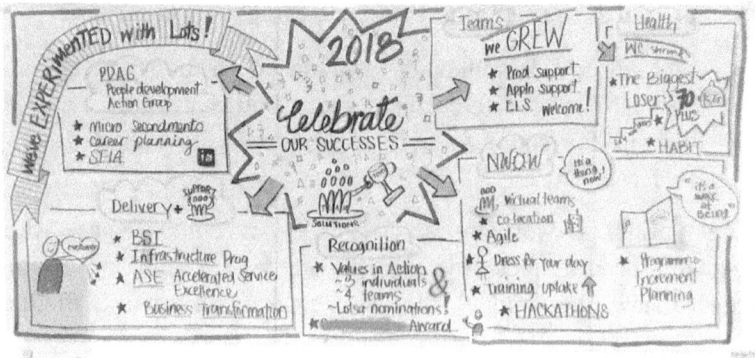

Prioritisation

The key to working on the right things is to have somebody who owns the work prioritise the work. It is important that everybody understands that the owner's prioritisation does not absolve them from ensuring we are doing valuable work. We all keep line-of-sight to the customer, and evaluate our work against their perception of value.

Prioritising work can be challenging. For example, in the real world there may be multiple product owners of the work that the team is doing. In this case, we want the owners to form themselves into a group with a single representative, so that they can collaborate amongst themselves to form a single voice for the team. This is often problematic. As another example, organisations want work prioritised based on some objective metric. This is often glibly specified as "business value", but assigning an outcome value in dollars to a small unit of work is challenging and possibly mythical[110], and an overhead.

"Cost of Delay", the cost of waiting for a piece of work, is becoming a popular way of prioritising. But cost can only be assigned in contexts where we know from experience what the delay costs. This isn't always true, especially when innovating. Allocating costs to small units faces similar challenges as assigning value, and requires significant effort.

The MoSCoW technique classifies work into Must Do, Should Do, Could Do, and Won't Do, which is a start but still doesn't sort the work within those categories.

If you map your stories to larger groupings of "features" and "epics", then prioritising those can drive the priority for the individual stories.

Some teams prioritise on effort, to do the smallest tasks first. Some prioritise whatever can confidently be done. These might seem odd, but they are low-cost heuristics that short-circuit arguments about more complex measures of priority. JFDI: just do something and, in the process, we will learn more to help with prioritising in the next iteration. And, hey, we will have done something.

There are other sophisticated techniques outside the scope of this book (and our experience). We offer these tips:

---

[110] See *The Art Of Business Value*, Mark Schwartz

- Use human judgement. Real priority is a complex mix of many factors that no algorithm is going to capture. But beware of biases and "common sense" (p68). Support with data.

- Use multiple voices. A collective will always do better than an individual, although one individual must have final say.

- Only the Clear-Fine work at the top of the backlog (p287) has to be well prioritised.

- Do whatever works for the team. There is no reason to enforce a method if the team is satisfied with the current way.

- Re-assess the method constantly.

Velocity

Velocity is a measure of how much work a team gets done in a given interval of time. Velocity is measured by a team in their own units of work estimation. The team estimates the effort of work, nobody else. Teams should not obsess about velocity. Try calling it Effort Budget instead, to make it less glamorous[111].

There is an elegant quid pro quo about velocity: the Product Owner agrees to respect it and not try to overload the team, and in return the team agrees to improve the velocity over time.

The team will adjust methods and units of estimation over time based on experience. Reporting and trending must cope with this: governance is not a reason to ossify process. It is up to the scrum-master to try to track velocity trend over time when units change.

Velocity is used to predict how much work can be done in the next iteration. Use it to prevent overburden: to limit work taken on. You cannot and must not use velocity to compare the performance of different teams. They work on different things. The moment you use velocity as a measure of a team it will get gamed, and lose its value. Therefore, there is no such thing as standardising velocity units across teams. Don't do it. Don't let managers do it. As soon as velocity becomes a KPI it is dead.

---

[111] This suggestion is from Diana Larsen

Estimation

Estimation of small units of work is useful at a local level to serve the needs of the team looking at work to be done soon, i.e. velocity. It is not useful to consolidate across a larger scale, or to predict further out in time, or to cost work.

It is amazing the human ability to estimate work without any precise units of measure. Is it small, medium or large? Most teams can answer this, and be close most of the time. There are a number of scales for such estimating, including t-shirt size: S,M,L,XL; and Fibonacci sequence: 1,2,3,5,8,13. We like[112] geometric progression: 1,2,4,8. (If it is a 16, break it up).

Estimation Poker is a useful tool for finding team agreement on an estimate.

There is heated debate over the validity of estimating Agile work. We regard the "No Estimates" movement as having some valid points but lacking pragmatism. Estimation of work is useful even if unreliable. The whole point of Agile is to accept imperfection of process in the cause of higher quality of product. Estimates become more certain, and hence more useful, the more familiar and predictable the work is. We can only argue against any estimates when pioneering into entirely new designs and technologies where novelty is high and hence predictability is very low. Even then, we have a "cone of uncertainty" which narrows as we proceed, making estimation more viable over time.

Agile on a large scale

Agile has been shown to scale, being used already at the organisational level in very large entities, managing hundreds or even thousands of teams. In fact, Agile naturally scales, thanks to the fluidity, network structure, and lack of hierarchy.

Agility is made easier if we can modularise our teams just as we break up what they work on. For example, layer them around customer experience, business processes, and technology systems[113]. As you break

---

[112] We think t-shirts don't have clear relative size, and 2,3,5 are too close together to get easy agreement

[113] *Agile at Scale*, D. Rigby, J. Sutherland, A. Noble https://hbr.org/2018/05/agile-at-scale

up the work structure into a "taxonomy" of work, you will identify hundreds of "products" for individual teams to work on. (Agile talks about "product" at the level of a single team of five people, whereas an organisation talks about much larger products, so we end up in the confusing situation where products are broken down into products.) Another aspect of Wardley's modelling (p274) is the concept[114] of pioneers, settlers, and town-planners, (or commandoes, infantry, and police) as another way of mapping the structure of your agile teams.

When we have many small teams all doing their work, managers get uncomfortable about coordination of it all. There are a number of methods for managing many small agile teams, such as:

- FAST Agile[115], using the OpenSpace technique.

- SAFe® Scaled Agile Framework[116] (If Scrum upsets Agile purists, you should see how they foam about SAFe. We regard it as the trainer wheels of legacy organisations venturing into Agile but not wanting to let go of structure and formality: it is a milestone when you outgrow SAFe)

- Disciplined Agile[117] (a less formalised structuring)

- LeSS Large Scale Scrum[118]

- Scrum@Scale[119]

- Nexus[120]

- Scrum of Scrums

- Kanban

Some of these are written for the IT context but all can be generalised for the organisation.

> "management is not just a team game, it is a game in which we have to fashion a team of teams, where the various individual teams exist in some suitable and mutually supportive relationship with each other."
>
> -   Andy Grove

---

[114] https://blog.gardeviance.org/2015/03/on-pioneers-settlers-town-planners-and.html
[115] http://www.fast-agile.com/
[116] Scaled Agile Framework and SAFe are registered trademarks of Scaled Agile, Inc
[117] https://disciplinedagileconsortium.org/
[118] https://less.works/
[119] https://www.scrumatscale.com/
[120] https://www.scrum.org/resources/scaling-scrum

Whatever we use, we must coordinate work across groups of teams somehow, in a collaborative manner, not by command.

There is a school of thought that if you need to scale Agile you are doing it wrong: that the work requirements should be sufficiently iterative and granular that scaling isn't needed: that you shouldn't make Agile bigger, you should make the work smaller. Perhaps once the whole organisation is behaving in an agile way this will be true.

Even further out, we should be able to define behaviours for teams in such a way that the macro behaviour of the organisation is emergent, in the same way that a colony of ants or bees work to a simple set of rules that create advanced behaviour on a large scale with no organisation. We aren't there yet, although concept like Promise Theory are getting close.

Collaborative ritual

In order to create a culture of sharing and collaboration, we need to connect across the siloes, the tribes, of the organisation. There are at least three general mechanisms to do this: communities of practice and of interest (p254); social communities and events; and collaborative rituals, which are more structured ways for people to work together to a result.

For example, a popular way to do Agile at scale is with "PIs". The term Program[me] Increments, or PI, comes from the Scaled Agile Framework® (SAFe). It refers to a slower broader planning cadence wrapped around a number of sprints, usually six two-week sprints giving a 12-week, or quarterly cycle. Once every PI cycle, there is a large meeting of all the teams with dependencies on each other, for a day or two, to plan the next 12 weeks, and especially to understand what everybody needs from each other. Bottleneck teams are soon identified.

Business, product, and strategy people make presentations, and programme managers pitch their initiatives. Then teams get down to planning, and more importantly agreeing, work for five sprints. The sixth sprint is an innovation and improvement sprint.

We believe such large-scale planning meetings are effective in large organisations with high levels of interdependencies. Modern organisations are supposed to be structured as many small independent units (divisions, teams, services, system, technology), but most established organisations don't have that luxury.

It is also an opportunity to have stakeholder groups "exhibit their wares", making the work teams aware of services and tools available.

However, there are other ways of planning and resolving dependencies. PIs are liable to become cumbersome and bureaucratic, especially all the planning and preparation leading up to them. Agile coaches joke that the best thing about SAFe is the day you don't need it any more.

The basic principle of bringing people together is a good one. Teal Unicorn have our own collective term for any such ritual: Community Collaboration (CC).

Our preferred ritual for large scale CC is OpenSpace Technology[121]. Don't be misled by the word "technology": this is about a self-organising CC, based on the observation that the break time is sometimes the most productive part of a workshop or conference. There are many variants collectively known as "unconferences". PI is useful for an organisation still taking its first steps into collaborative planning, but we should quickly grow to (or go directly to) OpenSpace as a more fluid, free, authorised method.

There is no pre-planned agenda, although we do gather information in advance. Participants dynamically set the agenda. Then we iterate through several cycles in parallel streams, addressing all questions on the agenda. Finally, we come together to discuss and close, and the participants write the proceedings.

There are other good models that we also use for participatory rituals, such as:

- Lean Coffee[122], a structured ritual to allow the participants to dynamically set the CC agenda.
- World Café[123].
- PechaKucha[124], Lightning Talks, or Ignite: each speaker gets a short time with self-advancing slides.

---

[121] Origin: https://www.openspaceworld.com/
Resources: https://openspaceworld.org
[122] http://leancoffee.org/
[123] http://www.theworldcafe.com/
[124] https://www.pechakucha.com/

- Kaizen (p271).
- Thinking tools such as brainstorming[125], pre-mortems[126], and Six Thinking Hats[127].
- Games and simulations (p199).
- Hacks (p246).
- Internal conferences (p252).

There is a J-curve (p190) with these rituals. Our rule of thumb is: all new activities take at least three iterations before they start to work well.

[125] Applied Imagination, A F Osborn

[126] "Pre-mortems" are a scenario planning tool: pretend it is a hypothetical post-mortem, and describe scenarios of how it failed.

[127] *Six Thinking Hats*, E. de Bono, (1985).

agile Product Management

The new ways of working want to align to the organisation's products, which drives increased demand for clear definition and good management of those products. Often, Lean or Agile thinking exposes the weakness in organisational Product Management (p294) and makes it no longer tolerable.

The roles of the product owners and product managers[128] become more important with Agile, to involve the organisation closely in work being done by teams servicing them.

Ironically, as we move to more distributed, autonomous, granular work, it makes it increasingly important to have centralised planning at the portfolio level across all the work. It is not enough to manage products; we must manage portfolios of products to prioritise and distribute resources across them. We can't do them all, we must manage and constrain demand.

agile Service Management

The Service Management (p294) community is moving fast to make itself more agile, in and out of IT.

The *VeriSM* body of knowledge[129] is the most notable non-IT agile Service Management framework, which is focused on digital products (Rob England, one of our authors, is a lead author of its core book[130]).

Within the IT community, its most famous service management framework, ITIL®, has released version 4 which embraces agility principles.

---

[128] What the terms Product Owner and Product Manager mean depends on who you ask and what reference they use. Good luck with that. We usually use Product Owner at the low level of the owner of one team's work, or a small number of related teams; and Product Manager as the owner of a higher-level aggregated product across many Product Owners. But whatever: go with what works for your organisation.

[129] https://verism.global/

[130] VeriSM - A service management approach for the digital age, Agutter, England, van Hove, Steinberg

Like Agile, another practice that came out of IT but now has much more general relevance is SIAM, Service Integration And Management (p116).

There is also a school of thought called "Agile Service Management" which refers to making our service management practices more agile, and doing that improvement in an agile way[131].

Project Management

It is important to address project management in the context of new ways of working.

In some sectors, the IT world for example, there is a particular problem with projects. Many of them fail. That is, they run over time or over budget or deliver poor quality outputs, or collapse completely. And IT is not alone in this. Many sectors struggle to do something new: military warships, medicines, railways, taxes, marketing promotions... Everyone building or changing anything should ponder this: the trouble comes when what we are building or changing is a complex system, when we don't know where it ends before we start.

If we are doing something simple, something where we can define the finished result fairly precisely (like a house, bridge, webpage, chocolate bar, this year's model of phone), usually because we have done something very like it before, then conventional project management looks like it works. Scope it, do a business case, get the money, requirements, design, build, accept and test, release/go-live, shakedown/warranty. Then we have little cakes and savouries for everyone, and we all go do something else. Information Technology calls it "waterfall" because each stage cascades irreversibly into the next, one step at a time, like a ...er... cataract, a series of waterfalls. IT people don't always do well at analogies.

Waterfall project management doesn't work for complex systems. In the real world, systems that look simple have a nasty habit of turning out to be complex when we get into them, especially anything with humans in it. When we impose fixed time, money, and deliverables, which is the classic project management formula, then the only other variable available to a project manager is the quality of the outputs. The moment

---

[131] Rob and Cherry are both Certified Agile Service Managers in this field.

they encounter anything at variance with the requirements and the business case (which they inevitably will, as these are complex systems), they either have to negotiate variation to time, cost, and scope, which is unpopular, or they compromise quality. The project cuts short testing, training, and documentation; and they start preparing a formal defect list to be heaved over the wall on delivery (we call it "dead cat syndrome" because it is just as unwelcome). We end up in the extraordinary position of being in the business of manufacturing defects which we formally deliver to our customer tied up with a ribbon, asking them to sign the defects off as delivered, then we deploy them.

This is clearly insane. So Agile changes the equation to say that we will fix the time, the money, and the quality; which means that the remaining variable is the deliverables. Traditional project management does not deal well with this: the fallacy of project management is that we are still building simple systems. It leads to the myth of "define/plan once and execute perfectly", which is impossible in the real world. Project Management led to the lunacy where you don't get your money until you commit to time, cost, and deliverables. All such business cases are theatre, ceremonial, a lie. We need to shed traditional project management ways of working for most things we do.

At its heart, agile Management is about redesigning ways of working from first principles to build without theatre or excessive ceremony. We build product where we iterate towards a hypothesis, exploring, failing, and incrementally growing a solution. That messes with governors' heads.

Here are some Agile principles that sit badly with conventional project management thinking:

1. No known defects - prioritise defects over new.

2. Bring the work to the teams. Stop disbanding and reforming teams.

3. Create a single stream of incoming work, a single backlog. Stop making workers prioritise across multiple backlogs with multiple owners – they can only lose.

4. Teams work to velocity. Don't overburden the work system. Limit WIP, never run people at 100% utilisation.

5. Delay making decisions and doing work until as late as possible – undeployed work goes stale.

6. Maximise the work not done.

7. Deliver in as small increments as possible.

8. Experiment and failure are how we work, all the time.

9. We don't know the end state until we get there.

10. You'll never get real quality built until those accountable for running it are those who build it.

Many arguments we encounter against this premise (that Project Management methodology sits badly with Agile) are ad hominem, about how only "juniors" or poor project managers have these problems. That may be the case but if only the strong survive your method, it's time you fixed your method.

The issue is not bad Project Management. It is that Project Management is an administrative tool, not an organisational construct. If you build an organisation out of projects, you build out of a construct that evaporates. All you have left is the droppings.

Product not project

The solution is to organise around product not project[132]. The conventional concept of a project has a number of dysfunctions which damage our agility. The generally-accepted better model is product flow: permanent teams aligned to products, who do streams of work for the lifetime of the product. We still manage surges of work through the organisation as projects, but they are events that happen, not work structures.

Organising around products has a number of benefits:

- it encourages a hub of people from all parts of the product lifecycle working together, instead of a linear model where each has their turn.

- it allows work in smaller, more frequent increments, increasing innovation.

- it enables continual improvement.

---

[132] Mik Kersten has written a very good book *Project to Product*, (Cherry has a signed copy!) although it is IT-centric.

- response is faster when a product unexpectedly needs to change.

- teams are stable, giving people a chance to learn to work together.

- it retains knowledge over the whole life of the product.

Build your organisation out of products. Don't change things in a big bang; do work incrementally over time. We need to have standing product teams, not temporary project teams. Bring the work to the team not the team to the work.

We consulted to a museum who embraced the principle of "product not project" right up to executive level. Their experience was of exhibits built by a project team who then disbanded, leaving nobody owning the specific exhibit, just functional managers owning slices of it; and no team accountable for maintaining and fixing the exhibit. Now each exhibit has an owner, and a team who maintain and improve it for its lifetime.

> "All systems are what emerges over its history of adaptation to stressors and how this cumulative experience positions / empowers each to be poised to adapt in near future = system-as-adapted, which never is the system as imagined in plans."
>
> - David Woods

Some work seems like it isn't related to a product, and still ought to be a project, but it turns out a standing team is still better. One client of ours made a capital investment to replace all the desktop computers. This would seem like a classic fixed-duration project, but it was much better executed as a standing Agile team who rolled out a small number of machines every week, working their way through locations, incrementally improving the process and the desktop design, and supporting the machines they had deployed. It took a little longer to complete that a waterfall project would have done, with a higher quality result at a lower cost, and they will never end: new staff, lost machines, and obsolescence mean the team is permanent. Big bridges often have a small standing team slowly painting them: when they get to the end they start again.

Another example was a project to upgrade server software that was long overdue for an update. Instead of doing it all at once, an Agile team worked their way through groups of the servers, improving and automating the upgrade process as they went. At the end of the servers, the team are now upgrade experts with automated processes they can repurpose to update other aging software.

One argument for doing things as projects is about recognising capital expenditure (capex) for accounting purposes: it's easier if projects are capex and everything else is operational expenditure (opex). Of course, it's never that clean when we do projects anyway, but capex can be realised without a project construct.

We do have particular problems with a lack of flexibility in government funding models, but governments are working as we speak to allow other models for assigning capex and opex. It's irrelevant anyway, it just means you need a funding buffer at some level between agile and project models. Solved problem.

The dysfunctions of Project Management are overcome by:

- pro**duct** portfolio management.
- good programme management.
- work organised by product not project.
- Lean/Agile ways of managing/working.
- Project Management becomes a tracking and coordination function.

Here is the final thought: waterfall project management doesn't work for building complex systems, but agile product development works just fine for building both complex and simple systems. Some people argue that you should do conventional project management when appropriate and agile product development when it's not. This bi-modal approach is

(a) wasteful: you have to maintain two sets of processes, skills and tools.

(b) toxic: you do great cultural damage when you have two such different ways of working, you almost force tribal behaviour.

Don't do it. Have one way of improving that works everywhere.

agile Project Management

"Product not project" doesn't mean we don't have projects anymore. Projects still exist - they are just no longer the primary building component of the organisation.

Projects are a transitory wave which passes through the product structure. A project is a surge in work, to deliver a defined outcome, a step-change in a product or products. Therefore, it is a surge in the number of people in the team(s) and in the velocity of the team(s) as we deliver the wave of change required by the project.

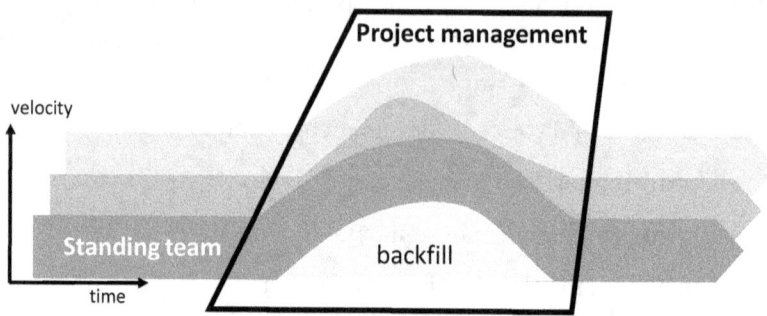

We still have project managers too. But they perform a logistical support function. Project managers no longer stride like gods, commanding everything: hiring and firing, making product decisions, and driving the priorities and structure of our organisation. Instead PMs provide services to the product teams, to organise timeline, money and resources; and to track capex/opex, benefits realisation, and work progress. You know, what project management used to do before it got out of hand.

Standing teams make sense. Project teams are a terrible idea: just when they have got through forming-storming-norming-performing and are actually starting to function as a team, the project ends, and we disband them. Individuals may come and go from a standing team, but as an entity it matures and improves.

Ideally, standing product teams should be Agile teams: small, autonomous, self-organising. So, we may be able to double or at most triple a team's capacity depending on the initial size, but any more than that, or if our teams are too big initially, requires splitting teams to stay agile. Keep the permanent standing teams small, say 5.

If we do scale to extra teams, make sure we either

> split existing teams and embed full-time staff into each team, or...

> redeploy an underutilised team from another value stream

When we bring in people to provide a wave in velocity, make sure you put the full-time staff on the interesting new work and back-fill the business-as-usual with contractors, so that the new IP doesn't walk out the door when the team shrinks again. Besides, why should contractors have all the fun?

The benefits include:

- accountability for the ongoing quality of the system rests with the team who built it, driving quality up.

- systems stay current and continue to improve for their lifetime.

- knowledge is held within the team over the lifetime of the product, reducing the need for documentation and reducing loss of knowledge.

- the teams have an incentive to do more innovation, and have more support to do so.

- the teams have an incentive to automate, because they will reap the benefits for longer.

- the teams improve work performance over time.

Even major one-off capital projects can benefit from agile thinking. A client was opening a hotel as part of a larger commercial complex. Instead of their plan to go live in a big bang by opening the doors one day, we recommended an incremental experimental approach: first allow a small number of junior staff from other parts of the business to stay, as a reward for performance, to shake down processes; then invite a larger number of more senior staff to stay with their families; with time in between to improve systems based on what we learn; and only then open the hotel to the public.

Buffering

The whole organisation doesn't switch to new ways overnight. So as the adoption of product-oriented improvement spreads out from some starting point, it runs into the established project-oriented ways of working and managing. There is a boundary problem where the "Product not Project" structure of standing teams and streams of work meets the project\business-case structure of programme/portfolio management and financial governance.

At that boundary, management needs to create white space to stop the two models clashing, and to mince up the money, turning big project gobs into steady team streams. This boundary moves out ever wider in the organisation, as our changing behaviour pulls change from those around or 'above' us.

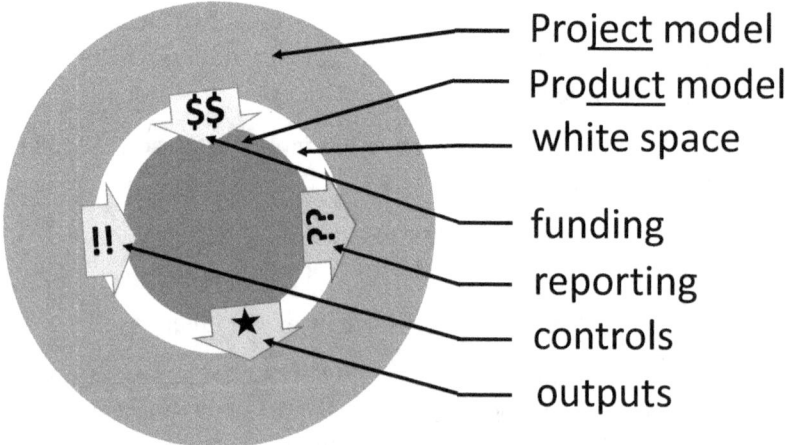

- Project model
- Product model
- white space
- funding
- reporting
- controls
- outputs

We need the support of managers at each of those levels to create the buffer zone and provide the conversion from one model to the other, or the old model will grind us to a halt.

There are four main interfaces across the white space, where we need to convert from one to the other:

- Money: it arrives in project-sized lumps and needs to be ground down into streams of funding for standing teams (p113).

- Controls: governance needs to be got out of the way to allow work to flow, or to be complied with in new ways (p110)

- Reporting: data is produced in new ways that often need to be translated to meet existing reporting requirements.

- Outputs: work arrives incrementally but the organisation expects it in big packages.

You will always have a boundary until society and government embraces agile thinking. In fact, you still will: at some sufficiently high level it is probably still a project.

One client of ours freed a team to pioneer working in Agile ways, so they published a list of existing controls and reports they were expected to deliver, and the corresponding ones they would be delivering instead to achieve the same outcomes. This caused some friction, but it also resulted in some governors working with them to come up with better proposals than their own.

---

1. D: "We need funding to promote these new ways of working; to support experiments, to educate, to coach".

2. M: "What are the measurable benefits, and when can we measure them?".

3. D: "I don't know".

4. M: "What? You have to know, to get the money".

5. D: "Well I don't. We've never worked this way. Give us some money and we will see what we can achieve".

6. M: ...

7. D: ...

8. M: "How much do you need?".

Review 3

Come to www.agilemanagers.club for answers, discussion, and more questions.

Revision

1. How can we deal with the complexity of our systems?

2. What are the pros and cons of automation?

3. What is the most important thing to get real value out of automation?

4. What does velocity mean?

5. What is the difference between a value stream, a value-T, and a value network?

6. How do we map the flow?

7. How do we visualise work?

8. Why can't we use team velocity to measure productivity?

9. What are product management and service management?

10. What are the issues with conventional project management? How can we overcome them?

Contemplation

11. How good is your organisation at decentralising command?

12. Would you say your organisation has a culture founded on continual improvement and/or learning?

13. How does work flow to and from suppliers? Are they working to the same cadences? How well integrated are they?

14. At what point does the scale of agile ways of working become an issue for you?

15. Where is your organisation on the project- to product-orientation spectrum? Which is the more important organisational construct?

16. Are you giving new ways the white space they need?

Action

17. What work can you visualise that is currently hard to see?

18. Where are the improvement registers/backlogs/databases?

19. Do you know what the value streams look like? If not, which is the most important to start with?

20. Who is blocked at getting work done and how would you know?

21. Do you know what the organisation's products are? Who does?

22. What automation of work is in use?

4. Getting to New Ways

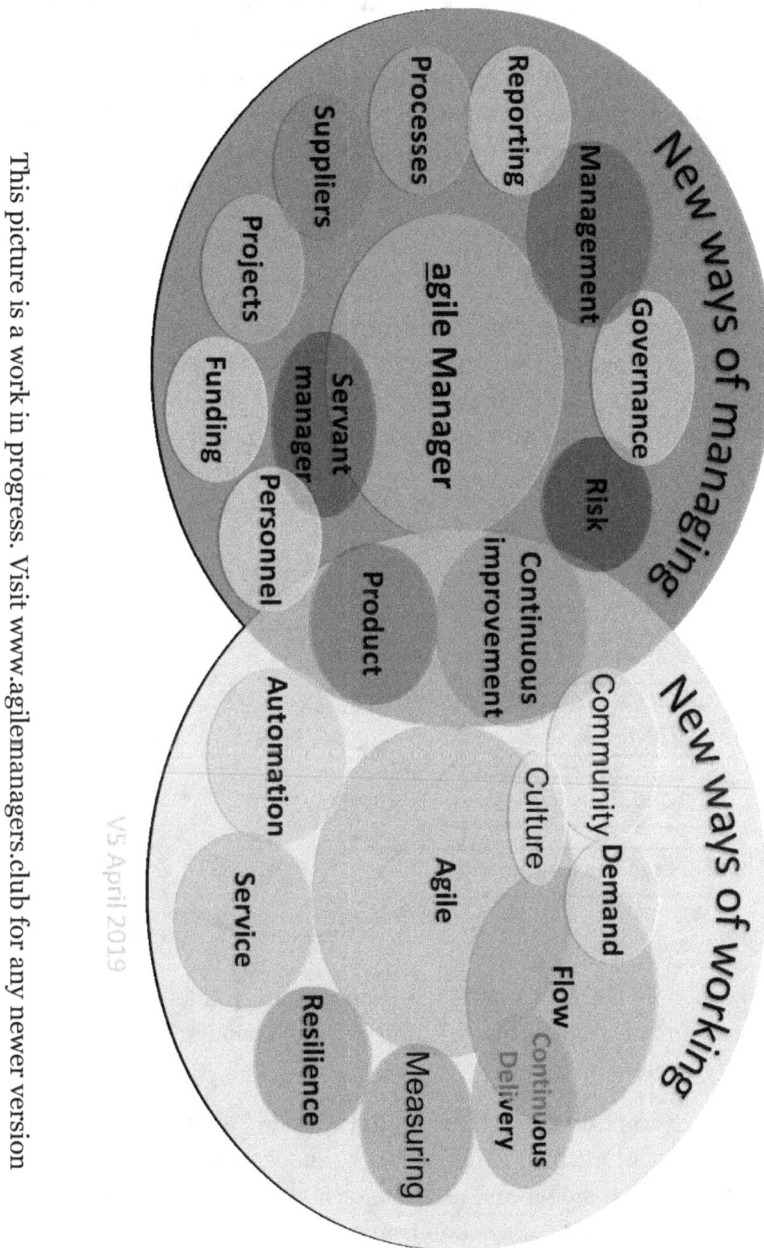

Now we know that improving management is key to changing our organisation; we have a set of principles to guide our journey; we have knowledge about new ways of managing that we can improve towards; and we have knowledge about the new ways of working too.

Use the ideas from this book to drive an advancement to new ways of working and managing. Do that advancement itself in the new ways: be agile! Don't create new overheads, new bureaucracy. The advancement should help people work better, not impede their work. It should be incremental and exploratory, knowing we can't predict the future states. It is founded on continual improvement – it never ends.

If you do it well, you will never need another big step-change "cultural transformation" again.

We start with yourself and your own personal journey then we look at how to grow agility. We discuss the insights we had that led to our own model for that journey, then how to develop managers in the new ways, how to change how you manage, and how to bring the organisation along.

Remember this?

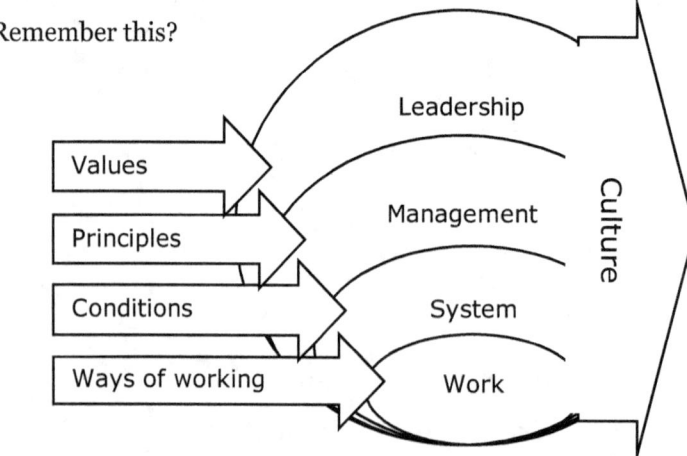

You should take a multi-level approach, influencing leadership, management, systems of work, and work behaviours; to try to create the desired emergent culture.

What we don't discuss is how to do the "new" ways of working: Agile, Kaizen, Lean, Kanban... There are other books on how to architect your organisation, systems, and technology; how to do those techniques; how to automate; how to coach and train people; and so on.

Advancing yourself

As we asked at the start of the book: do you get it? If you answered "yes", do you know what? The chances are that you actually don't. We see more unconscious incompetence than conscious competence. Start with yourself.

It is one thing to intellectually understand the concepts, and it is a far greater thing to internalise the behaviours as beliefs, so that you walk the walk naturally, without thinking, even when under pressure.

Remember that word "grok" (p7)? Do you grok agile Management? Examine yourself. Do some introspection, some self-testing. Validate your perception of your own behaviours with others.

It takes years to change your inner self from a command-and-control, hierarchal, scientific-management mindset to a collaborative servant gardener one. Connect with others trying to do the same thing. Find a mentor. Consult experts. Always be humble about your own capability, always be learning. We can all improve.

Every year Rob makes sure he can still walk 1000m up a mountain. If so, he is still fit enough. In recent years he has got better at it.

Test yourself

At the start of the book, we gave you some "Do you get it?" questions to test yourself. Here are some more to check yourself for "Command-and-Controlism", devised by Steven Shorrock[133], a little tongue-in-cheek, based on the Alcoholics Anonymous test:

☐ When you think of your organisation, is an organogram one of the first images that comes to mind (after the company logo)? YES / NO

☐ Is 'the customer' far from your mind, most of the time? YES / NO

☐ Does your division or department occupy most of your thoughts at work? YES / NO

☐ Do you lack a clear idea what other divisions or departments do, or even why they exist? YES / NO

☐ Do you think that most work can be prescribed in detail, usually with one right way to do things? YES / NO

☐ Do you ascribe to the motto, "If you can't measure it, you can't manage it"? YES / NO

☐ And when you see some quantitative data, is your instinct to set a quantitative target for where it should be? YES / NO

☐ Do you think that if only people would just do their jobs, everything would be alright? YES / NO

☐ When things go wrong, is your first thought "who screwed up?" YES / NO

☐ Is punishment your preferred response to procedural non-compliance? YES / NO

☐ Do you think that management always, or nearly always, knows best? YES / NO

---

[133] https://humanisticsystems.com/2014/07/17/facing-up-to-command-and-controlism-twenty-warning-signs/ Used with permission.

- ☐ Do you think that it is up to management to set goals and the process to achieve them? YES / NO

- ☐ Do you become anxious when things are not going according to a detailed plan or strategy, and seek to control behaviour to bring it back in line? YES / NO

- ☐ And in your mind, does changing a plan equate to personal failure? YES / NO

- ☐ Do people below you in the chain of command rarely or never argue with you or challenge you? YES / NO

- ☐ Do you think that reports up the chain of command give you an accurate view of the work? YES / NO

- ☐ Do you become anxious when there is communication outside the chain of command? YES / NO

- ☐ Do you think that involving staff in the investigation, design and management of work is usually a very bad idea? YES / NO

- ☐ Do you have frequent thoughts about controlling others' behaviour? YES / NO

- ☐ Has controlling adversely affected your social relationships with others? YES / NO

Did you answer YES five or more times? If so, you probably need help.

Continuing the Alcoholics Anonymous theme, Steven gives us a Twelve-Step Plan for recovery.

We:

1. Admitted that we were not in control—that our systems had become unmanageable.

2. Came to believe that a change in thinking could restore us to sanity.

3. Made a decision to involve the people who do the work in the investigation, design and management of the work.

4. Made a searching and fearless systemic inquiry of how the work really works.

5. Admitted to ourselves how the system was really performing.

6. Were entirely ready to remove adverse system conditions and optimise system behaviour.

7. Humbly worked with others to improve the system.

8. Made a list of the people we serve, and became willing to improve service to them all.

9. Improved service to such people wherever possible, except when to do so would harm others.

10. Continued to work on effectiveness, and when we sensed unwanted system behaviour, promptly addressed it.

11. Sought through observation and discussion to improve our conscious contact with ordinary work as we understood it, seeking knowledge of the system conditions and the power to improve them

12. Having had an awakening as the result of these steps, we tried to carry this message to others, and to practise these principles in all our affairs.

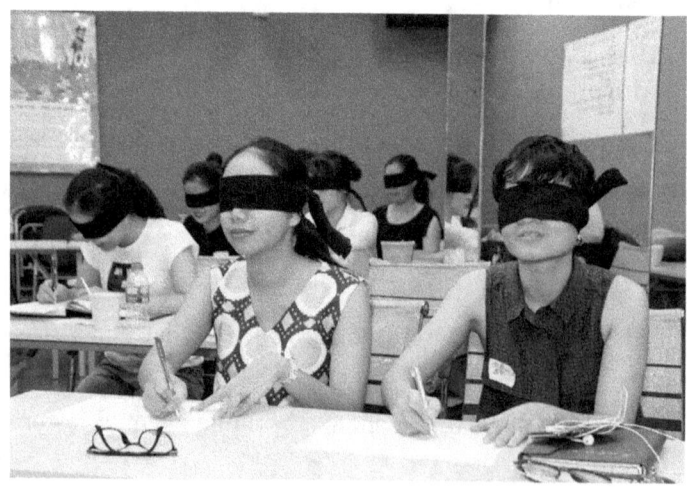

Personal development

A good general method for personal development is still Covey's *Seven Habits*[134], which describe a growth from dependence through independence to interdependence.

Focusing on growth as an agile manager, Teal Unicorn has devised the following <u>agile Manager's Personal Development Framework</u>[135], which is still in development. It is formed around two axes:

Mind (internal) <−> World (external)

Personal <−> Social

This gives us four development quadrants:

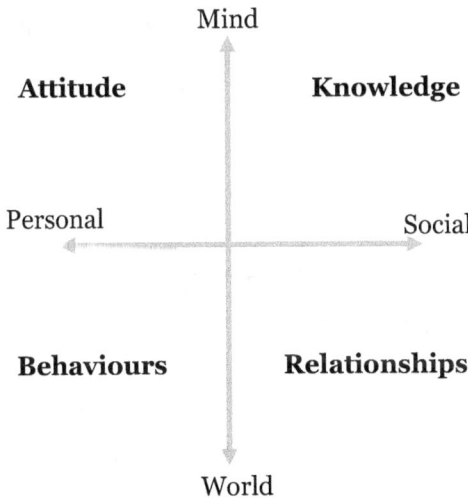

When you create a personal development plan, make sure you are thinking about your capability across all four quadrants to get a balanced view of yourself, and that you are taking learning actions in all four quadrants. Here are some suggestions:

---

[134] The 7 Habits of Highly Effective People, Stephen Covey, 1989

[135] Inspired by a bunch of influences. One that we can recall is Harold Jarche's "seek> sense> share" https://jarche.com/

Attitudes

Go find:	Ideas, principles
To develop your:	Beliefs
You need a:	Mentor
So that you can:	Support new ways

Knowledge

Go find:	Practices, tools
To develop your:	Skills
You need a:	Teacher
So that you can:	Know what to do, do the right things

Behaviours

Go find:	Exercises, experiences, experiments
To develop your:	EQ, situational responses: Org change Decision making Crisis Personnel performance
You need a:	Coach
So that you can:	Be a servant manager, do things right

Relationships

Go find:	Communities Your team Guild, peers
To develop your:	Feedback, learning, sharing
You need a:	Network
So that you can:	Give and grow

Emotional intelligence

The new ways of managing don't require you be smarter. They do require you to change emotionally, to grow your "EQ or emotional intelligence", to understand and deal with your own emotions and those of others. A lot is about developing empathy.

That journey is outside the scope of this book. Seek sources ranging from reading to counselling.

Dealing with change

One premise of this book is that management is usually the biggest source of resistance to change. As an agile manager, it is on you to detect, understand, and deal with your own resistant reactions.

You need self-awareness, mindfulness, to detect when you are pushing back, and why. Understand what the emotion is, and where it is stemming from within yourself – what belief is driving it. Be aware of your behaviours that result from this reaction, and the impact they are having.

Challenge your own beliefs. Get help from your supporters: your mentor, teacher, coach, and network. Try to change your personal narrative that is leading to these reactions: see the world differently.

Finally, try to see the positive aspects of the change, and don't get hung up solely on risks and worries.

Advancing culture

As already stated, culture is an output, it is emergent. So, it is a target, a matariki. For these new ways, we want to shift the culture to improve our beliefs and behaviours. We want to develop the following characteristics in how we deal with people, and how we do work.[136]

People	Work
Shared vision and goals	Continuous improvement
Free	Experimentation
Flow of information	Curiosity
Collaboration	Intelligent risk taking
Pride of workmanship	Learning and practicing
Respectful	Data-driven
Transparent	Recognition
Safe	Reflective

Overall, we need to create a culture of <u>trust</u>, of openness.

We want to get from "anti-patterns" (behaviours we don't want) to positive patterns of behaviour.

Anti-pattern	Aspiration
Status quo	Independent
Ceremony, theatre	Goals, customer value
Low-value controls, rules	Policy not rules
Afraid	Curious
Laying low, evasive	Blameless
Passive aggression	Safe
Functional	Professional
Obstructive	Exploratory
Resistant, cynical	Learning
Resignation, fatigue	Improving
Learned helplessness	Self-organising

---

[136] From the DevOps Institute's training course for DevOps Foundation certification, available worldwide.

(What do we mean by "Policy not rules"? The difference is not crisp, they overlap in meaning. Here we mean give positive affirmative policy, not negative punitive rules. Don't say "no jeans", say "dress appropriately").

This book isn't about culture change per se. This is about changing the ways we manage, in order that changes to the work system are unlocked, so that any culture change can emerge. We think management change is the key, the essential and often overlooked element.

Much can also be done to influence and shape culture in other ways. This book is about extrinsic change to the system; we can also influence intrinsic change of culture in individuals. You can guess from what we have said already that we believe intrinsic culture change should apply to managers as much as, or even more than, workers.

Plenty has been written about organisational change management. We draw your attention to one resource you may not be aware of: the "portfolio framework for embedding sustainability into organizational culture",[137] a tool devised by Simon Fraser University[138]. None of it is specific to eco-sustainability. It is a general framework for structuring your organisational change programme to ensure coverage of four fundamental aspects of change:

- Instilling capacity for change.

- Building momentum for change.

- Fostering commitment.

- Clarifying expectations.

It describes 59 formal and informal practices, for either delivering on current commitments or preparing for change.

---

[137] *Embedding sustainability in organizational culture*, S Bertels, L Papania, D Papania, 2010. Downloadable from the internet.

[138] Karen Ferris's book *Balanced Diversity* brought this to our attention. It uses this framework for an IT audience. If you are in IT trying to change practices, we recommend it.

Method

There are several methods for organisational change tailored to agility. We prefer to let the approach be emergent from circumstances and people, but we can see the value of some structure and methodology, especially a cadence to drive the work, and the power of ritual to trigger and resolve change. As we write this book, we are learning and experimenting with the OpenSpace Beta[139] approach, and its parent approach OpenSpace Agility, both part of the Open movement (p255). Their key elements are the ideas that advancement should be cadenced, on a 180 day cycle that they call a "chapter", with a Community Collaboration (p155) using OpenSpace ritual to open and to close a 90 day advancement.

Years ago, we created an improvement methodology called Tipu[140], which was similar. We are reworking it to incorporate these new ideas for a second edition of this book.

Other models include:

- ADKAR®[141]

- AgendaShift™ [142]

- Competing Values Framework[143]

- Lean (p280)

- Prime/OS™

- OpenSpace Agility™

- Toyota Kata[144]

We don't recommend any one approach. What is more important is that you obtain skilled help in advancement.

---

[139] *OpenSpace Beta*, Silke Hermann and Niels Pflaeging

[140] http://www.basicsm.com/tipu

[141] https://www.prosci.com/adkar

[142] https://www.agendashift.com/

[143] *Diagnosing and Changing Organizational Culture*, Cameron and Quinn

[144] *Toyota Kata*, Mike Rother

Volunteering

An essential aspect of change is that people sign up for it, they step forward, they choose it[145]. Imposing new ways or "voluntelling" people ensures disengagement. Practice the kata of always making an open invitation: the right people will come.

If the people you think are essential don't come, then either you can't make the change, or you are going to have to find a way without them. Mitigate against this by reaching out to invite people, by advocating for the new way, by selling. Many people have distaste for selling, but in reality everybody at work sells – so be good at it.

Whatever they come up with is the right answer: the solution lies within the people.

Liminality

To be liminal is to be in a state of change[146]. A liminal state can be exciting and challenging, with a sense of anticipation, adventure, and thrill. Equally, liminality causes discomfort and stress - even fear, anxiety and dysfunction. People want to go back.

Dealing with liminality is a key part of maintaining advancement. Exploit its positive attributes to inspire people to go forward: generate excitement, tell stories of possible futures, put up guiding stars to lead us. Resolve its negative aspects: reassure fears by showing how we reduce risk; use camaraderie and fun to defuse stress; and especially use rituals to give cadence and closure, to let that tension out and lock in a chapter of change.

Create momentum to carry us forward over impediments. Make the results so positive that there is no going back (if you're not making life and work better, you're doing it wrong).

---

[145] *Inviting Leadership*, Daniel Mezick and Mark Sheffield

[146] Liminal Cynefin is a recent incarnation of that model which maps and analyses the transitions between the Cynefin states.

Resistance

Remember people resist change for genuine reasons. You need to uncover those, empathise, respect their situation, find resolutions. It could be that they:

- are in an unreasonable system.

- have change fatigue from past badly managed change.

- think the new ways are unfair for themselves or someone else.

- think the ideas are wrong (always consider the possibility that they are correct).

- have tried something like this before, it didn't work then.

- fear loss of status, power, or value.

- don't like not knowing the answers.

- are in a position where they lack confidence.

- are accustomed to old ways, they are comfortable.

- like work to be quiet, easy, steady, calm.

- want it to be their idea.

Cynicism

When we talk about these cultural aspirations, the first response is commonly cynicism. They've heard all this before. Managers have put these presentation slides up with fine promises and nothing changed. We are left to deal with the culture debt of poorly executed change in the past.

Agile works. It makes an observable difference to many organisations. As we said at the start of this book "Do your research". People need to go look and ask, to see WDGLL - What Does Good Look Like.

And it works by changing behaviour, which leads to this new culture. So these aren't just fine words: we <u>have</u> to make this happen, it's how it works. We <u>invest</u>, we work hard at changing the culture.

Then the second response is "OK it works but it will never work <u>here</u>". It is a consultants' joke that all clients are the same because they all think they are different. We can point to similar organisations, but for many people we will only overcome this response once we create some early proof points internal to this organisation: run some pilots, get some early wins.

How do we do that? Read on.

Patience and perseverance

Processes, tools, and software might change in weeks, or even seconds, but the human rate of change is measured in years. Changing the culture of an organisation is a long-term undertaking.

Sometimes culture changes in sudden shifts, when it reaches a tipping point. It may even be possible to drive such sudden shifts: OpenSpace Beta[147] talks about "flipping" culture.

Make sure such rapid shifts are within the capacity of the group - don't start smashing everything. Bear in mind that revolution involves destruction and bloodshed, and a loss of productivity while society recovers. Gradual evolution is usually preferable.

We can make rapid early progress, and we can see quick changes in the external climate or "vibe" of the organisation, but fundamental shifts to new ways of working are a long-term commitment by the executive and everybody in the organisation.

Human beings are spread across a normal distribution of the rate at which they can assimilate change[148].

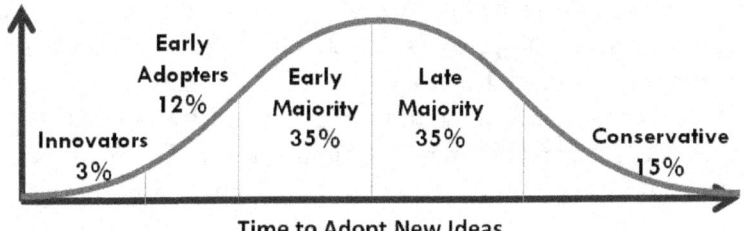

Time to Adopt New Ideas

---

[147] https://www.openspacebeta.com/

[148] This model is from *Diffusion of Innovations*, E Rogers, M Everett. Rogers used "Laggards" instead of "Conservative", but we think that is too pejorative.

A small number of people will be enthusiastic pioneers embracing new ideas, whereas the bulk of the population take time to absorb new ways of working. We must embrace the diversity of our personnel. Patience is required.

Likewise, there will be resistance. As you change a work system, it will build pressure to change back. Or - to use a different analogy - every organisation has its "immune system" that responds to irritation by trying to remove the irritant, smothering it with antibodies and ejecting it from the organism.

Sometimes the leaders themselves lose momentum, feel frustration and hopelessness, or even stray far from the original orientation. If that happens to you, stop and take time to ask yourself: What were the reasons for you to start this change?

We observe that many organisations lose their energy after the "honeymoon" period of enthusiasm and excitement for change, after a year or two. When we see this phenomenon, we often advise them to remember why they started:

- to satisfy customers, to bring best value in the fastest way.

- to be a pioneer, leading, bring new thinking, a new way of working and managing, become an agile business.

- to build a culture of continuous improvement; continuous development; response to the transformation of markets, society, technology, and management.

- to believe that you can achieve the above.

If you find yourself in this situation, let's consider (1) what you did and whether the achieved results are expected; (2) what you are not satisfied with, and what results are not as expected; and (3) what needs to adjust or change to make the progress better. Most of all, help everybody reflect on just how much has been achieved. Make sure the results are visible and proven: bring data, draw nice graphs. People don't see the wood for the trees, and they tend to get hung up on the negatives. It is important to show progress and accentuate the positive.

Don't be too despondent if enthusiasm does slump, and momentum gets lost. It is a natural cycle of a human system. Gather resources, rally the troops, re-plan, re-energise, and have another wave of advancement.

Make it real

The Lizard Brain (p121) wants everything to be tangibly real, to have an instantiation in the physical world. That's why paper-based kanbans are popular. That's why your advancement programme should have a physical location: a room or at least a wall, where people can go to see it, to experience it, to know it is real.

Some large organisations have a whole learning space, a dojo (p200). At the other extreme, we put our logo unicorn head up at client sites, not (only) for company promotion, but to mark the centre of mass for the advancement.

This one had a Christmas theme when it first went up:

And some sceptic gave this one a tinfoil hat:

This one is unadorned ... so far:

We also give out trophies and pins with a unicorn theme.

A culture book[149] is a great idea. Self-publishing websites like Lulu.com allow you to create single copies of high-quality coffee-table books from uploaded PDF files. We haven't tried a culture book yet, but we will. If it is well done, not corny, we believe it will be very effective to have a solid representation of our matariki.

Find a symbol, an icon, for the old ways of working[150], for culture debt, for negative baggage, things that have happened – something that people can identify with. Then lock it up in a cabinet, a box, a jar – where people can see it, can see that it has been removed, imprisoned. Or ritually do something to it: burn it, or throw it outside, nail it to a fence.

Whatever an icon is, it needs to by physical, tangible, not virtual, digital. Those things are good too, especially an intranet presence, but at some deep instinctual level nothing says this is real more than being real.

---

[149] *Organize for Complexity*, Niels Pflaeging
[150] We also got this idea from Niels Pflaeging in a workshop with him.

Advancing thinking

A common saying is "you don't do Agile, you be agile". It may have become a noun, but let's keep using it as an adjective: it describes behaviour, a way of working, not a state. Therefore, you never "implement Agile", "get to Agile", or finish. And you certainly can't measure how Agile you are.

You can't become agile with a project, and we beseech you not to try anything "big-bang". Anyone who does that clearly doesn't understand Agile.

It's a journey: it never ends, you're never finished. Agile is how you improve, and you will always be improving.

Our agility mantra is:

Work is to **iterate, increment, experiment, explore.**

Improving ways of working is to **reflect, and improve.**

The work of advancement to new ways of working and managing should be done in an agile way.

Explore what it means for your organisation. Be aware that you don't know where your organisation will get to or when.

Experiment constantly - all advancement is experiment. Nobody knows how a complex system of people, processes and technologies will behave when you change its conditions.

Therefore, **iterate** your way forward: make repeated small changes, (**increment**), and observe the result.

Then **reflect** on what the new ways are achieving, and how well you are transforming, adjust to **improve**, and go around again.

Expect failure

We have made it clear that failure is the basis of how we work in new ways. Failure is just as inevitable as we *move* to these new ways of working and managing as when we do the work. Workers will fail; managers will fail.

We will see such things as:

> Uncoordinated change in different teams means work fails to flow.

> Reporting is disrupted by changes to the observed data and its sources.

> Errors in new process design cause stoppages that we are unfamiliar with fixing.

> People take advantage of reduced controls in the form of ill-discipline and possibly even corruption.

> The confusion around changes to the process cause process failures.

Managers must walk the walk by welcoming failure and responding to it with the learning process. Of course, there should be consequences for bad discipline or corruption, but even a single punishment of *noble failure* or an honest mistake will have a negative effect on the progress in introducing new ways of working.

Beware of increased pressure: in times of crisis or looming deadlines, people revert to their old familiar behaviours. Managers will regress at these times: you will see doing work become more important than any improving of work; command-and-control management come back in; increased controls and reporting; and micromanagement of work. They need extra support and coaching to prevent this.

Effect of the J-curve

It is highly unlikely that any change to ways of working goes perfectly at first. (In fact, any change to any system is unlikely to go perfectly except when we can predict perfectly). Our entirely subjective rule of thumb is that it takes about three times for any new ritual or iteration to go well.

We should expect that when we change ways of working, performance will go backwards before it goes forwards, while workers get the hang of the new way, get the bugs out, and optimise the details.

This was discussed previously in this book as the J-curve.

Capability

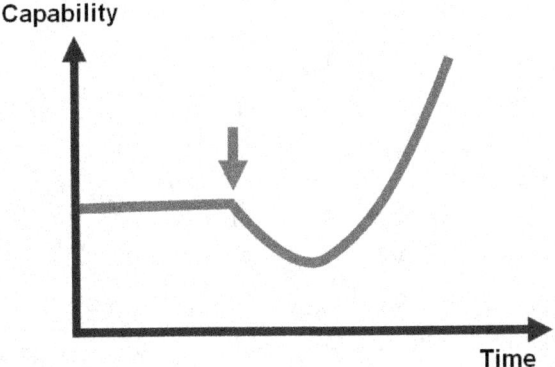

Time

When we make a change in ways of working and managing, there are three things that can go wrong on this J-curve:

1) We can lose our nerve when things start going backward and decide the changes don't work (it is entirely possible that this *is* true, or maybe we just haven't been patient enough), and we revert to the old way.

2) The improvement may never come, and the curve stays flat.

3) The performance dips so low that we go into a death spiral, we break the system entirely.

A strategy to minimise all three problems is to make many small changes instead of one big one (sound familiar? This is a fundamental principle of Agile), so that each "J" is small. We don't change much so we are unlikely to dip much.

Capability

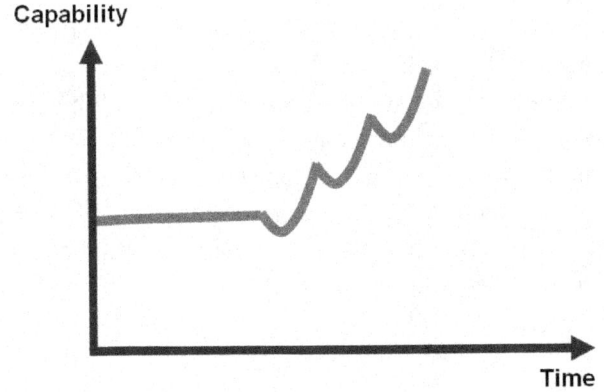

Time

JFDI

JFDI is a cheeky acronym for "Just Do It"[151]. The myth of the simple system - the fallacy of "plan once, execute perfectly" - leads us into analysis paralysis. We won't start until we have all the data, detail, steps, and resources.

This doesn't work, for many reasons described in this book. You need action to generate information.

Somebody needs to say "JFDI: somebody do something, so that we can explore and learn, and move forward." Always be doing - experimenting, incrementing - because only through doing can we learn.

We must learn to navigate ambiguity: to work with imperfect information, resources, or plan.

When a client of ours needed to move to new ways of working within IT, there was much discussion for years, until a crisis – a disastrous project which impacted the public – united everyone in a desire for new ways. A guiding coalition pondered for a few weeks, then the boss decreed a new way of deploying software changes, and announced it would start in six weeks' time. Nothing about how, and no compromise on when. There was much angst and even anger, but six weeks later, about half the work was deployed in the new way; and after a few iterations most of it was. The new approach slashed the defect rate to near a thousandth of what it had been previously, and created a predictability and cadence that had never been there before in the chaotic old approach. Little of the advancement was technological; most of it was change to practices, flows, and team structures. Automation will make them even better and faster in the future. That was a big JFDI, but the situation called for – and empowered – decisive radical action.

---

[151] Sorry if we anyone offended with profanity. Rob is half Australian half Kiwi, and the Vietnamese are fond of swearing too.

Crazy goals

A useful technique of ours is to set "crazy goals". Propose something ambitiously advanced, that seems crazy, that people say is impossible. Then challenge them with the wonderfully powerful hanging question "Impossible unless...??"

Use the answers to deconstruct the goal into prerequisites. If they say those prerequisites are in turn "impossible", repeat the process until you work your way back to something that we agree is achievable. Begin there.

At a client of ours, a generally conservative manager wanted to encourage new thinking, so he unexpectedly announced a desire to do away with a major change control. The reaction was shock that it came from him and consternation over the implications. However, it triggered discussion over what first steps could be taken, and opened the group to new possibilities. This opening up is important, as you will see.

Seek new ways with a product not project

We introduced the "product not project" concept earlier. As an example, consider the subject of this book: you want to get to new ways of working and managing. Don't do that as a big bang, don't launch a project with a finite timeline and funding. Don't bring in a team of consultants and contractors to do it all, to dump a pile of white ring-binders and mysterious new software and run away.

Don't start by reorganising everyone. One objective of new ways is to build collaboration and sharing across siloes. Changing from one set of siloes to another doesn't help. We can't "break down siloes", there will always be groups and tribes. It is not about how you slice the organisation, it is about making that structure not matter, by creating connections. Moreover, you don't know what organisational structure will work: you are guessing.

Getting to new ways of working and managing should be a "product" (internally) not a project. Create a New Ways or Advancement "Product Owner" for continual improvement. Do continual improvement forever. Fund it as a stream every year. Work from the backlog of improvements to ways of working and managing. Change incrementally, exploring and experimenting.

Collaboration

Everybody must collaborate in decision making, it is not a management function anymore. Let the people doing the advancement design the advancement. Bring people together to understand how they want to change, and what they think most needs improving. They're probably the best to judge. Even when they aren't, the fact that they feel inclusion and ownership is more important than perfection. Don't push change, allow teams to pull it as they require it. Use the Fair Process technique (p58) to be transparent and involve everyone in decision-making.

Create communities (p254), and collaboration spaces and events (p155) and social mechanisms like cafeterias, rest spaces, and clubs, to bring people together to consider new ways of working and managing.

How to move your boss

This is a common question: if the hierarchy above you are resistant to new ways, how do you change that?

Every person has different reasons to be resistant (p182). You need to work that out. Here are some tactics:

- Reassure them that risks are being managed. This is top priority for most managers.

- Create proof points within your scope of control. Show them off.

- If they like it, ask for mandate, support, and resources to go larger.

- What does good look like? Take them to other organisations. Bring in outsiders.

- Wait for a sense of urgency, a milestone, a compelling event, a crisis. Be prepared with the solution ready.

- Make them a hero, solve their personal challenge, deliver their KPI.

- Highlight some big current quality risks, and problems caused by slowness. Show how agility lowers risk and increases speed and efficiency.

- Show how agility makes staff happier and life easier.

- Explain that there are no patterns we can apply, only principles to apply to guide us. Find a way to teach the new ways of thinking, the new principles, so they don't think you have lost your mind.

Never waste a crisis

Just as every failure is an asset, even more so every crisis is a source of valuable motivation to change, and of experience of change. Harness chaos (p75). When things go badly wrong, people pull together to deal with the emergency. They come up with creative solutions as fast as possible.

In the last decade, New Zealand has been hit with earthquakes in Christchurch, Kaikoura, and Wellington which disrupted society (and in the Christchurch case cost lives – only immense good luck meant the toll wasn't much higher).

Christchurch central business district was destroyed and shut down. A new government body was formed to rebuild the city of 400,000. Creative solutions abounded: shared business hubs for organisations which had lost their premises; a new social welfare system built in a week to pay wages to those whose employer was out of action; pop-up shops in a street full of containers; a cardboard cathedral.

The Kaikoura highway (Highway One) was destroyed: we rebuilt it, opened just over a year later, giving us a much faster and safer highway[152] which never could have got past environmental approvals if it were not a national emergency.

---

[152] https://www.nzta.govt.nz/projects/kaikoura-earthquake-response/

Government departments and businesses after the Wellington quake (our government city) found themselves shut out of their buildings which had fractured and were ruled unsafe. No lives were lost but tens of thousands suddenly had no access to desks, computers, and files. Many organisations saw IT teams deploy hundreds of laptops in days to enable key workers, and security teams open restrictions on working from home.

These crises bring good things: open ways of working, willingness to take risk, opening of controls, and approval of creative solutions.

Seize the day. Turn a crisis from a disaster to an opportunity. Everybody is motivated. People rally. Risks have to be taken.

Be prepared. Always be experimenting and exploring, trying new ways. Build experience, capability, and proof points. When the crisis comes (and in many organisations we can foresee that it is "when" not 'if'), be ready with prepared new ways to propose. For more on how this fits with an overall model of growth, see p218.

A common reaction across these fast, creative responses is "Why can't it always be like this?" Use that thinking to motivate change. But move quickly: people fall back into their old ways within months.

Christchurch. Image: Lee Hanner [CC BY-SA 2.0]

Advancing management

We help the managers to understand new ways of managing, to change the management methods of the organisation. This changes the way the system is influenced, driven, controlled. This leads to the desired changes in work behaviour.

Unfreezing the permafrost

Managers with an appetite for risk tend to rise in the hierarchy; higher managers tend to be open-minded to new ways, and the daring pioneer middle-managers are on their way up. On the other hand, settled middle managers didn't get where they are by taking risks: they tend to be conservative and risk-averse. In fact, their primary purpose is often to manage risk, and that's how they are measured. That's why we see new ways of management as the key to unlock successful advancement. This view is also widely held in the Agile community, who sometimes referred to middle management as the "permafrost", the frozen layer between visionary executive leadership and willing practitioners.

Remember conservative managers resist for intelligent reasons, and remember to embrace the diversity of thinking, including risk appetites and rates of change. We must address concerns, so we need tactics to help them move. We want everything we do in advancement to help reassure them that we have risk in hand.

Proof points are essential, so that they can see the new ways working around them. When they see peers succeeding, it motivates them to do the same.

A sense of permission is important, especially if the previous management behaviours have punished failure. Reluctant middle managers need their superiors to demonstrate that failure is rewarded, that experimentation is encouraged.

Some middle managers suffer from "imposter syndrome": they feel they have risen to the limit of their capabilities (or beyond). When we tell them that they don't need to know the answers, that they don't have to be smarter than their staff, then this often comes as a relief to them.

Similarly, encouraging openness, transparency, and vulnerability allows them to confess and share their fears, and get the emotional support of their team; instead of the emotional loneliness of command-and-control.

If this book is making you uncomfortable as a manager, do what you can to reassure yourself: go see it work, practice the new ways, get hands-on experience.

Development programme

In our part of the world (New Zealand), professional training for managers is poor; some countries and organisations do it better. Don't leave managers to work it out for themselves. If you want to adopt new ways of managing and help other managers to do so too, then ensure there is a formal management development programme. Establish a programme, or modify the existing one, to transform ways of managing and ensure that all managers at all levels understand what is required of them as part of the advancement.

The programme should include:

- awareness training in Agile, Lean, and complex systems.
- manager-specific training in the implications and requirements of Agile, Lean, and complexity: what these new ways need from managers, and how they change leadership, management, governance, structures, systems, and teaming.
- training in **agile** management: servant manager, vulnerability, teaming, workflow, value...
- existing leadership/management development resources: exploit, integrate with, influence, and seek to modify existing programmes, courses, and support already available.
- coaching by expert coaches.
- mentoring by exemplars: establish relationships between managers already strong in the new management culture and those who are new or less familiar.

Training courses

There is not a lot of training specifically for agile managers (outside of IT). If you are in our part of the world, Teal Unicorn has courses and simulations. Consultants near you may do the same. However, there are many courses available globally for specific topics, such as Lean, Agile, Scrum, servant leadership, Situational Leadership, Cynefin, and Scaled Agile Framework.

Simulation games

It is a shame that there is not greater awareness of the power of "serious play" simulation workshops as learning tools. These take trainees to higher levels of learning than pedagogical classrooms [153]. By immersing and doing, they get insights and breakthroughs that don't happen by listening to lectures and learning theory.

We use games a lot, and design our own,[154] as well as using those from GamingWorks, Play14, Agile42, and others. We frequently see the "lights go on" for individuals, or new levels of energy and inspiration for those who already got it intellectually.

> "You can discover more about a person in an hour of play than a year of conversation."
>
> - Plato

---

[153] To Blooms Taxonomy's level three

[154] http://www.twohills.co.nz/diggers

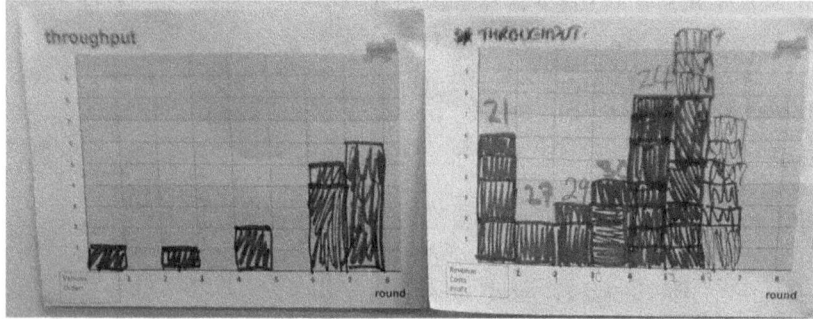

Dojo

A dojo is a martial arts term for a place to go to learn and master technique. In the Agile world, it usually means a place within the organisation where teams can go to do their work, assisted by a coaching team who introduce them to new ways on the job.

New Zealand is too small for most companies to afford such a model, so we modify it to have a dojo team who don't have a dedicated place but instead come to the regular workplace to work with a team for a fixed period for the same purpose.

The dojo provides expertise, resources, templates, and demo systems, so that they can coach a team in how to do their real work in new ways.

Coaching and mentoring

Coaching is advising and teaching on the job, with one or many staff.

Mentoring is personal career guidance one on one.

Neither coaching nor mentoring is done well in most organisations. If you want new ways of managing and working, significant investment is required in formal programmes for both.

Use a mix of internal and external people, to provide institutional knowledge and fresh perspectives. Create a mechanism to link people up for mentoring. Cycle coaches out or rotate them every year or two.

WDGLL

It is essential that your organisation understands "what does good look like" (WDGLL). We must see the organisation objectively in the context of other similar ones, otherwise an organisation can become quite delusional about its own capabilities.

You can achieve this by sending staff on site visits, study tours, conferences, sabbaticals, and secondments. These can be local or further afield. Or bring guest speakers into your organisation. People adopting the new ways seem to be generous with their time in support of others.

Seeing WDGLL provides an objective benchmark of just how good your organisation is. It creates a dissatisfaction with work system deficiencies when they get back to work, motivating people to improve.

Management Communities

Make sure managers have their own guilds to share and support. They need to get together regularly to understand challenges, celebrate successes, and spread good ideas. See "Communities", p254.

Advancing work

There are those whose work moves value through the value stream, and there are those whose work is necessary non-value work supporting those who move value.

Managers are generally a non-value function, whether they are managing people or managing work, and like everybody in that category they need to get out of the way of the workers trying to deliver value.

Management should not be an overhead on work, it should be a facilitator. Make work easier, make it faster. Get out of the way. Flip the management pyramid so that it supports the work instead of sitting on top of it.

Consider the cost – in money and time - of consultation, decision-making, informing, approvals, recording, and reporting versus the value of the work. It may be absurd. Especially as we move to smaller and smaller units of work, management and governance must find lighter cheaper ways to control work, or perhaps not control it at all.

Fix relationships

The relationships between organisational units at any levels can be dysfunctional. The more remote and formal the connection, the worse the relationship can be. In the worst case, one group can actively prevent or even undermine the work of another. More commonly, they are uncooperative or passive aggressive.

When the only connection is via emails or ticketing tools, the relationships can be particularly bad. Data in a ticket is useful, but the way they are used is sometimes toxic, as a way to abdicate and transfer responsibility, stall or hide work, procrastinate, over complicate, or be passively aggressive and obstructive. Ticket tennis ensues. As the Agile Manifesto states, there is no substitute for face-to-face.

Inter-group relationships can be one of the most important – and fertile – areas for improving flow of work. The managers of the teams can do a lot to encourage improvement. Tactics include:

- get the groups together in a room. Any excuse will do: training, social, workshop, hack.

- assign people temporarily to the other group.

- create virtual teams with people from both groups to work on a common goal.

- change the system so that work hand-offs must be face-to-face. Emails, tickets, forms and other mechanisms can only be used to confirm a conversation.

- getting them to cross-train each other, both ways, is particularly effective.

- co-locate them.

Lighter controls

Controls are essential to protect the organisation's assets. But achieving velocity through quality requires that all "necessary non-value work" get out of the way of value work. Minimise controls: just enough to control risk, ensure compliance, and monitor performance, with the least possible impact on value work. Experiment with less or lighter control.

Here is a checklist of tactics to minimise the impact of necessary controls on the flow of work, in ascending order of difficulty. Use this to get your own or others' management out of the way of the work. Make your way down the list until one gets the result:

1. Pre-approve certain types of work, e.g. police don't need a warrant to stop a vehicle.

2. Get an exemption, e.g. anything under 10 days or $10k.

3. Get delegated authority in the team, e.g. a research team member is authorised to do ethical review and escalate to an ethical review board only when necessary.

4. Aggregate the control, e.g. one work ticket for a group of tasks. Or a pool of budgeted money for a standing team to draw on instead of having to ask for money for each task.

5. Bring the control to the flow. Make work visible and have the controller observe the flow, instead of workers all having to go to the controller, often requiring some additional control artefact. A governor should observe the flow of work and express interest in

particular units of work (and stay out of it the rest of the time). For example, Occupational Safety should review all planned work in the planning tool and indicate which ones need hazard assessment, instead of requiring a special form be submitted for every single piece of work.

6. Substitute your own control, which delivers the same outcome as the existing control. E.g. we don't write this report monthly anymore because there is a report in our work tool that generates it on demand any time you want it.

7. Simplify the control, e.g. challenge the level of ceremony: do we really need all these forms? Or remove redundancy: document nothing which is already recorded in the work management software.

8. Make the control parallel to the flow of work, so that it happens while the work is happening e.g. financial approval which is incremental while work processes in stages; or quality assurance testing that is done while manufacture continues.

9. Make the control incremental, e.g. the design document starts as a photo of a whiteboard, grows to presentation bullets, then to a skeleton document, and finally is completed as part of the as-built documentation. Or compliance approval starts as a provisional light certification with growing levels of assurance to final approval when the product is turned on, ensuring no surprises near the end of the work.

10. Shift left: do it earlier in the workflow. E.g. risk and impact assessment can be done by the builders themselves, who self-certify.

11. Automate the control, e.g. credit checking; or scanning software code.

12. Remove the control. Show how the control is unnecessary or irrelevant to your work. Convince governors to have the control removed.

13. Ignore the rules. Go around the control. Seek forgiveness not permission. No, seriously. If you're prepared to make that career bet, make it: defy the control. Subvert it, go around it. Viva la revolución!

Getting those who own controls to modify them relies on reassurance, and reassurance only works with trust. That takes time and usually requires demonstrable success. So be patient and prove the changes.

Ultimately, changing the controls and governance is not a side issue to becoming agile, it is central. It leads to changing the operating model of the organisation (product not project, incremental funding, new capex/opex models...), and it doesn't get much more profound than that.

Challenge ceremony

As we work on improving a value stream, we should begin by looking at all the handovers between functional groups, and one of the first things we should do is to challenge the level of ceremony. Most of the rites and rituals accrete around handovers between teams, and these are the first points we map and optimise when looking at the flow in a value stream.

These handovers are the most likely points where three classic forms of Lean waste occur: unnecessary work, inventory pile-ups, and unnecessary waits.

Part of the impact of agile Management is to challenge the "level of ceremony" of these handovers, and try to reduce the complexity of handovers. Put crudely, we subject them to a bullshit test.

There is value in handover documents, where a template is provided with all the necessary headings, because this kind of documentation ensures that a team has at least given some thought to every one of the areas of capability which we want them to, before handing the work over. On the other hand, these artefacts are only necessary because of the dysfunctional relationship between teams, and the artefacts themselves often have little ongoing value after handover. Handover documentation is really a band-aid to try to repair the problem addressed by improved collaboration. And a checklist.

Handover documentation is a good example of the kind of high levels of ceremony which build up over time to try to address shortcomings in quality in the value stream. Each time something goes wrong, the downstream receiving team introduce new controls in the handover to protect themselves in future. Trust diminishes and ceremony increases.

Such ceremonial "crud" is a good indication of dysfunctional relationships. Is the amount of formality really justified? Are the artefacts produced really necessary?

To improve these handover points, we can consider such strategies as:

- simplify the artefacts.
- eliminate them altogether.
- integrate the communications.
- automate the whole handover from one team to another.

The goal is not to eliminate all ceremony entirely: it is to streamline. Make it as simple as possible but no simpler. Some definition and formality is required in all handovers to manage risk, and in fact to make them easier by setting clear expectations.

As an example, we saw an intranet development team who had to go through a complex process to approve the smallest pieces of work to change the internal intranet. The cost of approval and release of funds could exceed the cost of the work. So the manager "passed the hat around" business stakeholders, asking them to give the team the small amounts of funding they had in their budgets for intranet work. Then the team could deliver them twice as much value twice as fast by having a standing fund to draw from.

Nor does it help to mash teams together in order to theoretically eliminate the handover. The whole point of the new ways is to get groups to collaborate across organisational boundaries. Organisational reshuffles do not contribute to breaking down boundaries, they just create different ones. Reorganisation should come later in an advancement, once you fully understand the new ways of working and recognise the implications for the organisational structure (and it should happen incrementally). Therefore, we seek simply to understand where the handovers are and to make them as lean and collaborative as possible.

It's not just handovers. Challenge ceremony everywhere you find it. Even our own advancement rituals accrete ceremony over time. Agile meetings gather bureaucracy. Planning increases in complexity, formality, and detail. Reporting and record keeping grows. If you control it, tear it down. If you don't, call it out.

Eliminate theatre

Organisations are riddled with theatre: a performance which creates the illusion of something happening but which everybody knows is not real, yet we all tacitly agree to go along with the illusion.

Performance reviews. Many staff performance reviews bear no resemblance to the reality of what happened in the past year. Several organisations are now abandoning these as farcical theatre.

"Most corporate planning is like a ritual rain dance. It has no effect on the weather, but those who engage in it think it does. Much of the advice and instruction is directed at improving the dancing, not the weather"

- Russel L. Ackoff

Budgeting. So much time and energy is wasted on inventing magical numbers so the money can be doled out for the coming year. There are more efficient and realistic ways of doing this.

Security. Security experts will tell you that the most serious security threats come from within an organisation and yet much security energy goes into defending the perimeter. There is no better example of security theatre than the TSA show performed in American airports – there are richer targets than aircraft that don't get the same attention.

Operational change management. Surely nobody seriously believes that conventional "change control" produces value from reduced risk anywhere near proportionate to its negative impact on productivity and morale. It is a function whose primary purpose is to reassure managers that bad things are being prevented.

Project management. Formal project management was imposed on general work decades ago in an attempt to connect money inputs with benefits derived, but the benefits are doubtful, as we discussed (p159).

Do the non-value work

Once we have reduced controls to the minimum necessary, and got rid of ceremony and theatre, find ways for managers to do the non-value work instead of putting it on those trying to deliver value.

Managers can do their reporting for them. Don't make them produce reporting data. Go to the gemba, observe, and gather the data.

Likewise, managers can handle some of the controls; fill in the forms, go to the meetings, deal with the bureaucracy.

A favourite example of ours is timesheet recording. Nobody sees value in it, nor does it well. It is always theatre; the numbers are made up and gamed. It is bad for morale. Turn it off. Understand what value it provides (if any), then find other sources of data, and get managers to gather it.

Free the workers

Most "transformations" of ways of working don't succeed because they are done to people, not by people; and the transformation micro-manages people as clerical workers instead of freeing them as knowledge workers.

The priority of management should be on how people improve the way they work, not how they do the work. Create a learning organisation, a culture of continual improvement, and mechanisms for feedback and change. Let the work itself emerge from those who know best: those doing it.

Let the people doing the work design the work. For activities that are a process there is a hierarchy of ever increasing directiveness in how we tell people to do their work (see below); which should be modulated based on the capability of those doing it. Some only need policy guidance, others need detailed work instructions, and a full spectrum in between. This is the spectrum between knowledge workers (information masons) and clerical workers (information production line).

Define as little as possible as appropriate for their level of capability, and then free those doing the work to define the rest. After you throw out some of your documentation because it is documenting that which is not a process at all, or does not reflect reality, then review the actual processes and chuck out the documentation where you are patronising or treating your staff like children.

Layers of work documentation

Here is a model you may find useful: layers of increasing practice documentation, detail, and determinism.

When you document an activity, determine the competence, professionalism, and empowerment of those doing it. Then work your way down this stack documenting the minimum number of layers you need to in order to reduce risk and equip the people, *and no more*. Leave the rest to them.

So here they are, in descending order:

> Vision, strategy
>
> Goals, KPIs
>
> Policy: guidelines, rules, bounds
>
> Roles, responsibilities/accountabilities, relationships to others
>
> Plans
>
> Value stream, system
>
> Backlog
>
> Processes
>
> Procedures
>
> Work instructions

Within each layer we can simplify as well, for example:

- use checklists.

- embed documentation in the work "machine" in preference over written documentation.

Knowledge workers want only the upper layers; clerical workers need all of them. Knowledge workers are working in complicated and complex domains. They need freedom for Case Management. Clerical workers need all layers defined, for repeatability and precision in standardised transactional work. (This is not to say we would have zero documentation of work in the detailed layers for knowledge workers. In Case Management we still need descriptions of mundane tasks: templates, checklists etc. But the knowledge worker will assemble and work around them, to freely create the process in each case.)

Which brings us to our model we call Standard+Case (p278). Standardised work can be given to less experienced or less capable staff, because it has a high level of structure and prescription. Case work – complicated, complex or chaotic work – should be given to capable empowered knowledge workers, then get out of their way. Let them determine how to do the work and with what tools and methods.

Where you *must* define these layers, remember what we already covered. Go to the gemba, look at the work. Write for reality, not what is in your head (see "Platonicity", p85). And challenge the level of ceremony, eliminate theatre.

Fluidity

When we don't prescribe how to do the work, we can allow greater fluidity. Workers flow to the work where they are needed and they can add value. Workers assemble dynamically. As we said earlier (p108), it is possible to have long-lived standing teams and still organise fluidly around the work.

One version of this is called "swarming": getting the right people together dynamically as required to address a need, issue, or risk. An example of this is in support teams, responding to incidents. Conventional response is to have a service desk layer, who pass it to a back-room support layer, who if they can't resolve it then pass it to experts. This creates a lot of bureaucracy and delay (and buck-passing). Using swarming, the right people come together as quickly as possible to cut through all the process and just fix it.

One aspect of the highest level of Laloux's culture model, "teal", is this fluidity. People are self-organising. Under conventional management, self-organisation usually means a team plans and assigns work internally to meet goals given to them, and this feels progressive. But the ultimate teal self-organisation is self-assembly: a team find each other, determine their own makeup, identify the goal and desired outcomes themselves, source their own resources, and then do the internal planning and work distribution.

Maker schedules

Another way for managers to get out of the way and to respect knowledge workers is the concept of maker schedules.

Managers usually schedule their own time in 30-minute increments (or less), and expect everyone to behave that way. On the other hand, people doing actual work build intellectual models in their mind, which are lost every time they context-switch, incurring a productivity loss colloquially said to be 5-20 minutes, while they reload and re-engage.

The idea of maker schedules is to allow those doing productive work to schedule 3 to 4 hours of uninterrupted work time per day, at a time they feel most productive. That's about as long as the average knowledge worker can focus on sustained intellectual work in a day. And for managers to honour that. Managers should work around the scheduled work, not make everyone drop everything at a time that suits the manager.

Image © Phil Wade

Technology

Everybody wants technology to fix work systems, and it doesn't. Ever. Technology makes us more efficient or more effective, but on its own it never changes the way we work or manage work.

As we change the system - change the behaviours and practices - only then do we start to identify the need for technology where we are too slow or unproductive (efficiency), or we are error-prone or need super-human capabilities (effectiveness).

No tool can make good work, any more than it can eliminate bad work. They're only tools. We are the masters of our tools, not their slaves. We can do good work with pen and paper.

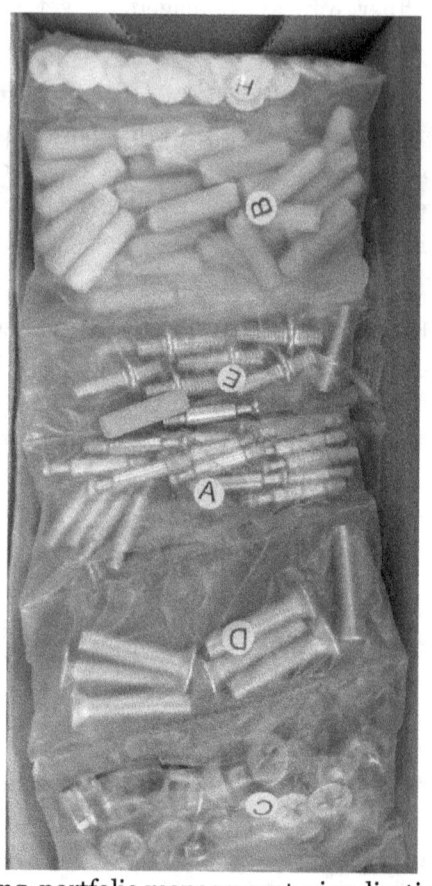

There are lots of tools for planning, portfolio management, visualisation of work, management of backlogs, automation of workflow, and so on. Wait until you know what you need and get that.

And that's all we have to say about technology. Tech is the easy bit. As the mathematicians say, it is a closed problem: you know a solution exists, you just need to find it. Human systems are an open problem; you don't even know if it is solvable. You may or may not get to an optimal system and a healthy culture. People are the hard part.

Unicorn Management Model

We have presented our ideas on advancing yourself, and the culture, thinking, management, and work. The Unicorn Management Model is our way of bundling those ideas. It's not a product, we don't sell it, it is public domain. It lives here: www.agilemanagers.club.

Three insights

The key to success in getting a legacy organisation to new ways of working, to agility, is understanding <u>how</u> to drive the advancement, and, in particular, understanding that the focus of the advancement has to be the <u>management</u> layer, more than the work. This is the nub of our <u>agile</u> Management approach: the insight that the most important aspect of new ways of working – the key to unlock advancement - is not the target state or some template solution or even distilling out a set of principles; it's the ways of managing.

The high-level executives are more likely to be risk takers and big thinkers and will embrace new ways of working more quickly than the middle management will. Likewise, the practitioners at the worker level are generally keen to do something better once you work them through their initial resistance to being changed.

> "Attempting to change an organization's culture is a folly, it always fails. Peoples' behavior (the culture) is a product of the system; when you change the system peoples' behavior changes."
>
> - John Seddon

But the conservatives amongst that middle layer, that permafrost, are usually the slowest to move in any organisation. So, while other bodies of knowledge emphasise executive support and new ways of working for the teams, we think that those two aspects actually sandwich the most important and most neglected area: moving the management.

The second insight that we have learnt is that you can't readily change the behaviour of individual people, whether they be executive, management, or team practitioners. People exist within a work <u>system,</u>

so we must extrinsically change the system, rather than intrinsically change the people or some amorphous concept of "culture".

Trying to change culture and work directly is futile (on its own). It works locally at a team level up to a point, if you can create enough white-space for change to survive. But beyond that point, change must be holistic at an organisational level: the work system, the ways we work.

> Every time I get asked "How do you motivate a team?", I challenge it because it's wrong question to ask as a leader.
>
> Motivation is not a thing that gets done to people – it's something people *do*.
>
> Ask instead "How do you create an environment for the team to motivate themselves?"
>
> - Claire Lew

And the third insight that experience and theory has taught us is that you can't change a human work system directly, they're too complex. "You can't change a complex system, you can only create the conditions for it to change itself." A complex system behaves organically[155]. You must change the externalities to extrinsically influence the system to change. Change the governance, policy, KPIs, products, services, and people development. In other words, change how we _manage_ the work. The culture and work will then change. Which brings us back to that management layer.

From these three insights, we created Teal Unicorn's approach to driving advancement to new ways of working.

We package the following components together as "The Unicorn Management Model"[156]:

- The improvement "paddle-wheel" model below.
- A four-tier growth model, p218.
- Principles, p219, and matariki, p221.
- An Improvement Machine model, p226.
- A management development programme, still in development.
- An experiment programme, p241.

---

[155] Its not actually alive, so don't get carried away with the analogy.

[156] The model is shared under a Creative Commons Attribution-ShareAlike 3.0 Unported License. Please credit "Two Hills Ltd"

Advancement model

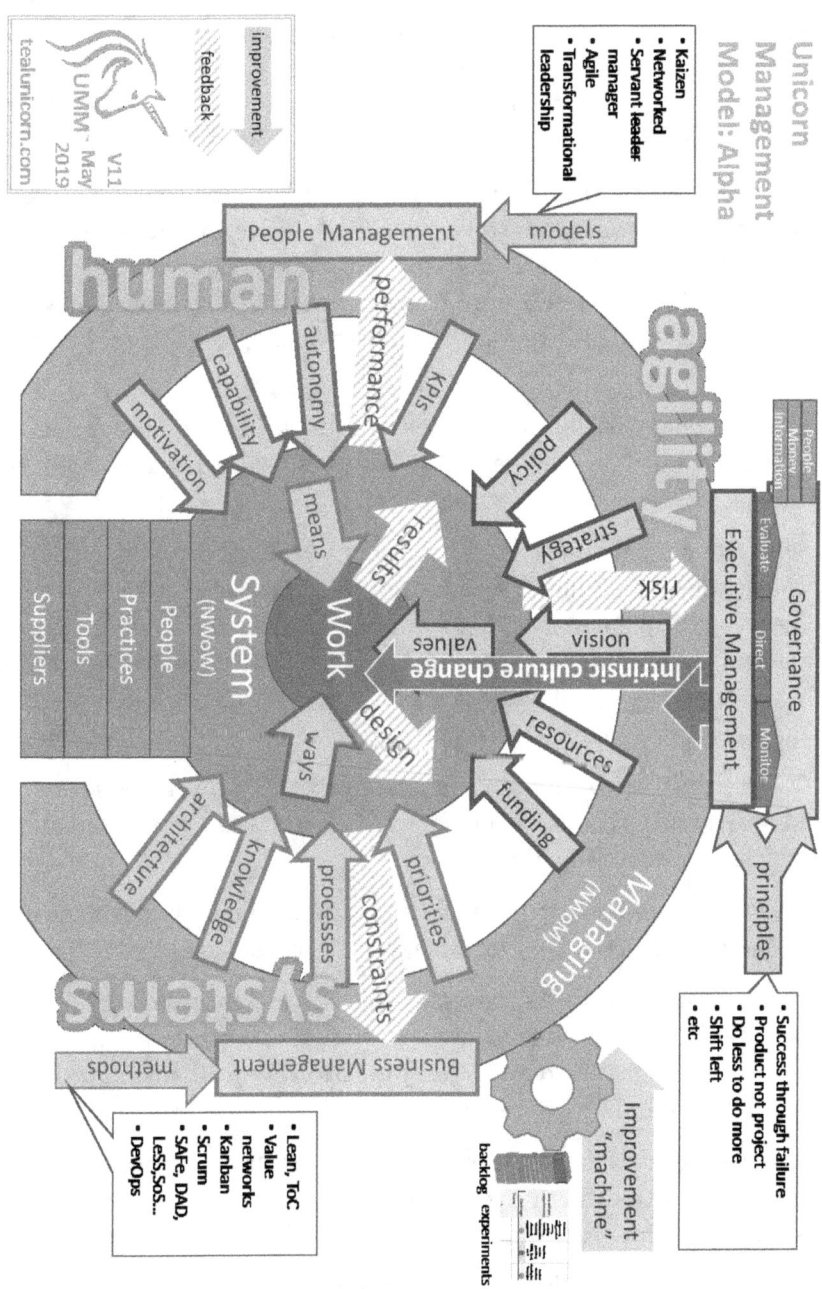

For a full-colour digital version of this diagram, go to http://www.twohills.co.nz/umm

This diagram summarises the Unicorn Management Model: this advancement model is how you can make improvement actually work, to achieve behaviour change and eventually culture change, to get the organisation into new ways of working and managing, to achieve organisational agility. It seems like every model has to have a complicated picture so on the previous page is our "paddle-wheel" diagram. It tells us:

Trying to directly change the way people work is futile: you can't order them to be different. It is still worthwhile to drive **intrinsic cultural change**, to both managers and workers, but it won't succeed until you also create **extrinsic change**. They work within a **system**. The work system must change, to allow the people to change the way they work.

The work system provides them **values** to guide them, **ways** of working to shape what they do, and the **means** to do their work. In return those doing the work provide design of the work (procedures, techniques, standards), and results from the work.

The system is built on people's behaviour, practices, artefacts and tools, and suppliers / partners. We **change the system** in order to change these inputs to the work. The way we change the system is by changing the way we **manage the system**. We do this in three primary areas: we change the people-management, the governance and executive management, and the business management.

The **executive management** provides the **policy, resources, vision, strategy, and funding**, which in turn sets the values that the people use when doing their work.

We exclude **leadership** from this list: leadership comes from managers and non-managers alike. Not all managers are leaders.

The executive are themselves directed and monitored by the **organisational governance**, who should be concerned primarily with three system resources: **people, money, and information** - which they should govern equally.

The executive management receives feedback from the work system, especially but not exclusively feedback on the **risks** present in the system, in order to allow them to manage risk.

In order to change the way executive management and governance think, we coach both governors and executive managers in the new **principles** guiding the way they manage. There are primary management principles that we use, and a number of subsidiary principles derived from them. For example, these principles include the ideas that success comes through failure, we should organise around products not projects, we need to do less in order to do more, and let the people doing the work design the work.

The **people-management** function influences the work system through **KPIs, capability, performance management,**. These shape the ways for people to do their work. People managers receive feedback from the system primarily around the **performance** of the work.

The way that we influence people management is through introducing new **models** for behaviour, including kaizen cultural improvement, network management structures, servant manager (we don't like the term servant leader), agile management, and transformational leadership.

The **business management** function provides **priorities, workflow definitions, process designs, tools, and architecture**, which practitioners use as the means to do their work. The business management function receives feedback from the work system primarily but not exclusively around what are the **constraints** in the system that management can help remove.

To change the way business is managed we introduce new **methods** such as Lean, Theory of Constraints, value networks, kanban, Scrum, Scaled Agile Framework or Disciplined Agile or Large-Scale Scrum or Scrum of Scrums, and DevOps.

An improvement "machine" drives a **continual improvement programme** to keep the whole thing alive and moving.

The paddle-wheel diagram is labelled "Unicorn Management Model: **Alpha**". One day you will transform to a Beta organisation(p48), or - to use another model - a "teal" culture (p10). This UMM is for working in an Alpha world. It is how we drive the advancement towards Beta culture. As we advance, there will be less influence from management on the system, and more from the people doing the work. There will be a different picture, the Unicorn Management Model: Beta. Look for that in a future edition: we all have to get there first.

Growing to new ways

The Unicorn Management Model honours the principle that you can't change a complex system, you can only create the conditions for it to change itself. Management creates and manipulates those conditions. The model also follows the Agile principle of "Let the people doing the work design the work". The work system gives them the values, ways, and means, and lets the work be emergent.

Don't rush to blame the individual. Unreasonable systems make unreasonable people. Fix the system. Staff get labelled as lazy, negative, or obstructive, when they're actually frustrated, bitter, disengaged, tired, afraid, unsafe. Most people blossom when you get the work system off them.

Nor is it the process that is the problem. Trying to improve a process is like fixing one cog in a gearbox. Even if you overcome that analogy by making a process more efficient, effective, and usually easier, that will often be a local optimum which degrades the overall system flow.

And of course, improving tools never fixed anything, in isolation. Tools are a lower priority than systems, people, and practices. Improve the system to free the people to improve the processes to identify tool requirements.

We see the improvement growing through four tiers or modes of advancement activity. This is not a project plan, these are not phases. Nor is it a maturity model. We just improve in more ways over time as circumstances change

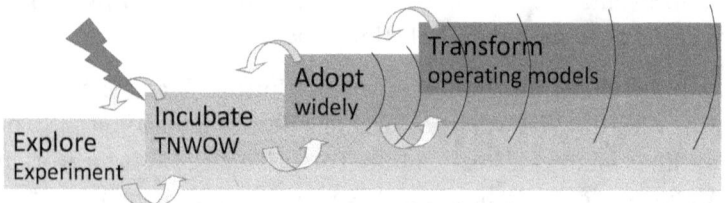

So long as the organisation is in an **explore** mode, you can advance in the grassroots, below the radar, guerrilla-style (maybe with localised management support). But in order to move to "The New Way Of Managing For Our Organisation", you need executive support: a mandate to **incubate** that new way. We come together to grow new ways for our organisation, triggering new exploration.

Once we feel we have a minimum viable model tor TNWOW (the new way of working) we then begin to **adopt** it widely. For goodness sake, adopt in an iterative incremental manner, with feedback to continually improve what we have incubated. Test different options for each iteration as you adopt, and use selection to eliminate options and evolve new ones as you iterate.

As we adopt the new way of working, we pull new behaviour from the rest of the organisation, and we start to **transform** the operating model of the organisation and its suppliers and customers: new funding, strategy, planning, prioritisation, portfolio management, engagement between functions, governance, audit, measurement, reporting... We do so collaboratively, so this also alters how *we* work.

Practical principles

There are many principles we can derive from the thinking of Agile, Lean, DevOps and other bodies of knowledge. There is no template for any organisation – you must agree together which principles drive and guide your organisation.

We make these principles more guiding and less abstract than the principles in Section 1, p88 (we don't want to sound like a Zen master). Remember the groups we had for those principles? They are organised into three groups:

> **Human**: People, Customer, Culture, and Trust.

> **Systems**: Transparency, Slack, Flow, and Science.

> **Agility**: Complexity, Agility, Failure, and Improvement.

Using those groups again, some principles of the new ways which are likely to work for you are:

Human

✓ The customer determines what is valuable, whether we are doing the right things.

✓ We are all on the same side.

✓ Quality is everybody's responsibility.

✓ Our people are adults, professionals, with good intentions.

- ✓ Management exists to grow people; to grow the work system; to make work more agile; and to ensure maximum value is delivered to the customer.
- ✓ People flourish: they do well here, they blossom. We care about growth, engagement, and mental and physical health. It is better (and usually cheaper, and often just as fast) to grow somebody than to replace them.
- ✓ Whenever possible, we communicate face-to-face.
- ✓ We embrace diversity. Mixed groups make the best decisions. A collective view from a wide range of perspectives is the most valuable qualitative data.
- ✓ People differ in how quickly they change - we value conservatives. People aren't positive and upbeat all the time.
- ✓ Collectively, we hold the solutions. External and internal experts provide knowledge and ideas; together we find the answers.
- ✓ Ways of working are designed by those doing it. Change is pulled by them not pushed by the organisation.

Systems

- ✓ We are holistic, we understand and improve the whole work system.
- ✓ Agility, velocity, and efficiency are outcomes from quality in what we produce and how we work: focus on lifting quality.
- ✓ Shift left: ensure quality as early as possible, as integral to the work as possible.
- ✓ Work is sustainable indefinitely without accruing cultural or system debt.
- ✓ Maximum throughput does not come at maximum utilisation of resources or people. There is slack capacity.
- ✓ The answers lie where the work is done – we go to the gemba often.
- ✓ Managers and governors go to the work to get their own data, and do their own reporting of what they observe.
- ✓ Work must flow out to a customer to have value.

Agility

- ✓ Failure is embraced as an asset of the organisation. We extract maximum value from failure. Failure makes us stronger. We don't punish failure. We reward information about it. Failure is met with curiosity not controls.
- ✓ Fail well. Fail fast, early, small, often. Minimise blast radius. Be immaculate in what you do: only noble failure.
- ✓ Planning is essential but plans are expendable. Plan only enough.
- ✓ We navigate ambiguity. We don't know the end when we start. We cope with imperfect information.
- ✓ The only way to know is to do. Opinions are interesting, but validating the hypothesis at minimum cost and risk is much more useful.
- ✓ Agility is about how fast you can change how you work, not how fast you work.
- ✓ Continual improvement is the way we do things around here. We are a learning organisation.
- ✓ It is more important to improve work than to do work.

Check our website www.agilemanagers.club for the latest versions of these.

Matariki

Applying the Improvement Kata, what's your vision for New Ways of Working and Managing? What are the far-term goals? As explained earlier in the book, we call these navigational stars "matariki".

Try to separate matariki from principles: principles are abstract and can be applied anywhere, matariki refer to specific aspects of our work. We also separate matariki from goals: matariki give a specific direction, but goals should be SMART: specific, measurable, achievable, relevant, and timebound. Goals are specific enough to know when we get there (though these vision goals are set so far off that we are not expecting to get there any time soon). Matariki are far out.

Remember there are no neat templates or formulae to New Ways of Working. We have stated some aspirations throughout the book. Here they are and some more. Start with this list as examples, and decide your own as an organisation. They're not fixed in the sky, they move, so you can revise them say every year, or more often in a fast-moving world.

Your organisation's choice of matariki and specific goals is enlightening. Step back, take an objective outside view of the result, as we do as consultants. Are they consistent? Do they all point back to a common vision? Or are they all over the place, a grab-bag, contradictory, indicating lack of cohesion?

Human

★ Our value is measured by what is delivered to customers.

★ The Voice of the Customer is present in all decisions.

★ Teams work together focused on the customer value.

★ Out of hours work is exceptional, never normal.

★ All important communication is face-to-face.

★ Managers are servant managers. The hierarchy supports the work, management is a foundation not an overhead.

★ People want to work here. We get all the good staff we need.

★ Teams are stable and long lived.

Systems

★ We optimise whole value streams, not local activities.

★ Quality is built into the work systems, as early as possible.

★ Cultural debt and system debt are falling.

★ Value streams are run at maximum throughput not maximum capacity. We ensure that people are not utilised 100% (or more).

★ We work in networked ways: we create connections, our communities cut across silos, we are fluid, we come together in virtual teams, we swarm to get stuff done.

★ Controls are as light as possible, as early as possible, parallel where possible, and incremental. All non-value functions are focused on getting out of the way of the value flow.

★ Information flows freely and widely. Feedback loops are strong and fast.

★ All work is visible.

★ When we want to find out, we go to the gemba: performance, status, design of work, feedback, morale... Managers do reporting.

Agility

★ Productivity (velocity through quality) always increases.

★ All culture and operating models are based on a foundation of continual improvement.

★ Everybody works in cadenced iterations.

★ Experimentation is how we work. All iterations are an experiment. We re-plan often based on what we learn.

★ We are organised and architected to minimise dependencies between teams. We align and manage the remaining dependencies with minimum surprises.

★ All teams are small (<10) and self-organising.

★ The organisational structure is pulled by the teams not pushed by the management. It usually happens incrementally, not in big reorganisations.

★ Teams pull from a single stream of work.

★ Work is prioritised by those owning the value produced.

★ Work is broken down small enough to get done. We scale work down, not teams up.

★ We build our organisation around products not projects. Projects are a logistic construct to manage large scale work, not an organisational structure or a work structure.

★ Our systems are built to expect human error, to be resilient in failure, and to respond to stress by improving.

★ We balance the efficiency of standardisation and automation with the agility of diversity and human work.

★ We can change the way we work quickly.

Check our website www.agilemanagers.club for the latest versions of these.

Branding

It is good to have a name for the new ways of working, and for the role of the person owning that. We don't have strong recommendations. Something like Velocity Improvement, New Ways of Working, nWoW!, or The Agility Programme. It needs to be something that resonates for the organisation. It may link to existing ideas, movements, or initiatives within the organisation.

Whatever you do, don't call it "Agile" or "Lean", or any industry labels. They come with baggage. "Oh X? We tried that; it doesn't work". Use a name that describes what you want to achieve, in the language of your organisation (remember the suggestions at the start of this book on p12).

Use iconography: we like unicorns (p187). A visual theme is useful to build the branding. Many people are pictorial, not narrative in nature. It needs to be an iconic concept that works both in words and pictures. Teal Unicorn has chosen the unicorn because it is an established Agile trope, funny, light-hearted, open to puns and jokes, richly visual, with a wide variety of available merchandise. It makes people smile.

Andrew Hood
security good guy

Invest

To make advancement happen, you must invest: time and money.

You don't change the management-system-behaviour-work just in everybody's spare time. It takes effort and cash to improve culture, promote sharing, develop people, create automation, and most of all to give managers and staff some time capacity to even think about improving how they work.

When we make these improvements to create advancement, it is usually investment outside any project structures: projects have no incentive to make improvements if they have a fixed deliverable and an end date. It is often outside of any business unit, where you are making improvements to a shared service to change workflow. In every case, it is hard to find anyone willing to pay for it all. You usually need a dedicated discretionary fund to make advancement happen.

Even more than money though, it is essential to give people time. Manage demand, reduce utilisation to 80%, give permission to improve, reward improvement over throughput. The better we get, the faster and more efficient we get. We reap rewards in future, and we buy ourselves even more headroom to improve more. It becomes a positive feedback loop.

The Improvement Machine

No artefact in business has any value without an active practice to keep it "alive": evolving, improving, relevant. That practice includes people with roles and responsibilities to maintain the artefact, and tools and procedures to do so. This is true of portfolios, knowledgebases, handbooks, anything at all. Artefacts that are allowed to get out of date or into disrepair soon fall out of use. This is also true of this advancement to new ways of working and managing. Without staff dedicated to keeping a backlog alive, it soon dies out.

We call the practice to drive an advancement the "machine". Here's how the machine works:

As we evolve our work, we identify improvements we want to make. These need to go into a backlog to be prioritised otherwise we soon become overwhelmed by all the improvement to be done. This backlog is maintained by an "Advancement Product Owner".

An agile team, the "Advancement Office", drives the advancement. They keep the backlog alive. They:

- help formulate the vision and matariki.

- evangelise the new ways.

- encourage other teams to make the improvements from the backlog.

- encourage other teams to come up with their own experiments in new ways of working.

- resource and support those improvements and experiments.

- track the impact and benefits of new ways.

Often, multiple other advancements are happening outside the scope of this New Ways improvement, or overlapping with it, which are themselves transforming how we work. This will require coordination and the resolution of differences, but it doesn't necessarily require central planning, which would be counter-productive to agility – what is required is alignment and collaboration. It does mean that the scope of the New Ways improvement machine needs to be clearly defined (and may grow over time).

Model

As we have discussed, there are no templates. Every organisation lands somewhere different. But here is a model that has worked well for us for the "Improvement Machine".

Just as we advised "don't call it Agile", we are not suggesting you use these names we use in this book, only these concepts. Use existing roles and groups where you can; or else use existing organisational naming styles and conventions so they blend in.

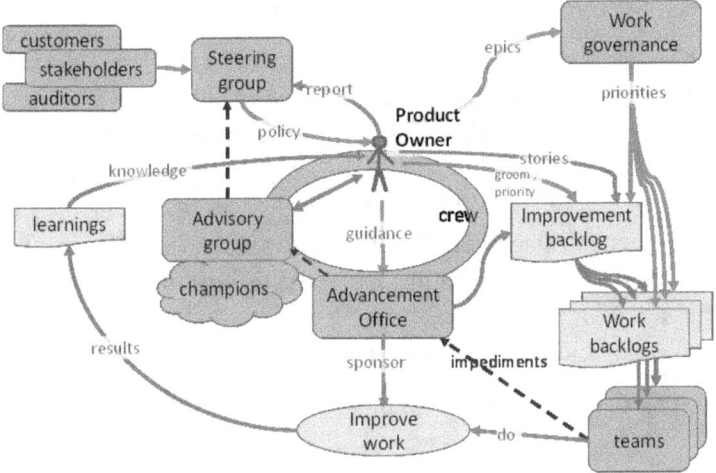

Product Owner

For the purposes of this model, we call the person who owns responsibility for making the advancement happen the "Advancement Product Owner, APO". The advancement is not really a product, but the role is a lot like a Product Owner as they define it in Scrum (p291).

You wouldn't actually call it Advancement Product Owner (we hope). Advancement isn't a "product". And "owner" implies authority and accountability, which either makes others see the role as a power threat; or allows them to transfer accountability, to think this person is going to do everything. Perhaps call the role a {Your initiative's name} Champion, or Steward.

The APO has three primary **activities**:

- gathering the **vision**, goals, matariki, and roadmap for advancement.
- **organisational change management** within the scope of advancement: communication, celebration, collaboration, motivation.
- **metrics**: making systems behaviour and performance transparent (evidence), and communicating the progress of advancement (feedback).

The APO has three primary **tactics** to achieve this: **catalysis:** trigger change; **intervention:** "nudge" to redirect energy when required; and **support:** provide advice, assistance and encouragement.

The APO owns the advancement, not the work transformed. This means that new capabilities created by the Advancement Office will be handed off to other functions to own them. The Advancement Office serves their APO. The Advancement Office would only create a capability where nobody else will, but - as soon as they can - they find someone to give ownership to. This prevents the Advancement Office or the Advancement Product Owner becoming a growing empire, and removes any threat to anyone else. Usually a potential owner volunteers themselves by complaining about the new creation.

For example, we started a small group of roaming Agile coaches, fostering Agile thinking in teams all over the place. The Training Department soon complained so we handed ownership over to them. Other examples might be value stream mapping, software lifecycle automation, dojo, work management tools, or agile funding. Start working on them until somebody wants to own them.

It also means that the APO is **not accountable for changes getting done**, (no accountability without authority), only for identifying and tracking them; and putting them into work management epics, so that governance will prioritise them and ensure they are accepted into backlogs of those who own the functions where the improvement is to be done.

These changes must be prioritised and executed by those accountable. Whatever existing "Work Governance" function your organisation has must communicate the priority and make sure the changes happen. We depend on everybody honouring the fundamental principle that it is more important to improve work than to do work.

Crew

Somewhere between the Advisory Group, the Advancement Office, and APO, an inner circle of passionate people will emerge who want to work together to make this happen. We call it a Crew, an informal Agile-sized team – 3 to 7 people - who provide the energy to "the machine".

Take care of the people at the core of the advancement. They get passionate, they see everything to be done, and they get called on a lot. It is easy for them to get burned out (p134).

Champions

"Champions" is our term for a looser and wider group of people distributed across the organisation, who provide local enthusiasm and support, promote the ideas, advance the cause, and provide feedback. Keep track of who they are, support them, reward them, and bring them together at times.

We use the word "champion" in the sense of supporting and promoting, not winning, but it might sound too elitist to you[157]. How about "pioneers" or "league"[158]?

Advisory Group

There will be an ever-changing group of people who are early adopters of the new ways of working and managing, including some who are passionate, who want to champion the new ways, and those who are just curious (including some who are attracted by noise and success).

We harness this energy in an advisory group who meet regularly to hear progress, and to do what they can to advance our cause, adding resources and removing impediments. The group is open and voluntary, and fluid. We do reach out to key stakeholders to encourage them to join in. Try to develop a diverse (p56) community of people. In some contexts, you can bring in outsiders to advise and help. If the size gets unwieldy, don't shut people out: split it into more focused groups.

---

[157] We used to say "Circle of Champions", but that *really* sounds elitist.

[158] or "Rebel Network".
https://transformingtogether.blog.gov.uk/2019/03/21/creating-a-rebel-network-to-deliver-transformation/

Steering Group

John Kotter talks about the need for a powerful guiding coalition[159]. Either bring together the powerful stakeholders who will help to make this happen, or find an existing group that this initiative can back into, as one of its goals, as an agenda item.

The steering group will:

- give a powerful mandate, and keep executive support.

- provide direction: goals, policy, bounds.

- make decisions escalated to it.

- deal with impediments escalated to it, usually after the advisory group can't deal with them.

- usually be the source of funding and other resources for the "Machine".

Advancement Office

We call the team who do much of the work driving the advancement "The Advancement Office", because there are some similarities to a Project Management Office, of the type where PMOs don't have any project managers working for them directly but do:

- provide guidance, resources, supervision.
- provide a centre of expertise.
- evangelise the practices.
- monitor improvement of the practices (and possibly audit).
- plan and promote improvement of the practices.

They might be a specialist team solely for the advancement activities moving us to new ways of working and managing, or they may be part of a broader Continual Improvement function, if you already have one. Again, whatever works.

You probably won't call them a "Advancement Office". That is a term for the purposes of this book, it is not in general use. Call it by your own terms (if it is a distinct entity – it may be part of something else).

---

[159] https://www.kotterinc.com/8-steps-process-for-leading-change/

The following general description of an Advancement Office provides their aspirational goals (matariki).

The purpose of an Advancement Office generally is to:

- create a consistent vision and understanding of new ways of working and managing across the organisation.
- create models of what new ways mean for the organisation and how they work.
- provide a central point for the dissemination of knowledge on new ways of working and managing.
- promote the adoption of new ways across the organisation: Agile, Lean, servant manager, and other practices.

Activities will include:

Vision

- help the APO maintain a roadmap and matariki for future evolution. This is not a programme plan – it's a shape, strategy, and direction for advancement to velocity through quality.

Models

- create models, policies, standards (not too many of these), and templates for lifecycles, as part of design of lifecycles and value streams.

Knowledge

- provide a programme of training in these new ways.
- create an inventory of existing New Ways practices, tools, skills, and experiments.
- maintain value stream maps, and continually look for opportunities to remove constraints and improve flow.
- provide an incubator for new ways: a common space where people can go to experience them, to get a demonstration of software, and to talk to coaches (a "dojo").
- facilitate sharing with other organisations.

Adoption

- run an Advancement Continual Improvement Programme (or inputs into a more general Continual Improvement Programme).
- create and promote collaboration across teams.
- encourage and facilitate forums, communities, and guilds of expertise.

- measure and report improvement, and provide dashboards to teams and to managers.
- review and possibly audit practices.
- provide support and possibly funding for work automation.

We recommend the following initial Advancement Office activities (and there will be plenty more), in roughly this order:

1. Establish an improvement **backlog**, or find an existing backlog to use.
2. Identify your Advancement **Product Owner**, if that is not already clear.
3. Assemble an **Advisory Group**, or identify an existing group that can fulfil the function.
4. Assemble a **Steering Group**, or identify an existing group that can fulfil the function.
5. Identify the **Work Governance** function that can set and drive work priority for you.
6. Understand your customers, auditors, and other **stakeholders**.
7. Create the **flow** of improvement work, p234, connecting all the functions: the roles, processes, data flows. Get everybody involved and engaged.
8. Establish **funding** for the APO (which will fund the work of the Advancement Office, amongst other things), usually via the Steering Group.
9. Establish a **manager coaching programme** to transform manager behaviours and ensure that all managers at all levels understand what is required of them as part of the advancement.
10. Establish an **experiment programme** to encourage all individual teams to experiment with new ideas and techniques.
11. **Support** teams and functions to evolve out of experimentation through incubate/adopt/transform into the new ways, and track the heatmap.
12. Do **value stream mapping**. Bring in expert help to analyse and improve the value streams, to give a holistic view of flows of work, to bring transparency as a foundation for improvement in velocity and quality.
13. Establish a **dojo team** (p200), to build NWOW expertise amongst teams in a targeted manner.

Roles

Here are some roles within the Advancement Office. These roles <u>don't</u> mean job positions. In Agile we don't have roles for individuals, just skills. One person may wear multiple hats, and some of these roles may be fulfilled outside the Advancement Office.

Role	What
Advancement Product Owner APO	The person responsible for the advancement towards new ways of working and managing. Has the powers and responsibilities to direct, prioritise, and assign value to work. Represents the advancement to the rest of the organisation.
Advancement Programme Manager	Manages the flow of work, timeline, logistics, and funding for the initial set-up of the Improvement Machine until improvements are flowing smoothly.
Continual Improvement Manager	Liaises with teams doing improvements, (including innovations and experiments). Coordinates the backlog of stories allocated to other teams. Reports on the portfolio of improvements (including burndown)
Advancement Office Scrum Master	Keeps us working agile. Runs interference. Removes impediments.
Cultural Change Manager	All aspects of cultural change: communications, learning, coaching training, creating, communities, encouraging, collaboration. Connect up with other intrinsic cultural change initiatives.
Advancement Strategist Get an expert: bring in external knowledge and experience.	Provides high-level conceptual view. Maintains a holistic perspective of the advancement, the big picture. Advises on strategy. Teaches and coaches theory on new ways of working and managing.

Role	What
	Identifies strengths, weaknesses, opportunities, and threats.
	Liaises with senior managers.
	Grows others, to become obsolete.
New Ways Evangelist	Challenges conventional thinking.
	Promotes concepts.
	Maintains enthusiasm and positive energy.
	Marketing.
Agile Evangelist	Promotes Agile thinking.
	Teaches Agile methods (Scrum, Kanban...) and tools.
	Coaches teams adopting Agile.
	Runs an Agile Coach Guild for all coaches across the organisation.
New Ways Architect	Owns and coordinates design and documentation of new ways of working and managing.
	Maintains the big picture and the dependencies to ensure a consistent new system of work.
Workflow Engineer	Maps value streams.
	Advises on and designs flow improvements (practices, tools, teams...).
Tool Coaches	Support for teams adopting organisational tools, to help with setting up work, and designing dashboards and reporting.
Administration	Organises events and training, Logistics.
	Maintains knowledge base of learnings, heatmaps, record keeping...

Growth model

As you grow through the four tiers of advancement (p218) - Explore, Incubate, Adopt, and Transform – this Improvement Machine model will evolve too. If you get the luxury of starting early on in the growth model, back at Explore, you can start simpler and grow over time.

Explore

Initially, if you are in Explore mode, you don't have a mandate to transform, so there is little or no funding. You don't have the executive support to go to Work Governance for prioritisation, and you probably don't have a steering group. You often have a sponsoring senior manager.

In Explore mode, we use a model like this:

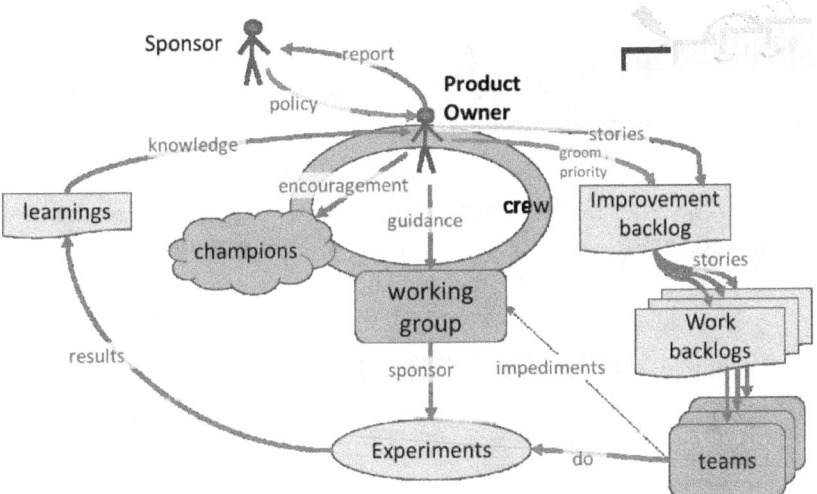

Working Group

Without funding, you don't have a team yet, so you assemble a Working Group of people from other teams who are early adopters, champions of the new ways, or curious and supportive. They volunteer to take on the improvements you suggest, doing them as part of the Experiment Programme, which you do get support for.

Like the later Advisory Group, membership is fluid: we invite some and others volunteer themselves. Some come along out of curiosity. Some realise they don't fit or don't have the available bandwidth, and they drift away. This group is expected to have more skin in the game than an Advisory Group: we have greater expectations that they will help out, take on some of the work that an Advancement Team would do if we had one. The Crew and the Champions will naturally appear out of this community.

They generate and track experiments, building knowledge and proof points, in preparation for evolving to the Incubate mode.

Incubate

Once you get a mandate to incubate "The New Ways Of Working and Managing For Us At Our Organisation", whatever you choose to call it, the model changes.

You start to grow an advancement team. They might be the informal Crew, they might be a more formal team, mostly drawn from the Crew. They do the initial work of the Advancement Office described above, including finding the Steering Group to direct the development of new ways, and the Advisory Group of involved stakeholders.

Many of the people in the Working Group will move to the Advisory Group. You will want to bring in the roles (p233) of a Workflow Engineer at this time, and a higher level New Ways Architect if you are going to have one, to own and coordinate the design of new ways of working. Also, an Advancement Strategist if you don't already have one.

In Incubate mode, we use a model like this:

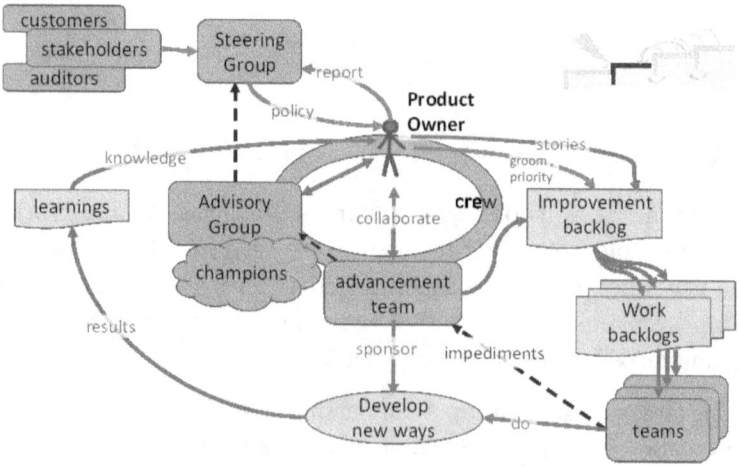

Adopt

Then once you gain agreement via the Steering Group to start to adopt the new ways of working and managing, you reach the final model we saw above. All roles (p233) are now present (remember they don't represent headcount, jut roles that people perform).

The picture is repeated here:

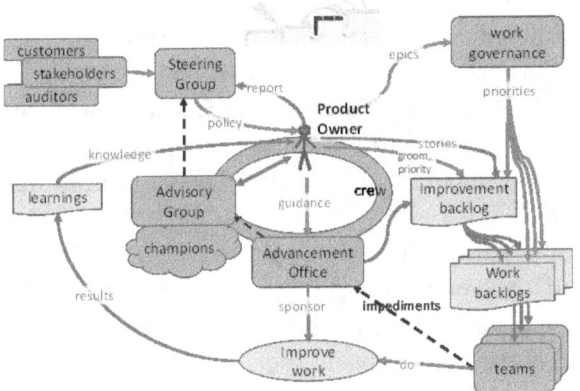

Transform

Once you reach the Transform mode, and start influencing the whole operating model of the organisation and its suppliers and customers, the model doesn't change, but the entities such as Steering Group and Advisory Group become wider and more prominent. There will be other advancement teams working across the organisation, for you to collaborate and coordinate with - agility at large scale.

"higher levels of tacit functional capability in organizations are invisible by definition. For an industrial imagination, an organization is a set of explicit and legible systems and processes. If you transcend those, what even are you talking about?"

- Venkatesh Rao

The destiny of the Advancement Office is to become obsolete: to consolidate improvement behaviour into the culture of the organisation to the point where it is no longer necessary to maintain a "machine": where everybody improves all the time as part of "the way we do things around here".

Challenges

This "machine" is designed to overcome some common challenges to advancement. It does so in these ways:

- stakeholders are self-selecting: all are welcome in the Advisory and Working Groups.
- everyone gets heard: there are multiple feedback loops from the teams and from the groups.
- executive support is promoted and maintained by the Steering Group.
- funding is drawn from the Steering Group who have visibility of and involvement in what the advancement is achieving.
- work is prioritised for all the teams by the same governance as other work, so that advancement doesn't get lost.
- the champions maintain the energy in the field.
- as the organisation shifts to different tiers of advancement, the machine adapts.

Scaling

Any team can do experiments themselves within their domain. Any manager can encourage and protect that, creating a buffered bubble of safety. But, until we have a mandate to incubate The New Way Of Working, how do we ever scale beyond isolated teams?

The Working Group (p235) provides a way for like-minded individuals to find each other and provide mutual support, but it is loose.

A stronger construct is to form triads[160] of peers: three people with a shared vision, roughly equal status, and an agreement to look after each other. Their three groups will collaborate and form a tribe of people working towards new ways. Then you can jointly take them on a journey of Tribal Learning[161], to create larger pockets of new ways within the organisation. This is the intermediate stage of growth between team-level experiments and adopting a new way for all.

---

[160] This concept comes from *Tribal Leadership*, Dave Logan and John King. The triad technique is not obvious. It is described in detail in *The Culture Game*, by Dan Mezick.

[161] Again *The Culture Game*, Dan Mezick

Measure progress

As part of the Improvement Kata (p271) we set our aspirational vision. One often uses the language of navigational stars, points of reference for sailors when navigating. As already discussed, we at Teal Unicorn use the term matariki for navigational goals.

To extend the sailing analogy, we often coach clients to measure progress from your wake behind, not the stars ahead. If you measure against the stars, against an ideal model, you will always be disappointed. If you measure how far you have come, you will hopefully always see an advance. If you are not moving forward, you have a much bigger problem than measuring progress.

You need a high-level indicator of progress on new ways of managing. It is important to focus on outcomes, and not to have too few metrics. No metric is perfect: they all distort behaviour as people optimise to the indicator, not the outcome. Portfolios of multiple metrics smooth out this effect. Teal Unicorn prefers a Balanced Scorecard: multiple portfolios (there are usually four quadrants) of metrics.

Here is our preferred balanced scorecard:

Value throughput	Sustainability	
•User-story effort "points" •Percentage of work which is creating new features •Amount of money spent/period •Benefits realisation	Culture debt •Staff satisfaction •Churn •Health	System debt •Improvements •Problems •Risk
Quality	Improvement	
•Customer Satisfaction •Defects •Ease of obtaining funds •Reliability of services •Fitness for purpose	•Hours spent on improvement •Improvement results •Innovation •Learning	
Narrative		
All reporting should come with a narrative of what we are seeing and why, prepared by those close to the work. Don't leave it to recipients to spot and infer what's happening.		

The metrics above are only examples of suggested measures. Start with what you can measure now. We believe bad metrics inspire better metrics, so long as we are clear about the quality of the metrics.

One would want to have a portfolio of metrics under each quadrant of the scorecard. Be constantly improving and changing them - dashboards are a dynamic activity, not a static artefact. We also create a spreadsheet of measured, needed, desired, and rejected metrics, to direct development of the scorecard over time.

Quadrant	Topic	Measure	Metric	Status	Source	Owner	Weight	Units	Target	Upper bound	Lower bound
value	lead time	Jira xyz - abc	average lead time per feature	reporting	Jira		3	days	lower	20	
quality	access to funds	Working account balance	business funds committed	available	Working acct		0.002	$k	higher		
quality	satisfaction	Monthly score	customer satisfaction survey	feasible	NPS		8		higher		6
value	throughput	Jenkins sum(xyz)	features per release	needed	Jenkins				lower?		
value	throughput		total value delivered	proposed					higher		
value	throughput		average cycle time per feature	not possible					Lower		
value	cost of delay		business cost of backlog	deprecated					Lower		

Remember, no artefact like a scorecard has any value unless you also build a practice of people and processes around it to keep it alive. Find some smart data kids: they work wonders with big data these days.

Value and Quality are lagging indicators of how well we have done at improving work, how far we have come, our "wake". Sustainability (systems and culture debt) and Improvement are leading indicators of how well equipped we are to improve in the future.

Balanced Scorecard is like an advanced game of Whack-a-Mole. It is about keeping all four quadrants advancing. If you push Value too hard you may degrade Quality. If you improve Value and Quality too hard you may reduce Sustainability by neglecting pay-down of system debt or grinding your people, and you may forget to Improve.

> We don't want to define "done." In an ongoing system, a symmathesy, there is no "done" except death.
>
> Instead, define "better." Then you can know you accomplished something.
>
> - Jessica Kerr

Experiment

Our assertion is that all real-world systems of work are complex. By experimenting we explore our way towards new ways of working. Cynefin (p273) talks about the need to "probe, sense, and act" to find a way forward in a complex situation. We don't know the end when we start, we don't know the answer.

The way forward doesn't need to be a single path of exploration: send out many scouts. In other words, run parallel experiments in different directions. Create diversity, then select for success. Use evolutionary natural selection.[162] Keep doing what works and stop doing what doesn't.

A programme to encourage experimentation in teams is a successful way of creating grass-roots enthusiasm. It "lights a grassfire".

Benefits of experimentation include:

- ❖ create proof points for the organisation.

- ❖ give staff time and opportunity to change their understanding and attitudes and behaviours.

- ❖ develop a knowledge base of innovation in order to understand what works here in this organisation (and what doesn't), and how it works.

- ❖ give experiments an opportunity to fail fast on a small scale with low impact in order to maximize the probability of incubating a good model.

- ❖ learn to fail well. By definition, some experiments will fail.

- ❖ test whether an idea works in one team's context.

- ❖ make useful improvements (note this is not top of the list).

- ❖ get people involved and enthused with new ways.

- ❖ contribute to team-building.

- ❖ learn new skills.

---

[162] It is a valid use of the Darwinian model here: weak ideas die out.

Outcomes of experimentation include:

- ☐ develop awareness of new concepts and principles and allow the staff time to absorb and understand them.

- ☐ discover, foster, and initiate innovations across the organisation.

- ☐ remove impediments to innovations/experiments:
    - ○ find owners for impediments.
    - ○ protect the team: "run interference", provide "air cover".
    - ○ negotiate and arbitrate solutions.
    - ○ fund solutions: e.g. additional software licences; training "scholarships".

- ☐ map innovation to ensure we have coverage of all the areas of new ways of working.

- ☐ foster an ad-hoc informal "Crew" (people who will provide support, advice, evangelism, and enthusiasm, p229) for the Advancement Product Owner (p227).

Deliverables of experimentation can be a stocktake of current innovation (p249); a presentation of proof points and learnings from experimentation/innovation cycle: results, outputs, and value from innovations; and/or a simple governance engagement model for innovations to exist within, to interact with the existing organisation.

Approach to experimentation

Experiments seek to see if the ideas will work, to generate proof points, and to develop awareness and experience. The experiments should have a purpose and testable conditions.

There are boundaries around experiments including decisions as to what success will "look like" and when it will be done. Experimentation can be done with subsets of innovation, ideation, etc. Try a thing.

The Crew create an inventory of who is doing what - this includes people, process and automation - and create a repository of learnings which will feed the backlog of improvements. Make a heatmap of experiments (p249) to ensure you have coverage of all areas of interest, and encourage experiments where you don't.

Experimentation does not require executive or even management support: it can happen guerrilla-style, grassroots, bottom up. Executive permission is useful. Executive leaders at the CXO level can communicate that experiments are mandated, encouraged, and resourced: it's OK to experiment as part of (improving) work.

Experiment critical success factors

Managers need education on experimentation: a 1-hour session on the ideas and method. Coaching as well as needed.

Teams need training on the new ways of working; and a 60-90 minute session for each team to coach what and how to experiment; and good policy: what the rules and bounds are.

Once they start experimenting, teams need ongoing support; coaching; access to the right people; removal of impediments; money, white space, resources.

The owner of the programme needs a mandate to encourage experiments; air cover from those who might oppose the idea; and discretionary funds.

How to do an experiment

To decide if it is a good idea or not, ask yourselves:

1. Do we have responsibility over the domain of the idea?

2. Is the human, financial, operational, and reputational risk below the acceptable threshold? Do we know the threshold?

3. Do we have the necessary approvals? And agreement from impacted stakeholders? (Don't go wider than we need to).

4. Have we made the experiment as small as possible and minimised the blast radius?

5. Can we stop partway through if need be? Can we go back?

Do what is required to define and plan the experiment: a workshop, an A3 description, trying an even smaller experiment first...

Put the experiment on your backlog along with other work. Don't try to do it in "spare time". Let the team promoting experiments know what you are doing. Experiment for a set time, then review and decide whether to keep the idea. Feed back the results to the APO. Share your learnings - good and bad - widely.

What experiment

Each team should discuss it amongst themselves to choose and agree experiments. You don't need to transform a project or process or team to all aspects of new ways of working in order to experiment.

You can try any one idea such as:

Customer alignment, business relationships, product owner, portfolio, services, business value streams, demand, engagement.

Suppliers, service providers, anything-as-a-service.

Product structure, standing teams, "no projects".

Agile thinking, experiment, fail fast, less ceremony, self-organising teams, standing teams, skills not roles.

Agile methods, cadence, sprints, user stories, backlogs, kanban, Scrum, hacks, agile on a large scale.

Automation of work.

Flow, Lean, workflow, value stream mapping.

Visibility of work, kanban, obeya.

Shift left, bake in quality, lighter controls.

Service management, service levels, end-to-end, support.

Measurement, feedback, improvement, kaizen.

Sharing, community, guilds, events, development, training, celebration, showcases.

Collaboration, chat, virtual teaming, colocation.

Management, empowerment, virtual teams.

Funding, fixed teams, budgeting, estimating, business cases.

Governance, policy, strategy, planning.

Looked at another way, consider opportunities to do these kinds of activities:

Pay down **system debt**: fix, improve, replace, clean up....

Encourage **continual improvement**: incremental changes to process or tools, so we are more efficient or effective or flexible.

Optimise the whole flow of work, not just your team's part of it. Help people get work done, get out of the way.

Simplify the flow of work. Remove waits, piles of work, running around, redundant work, higher standard than necessary for value, double handling, errors, rework.

- o Simplify handoffs, challenge ceremony, get out of the way of the flow of work.
- o Give people what they want to get their job done. Don't force them into your models.

Automate menial tasks, toil (defined and repeatable: we know what to do and we get the same results every time).

- o Then make it self-service: Improve that automation so that it can be entrusted to those who ask us to do it, so they can do it themselves without waiting.

Collaborate more closely with other teams, open up communication, form communities/guilds. Communicate face-to-face instead of by emails or tickets (use those to confirm arrangements).

Form **virtual teams**: they report to different managers, but they are committed to a common piece of work. Note that "virtual team" doesn't mean "do your day job and do this other thing somehow in your spare time": it is a temporary re-assignment, not an additional assignment.

Share **knowledge** (amongst yourselves, with others).

Hacks

Hacks are an effective way to cut through the noise to get to a resolution. They are a structured version of swarming.

1. Find a problem, need or risk to be solved.

2. Assemble a cross-functional team(s) of the right people.

3. Put them in a room for a day or two with everything they need.

4. Give them the goal of coming out with a solution.

There are four kinds of hack:

Open hackathon

Run an "open house" providing resources and a backlog of problems to volunteers and invited participants in an open space: invited to play, usually lured by food and drink and glory.

-   o Varying levels of guidelines as to outcome, from "anything you like" to "make x better".
-   o Measured by results: best to nail it on the day, though some will create ongoing work.

Formal hackathon event

Form multiple cross-functional teams (invited or volunteers) to address multiple selected problems in a structured way.

-   o Needs prework by the teams. This needs to be structured to ensure it happens.
-   o Often generates ideas not results.
-   o Present outcomes to a "Dragon's Den" panel to get more resources.
-   o Work often happens after. Needs a strong lead, and plenty of follow-up and support.

Team Hack

For a single team to attack a set of their problems.

They will often need support to have access to the right resources, and will need to bring together a group from other areas to have all the right people.

Problem hack

Work to a defined requirement, a single need e.g. "we need to automate task x".

- o Ad-hoc as a need and a willingness come up
- o Recruit a team with the required skills.
- o The owner is a manager who will benefit from the outcome, and will run around to recruit/beg resources and to remove impediments.
- o The goal is to nail it on the day, so manage scope well.

General principles and techniques for hack include:

- Always have warm up activities.

- Coach not teach: a bit of inspiration then get on with it.

- Have reflection at intervals and at the end; also coaching opportunities.

- Mix up existing organisational teams.

- Create an atmosphere of "different".

- Provide them with
  - o Food and materials
  - o Support staff
  - o Coaches
  - o Senior managers to remove impediments

- There is value in the show to the organisation, and the experience for the participants, as well as the actual results.

- Integrate hacks with Continual Improvement programmes: they should ideally draw from an improvement backlog, and their learnings can feed back into the same backlog.

Pilots

We can run larger, more structured experiments: pilots, prototypes, or proofs of concept. Find teams or small projects or pieces of work where we can try as many new ways as possible in one place. If possible, we want to run several pilots: diversity of people and ideas will find the strongest ways. The objective is to create a proof point showing that putting the new ways together will work here in our organisation. This is moving out of the Experiment tier of our journey and into Incubate, as we define and prove the new ways together.

We want to choose pilots (1) suited to agile ways of working: uncertain outcomes, changing conditions, cooperative customer willing to work closely, creative solutions welcomed; (2) with minimum blast radius: low visibility outside our domain of control, low impact on customers, low reputational risk; (3) with low dependencies to other work; and (4) where we can create white space: we can de-couple it from the rest of the system as much as possible, to allow it to work in new ways unimpeded: funding, controls, bureaucracy, reporting, compliance, audit... even goals, measurement, deliverables, and benefits realisation.

Before we embark on a pilot, we should do some smaller scale experimentation first to build experience and skills. Nevertheless, pilots will fail. Ensure we are going to judge the experiment on what we learn, not what the outcomes are.

Look for opportunities such as:

- a small project to improve internal infrastructure.

- a new service to an existing (not new!) customer which is fairly independent, and where the client is expressing a desire to see new ways of working.

- a team brought together to do something entirely new internally, a "special project".

Results of experiments

Encourage everybody to provide feedback to the owner of the experiment programme on who is experimenting with what. Give those willing to experiment the incentive to tell us by giving them access to support and resources in return.

Track experiments on a matrix map of experiment topics versus parts of the organisation. Indicate overall status for each topic, showing how good the coverage is for the organisation, e.g.

Green 😊 = lots of teams trying it, with success

Yellow 😐 = not many trying it

Red 😟 = teams are failing

Grey 😶 = not enough trying it

	A	B	C	D	E	F	G	H
2		**Innovations, experiments**	Customer alignment, BRM, product owner, portfolio, services, business value streams, demand, engagement	Suppliers, service providers, COTS, SaaS, xaaS	Product structure, standing teams, "no projects"	Agile thinking, experiment, fail fast, less ceremony, self-organising teams, standing teams, skills not roles	Agile methods, cadence, sprints, user stories, backlogs, Scrum, agile at scale	Testing, automat TDD, conti testin;
3		**Coverage:**	😐	😟	😐	😐	😊	😐
4		**Teams**						
5		A						
6		B				✓		
7		C				✓	✓	
								Exploratory testing lead

Barcham Map

We can use the growth model on p234 to develop an alternative map[163] of our experiments:

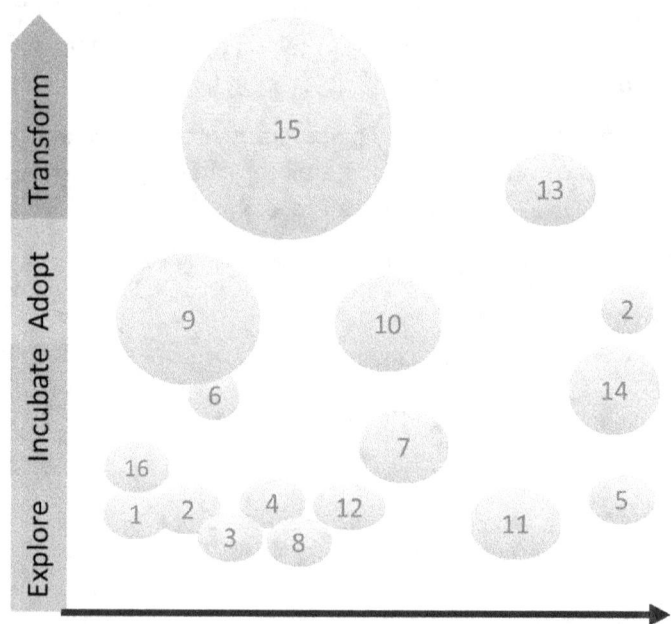

The numbers map to a key of what experiment each one is. You can try colour coding, and different dimensions on the graph, e.g.

X axis:

- visibility to customer
- risk, out-there-ness
- business value
- learning/improvement

Bubble size:

- number of experiment categories covered
- business value
- effort, number of people

---

[163] based on ideas from our friend and colleague Dean Barcham

Celebrate and share

An essential part of consolidating change and maintaining its momentum is to celebrate and share success. It is amazing how many people in an organisation can be unaware of the progress already made and the resources already available. And those involved in an advancement need to step back from time to time, to see and feel how far we have come.

As we discuss elsewhere in this book, it is essential to measure progress by looking backwards not forwards. Perfect is always a long way off, and progress to date is always more than people realise until it is pointed out to them.

Storytelling

Telling stories is one of the most persuasive tools we have. No meticulously researched data or beautifully drawn graphs are as powerful and compelling as an individual telling their story of their own journey to new ways of working.

Capture these stories in text, video, and posters, as well as encouraging the subjects to tell them publicly - especially to senior managers.

More generally, tell stories of other organisations too.

It's more powerful if stories are real, and doubly so if told first-hand. But fables work too – we used one in this book – so long as they are credible, with foundations in reality. We can also tell the real story so far then extrapolate to build the vision.

Stories allow us to communicate vision and values, to inspire, to overcome hesitation and rumour, and most of all to reassure that what we envision is possible[164].

---

[164] *The Leaders Guide to Storytelling,* Steve Denning

Showcase

It is important to have internal events to showcase the progress with advancement. Smaller lunchtime events are useful, but you should also consider a larger internal conference open to all staff, with invitees from other organisations and external stakeholders.

The event should generate attention and excitement: it's a show, a carnival, a celebration, fun; not a sober meeting. A little razzmatazz is good - some showmanship. Send the message: new ways are different.

These events are good to have at least twice a year. Half a day could be sufficient, but a full day is better.

We call them a DoSho, a portmanteau of dojo (p200) and showcase.

The **purpose** is primarily to look backwards not forwards, to:

❖ prove it is real, it works.

❖ celebrate success and progress.

❖ create awareness of what has been achieved and what is available.

❖ market to create a pull demand for the capabilities developed, such as coaching, templates, designs, documents, tools, and automation.

❖ show this is not an old-school organisation.

The **objective** is to present the current state of:

☐ tools.

☐ practices and processes.

☐ flow optimisation.

☐ changing behaviours, ways of working.

☐ improving measurement and feedback.

☐ improving collaboration and sharing.

Suggested content:

• the Advancement Product Owner (p227) presenting on what we have so far. Only a brief slide on the future.

- business speakers (champions, sponsors) presenting on what advancement has achieved for them.

- senior leaders invited to speak 5-10 mins each on what it means for their area. Step up, walk the walk, commit.

- personal stories from staff. Often the most important element. Essential.

- demos of things built.

Other events communicate future strategy roadmaps and do planning, but that's not the intent of a showcase. Don't fall into the trap of making a forward-looking promotional event with visionary speakers and plans etc. We want to look back and show what we have achieved.

It is important to have speakers from the business/customers, but they should be providing feedback on the benefits they have seen so far more than painting pictures of the future.

It is also important to have an "exhibit area" where all of the entities who have achieved something get an opportunity to show and discuss with individual attendees just as a vendor would do at a conference.

Automation developer/toolmakers need to understand that they are marketing to their consumers: that they have to create a desire for the innovations that they are creating, that a "build it and they will come" approach is insufficient.

Other entities should also exhibit, in order to establish relationships and awareness with the attendees, e.g. Finance, Procurement, Audit, HR, Risk, Security ...

Finally, it is essential that leaders show up: that they participate and demonstrate the new ways, to provide support and show commitment. And to learn something.

This paragraph is unrelated to any other in this book: it is here to give you something to serve as a secret code, telling others that you have thoroughly read this book. Why is a unicorn fantasy and a giraffe real, when a unicorn is just a horse with a horn and a giraffe is a horned camel-antelope with a 2-metre neck? Just say "camel-antelope" and anyone who has really read this book will know you have too.

Communities

Develop communities within the organisation to ensure networked relationships and free flow of knowledge (the "water cooler" effect: things learned incidentally while mingling; serendipity of connections).

Communities should especially connect across the silos and tribes, and across the flows of work. Turn streams into networks. Create formal and informal communities.

Communities should be regarded as organic: they are born, grow, and die according to their own natural dynamics. You can nurture them but there is only so much you can do.

We divide communities into two types:

Communities of Interest assume no prior knowledge. People come along out of curiosity, to find out. E.g. talk about data, wellbeing, Agile, marketing, or customer experience.

Communities of Practice, also known as guilds, expect expertise. Discussion will be advanced and jargonistic. The intent is to share new ideas and developments, to keep the group on the same page, and offer support for difficult challenges. E.g. guilds for scientists, coaches, people managers, widget engineers, data analysts, maintenance staff, facilities, security, or scrum-masters.

Beware communities as sources of information: it should be filtered or validated by experts. Communities spread accepted wisdoms and obsolete workarounds. The extreme example of community information is the World Wide Web: this is how we know the earth is flat. This is where a Centre of Expertise is useful (we prefer that term to "Centre of Excellence"), to be a curator and hub of accurate information.

Communities can have other issues too: they spread toxic attitudes faster than healthy ideas; rumours fly; self-appointed experts mislead.

But of course, the benefits outweigh the negatives. Networks develop across siloes, information flows freely.

The future of agile Management

If you have been paying attention you know that nobody knows, and our best guess constantly changes. You must use the Improvement Kata: regularly re-assess your vision, your desired state, your matariki.

Here are some indicators to watch:

Business Agility Institute https://businessagility.institute/

Drucker Forum https://www.druckerforum.org/home/

Forbes https://www.forbes.com/leadership-strategy

Harvard Business Review https://hbr.org/

Institute for the Future http://www.iftf.org/

Knowledge@Wharton http://knowledge.wharton.upenn.edu/

Open Leadership Network https://openleadershipnetwork.com/

XScale https://xscalealliance.org/

Agile is a dynamic area with some big personalities taking it in different directions. This is fine: in this context we can properly use the concepts of natural selection and evolution. Some of these ideas will survive and their descendants will be even more interesting.

Whatever happens to agile Management in the future, it will be exciting. By embracing diversity, moving from Alpha to Beta management, growing towards teal culture, we just might fix a whole lot of work, organisational, and societal problems that currently look difficult and depressing. This really is a social renaissance.

The Open movement

We can't predict the future, but we have a strong feeling that the Open movement is a pointer to it. In an open system, agents are open to send and receive. Open sending means having an open nature: to know and disclose what you think, want and feel. Open receiving means being open minded: accept the best idea available.

This loose international affiliation of thinkers is evolving new ways of working and managing around a common thread of the OpenSpace

Technology technique for self-organising collaboration, and other sources of fundamental work thinking such as Promise Theory[165], Core Protocols[166], Invitational Theory[167], and Clean Language[168].

The underpinning principle is opening an organisation to freedom, self-organisation, the application of principles not rules, and an embrace of the complex organic nature of human groups.

There is a set of core Open Patterns and Practices of Business Agility[169]. We also list their antipatterns[170] to understand by contrasting to what they are not:

1. **Leadership Invitation**, *instead of* Imposition,

   Open methods favour an opt-in ("pull") approach rather than an imposition-based ("push") approach to organisation-level change.

2. **Proceeding By Explicit Agreement**, *instead of* Delegating or Dictating.

   An organisation of individuals is largely defined by the implied and expressed agreements that those individuals enter into. Open methods make these agreements explicit.

3. **Clarity of Authorisation,** *instead of* Lack of Clear Authority.

   In the Open approach, the delegation of responsibility always includes the clear and explicit delegation of the authority that is needed, to actually execute and deliver.

4. **Boundary Management,** *instead of* No Clear Boundaries.

   Especially with respect to authority and authorisation, when using Open methods, boundaries are clearly defined by executive leaders, are open enough to generate self-organisation, are explicitly communicated, and are carefully maintained.

---

[165] *Promise Theory: Principles and Applications*, Mark Burgess, Jan Bergstra (2014)

[166] https://liveingreatness.com/core-protocols/

[167] An Introduction to Invitational Theory, William Purkey and JohnNovak (2015) *Inviting Leadership*, Daniel Mezick and Mark Sheffield (2019)

[168] Developed by David Grove in the 1980s https://en.wikipedia.org/wiki/Clean_Language

[169] from the Open Leadership Network https://openleadershipnetwork.com/

[170] This list with the antipatterns is taken from an Open presentation by Heidi Araya.

5. **Use of Protocols,** *instead of* Lack of Shared Signals.

   Open approaches clarify communication and understanding via protocols, which are small, shared agreements about how essential interactions are structured.

6. **Whole-Group Process,** *instead of* Closed Door Decisions.

   Open methods favour whole-group process over closed-door decision-making. To the maximum extent possible, Open methods have a bias towards "getting the whole system in the room" to validate assumptions, gauge overall group readiness, and obtain validated, organisation-level alignment before proceeding.

7. **Empirical Approach,** *instead of* Ad Hoc Approach.

   Organisations are more like living systems than they are like machines. Acknowledging this reality includes recognising the need for frequent iterations of experimentation and "learning-by-doing."

8. **Common Knowledge,** *instead of* Siloed Knowledge.

   Often associated with transparency, common knowledge is up-to-date shared information that everyone in the organisation knows. The generation of common knowledge is essential to coordinating very large groups at scale.

There is a rich community of Open models:

- AgendaShift
- BetaCodex
- Coaching With Consent
- FAST Agile, now Fluid Scaled Technology
- FailAgility
- FutureSearch[171]
- OpenSpace Agility
- OpenSpace Beta
- Scrum@Scale[172]

---

[171] *Productive Workplaces*, Marvin Weisbord
[172] https://www.scrumatscale.com

Some of these models will grow and some will fade - it is a dynamic evolving community of ideas - but the Open Movement is likely to shape future ways of working and managing.

This book talks about Beta ways of managing and working to give us an aspiration, but mostly we focus on how to start the journey within an Alpha organisation: this book is about conventional Alpha wanting to get to open agile Beta. We accept the reality of where we are and what we are working with in most organisations.

The final key to unlock Beta is Open Leadership, opening our executive leaders to accept the renaissance in culture, in ways of working. Our executives must let go of power as they perceive it, to accept a new power, the power of the gardener - or even think of it as the power of the creator of worlds. The future lies in self-organising organic ecosystems of people, in which there is no centralisation or hierarchy of power. Most bosses are open and willing to rising out of Alpha, but many will be challenged as we get closer to Beta. That last lock-and-key is beyond the scope of this book.

Your next steps

This book is intended as an introduction to new ways of managing. It serves as a signpost to all the directions you can go from here, depending on your own interests and capabilities. That's up to you.

We looked at the renaissance in work - the new ways of thinking, of managing, and of working - and then at ways to get there. Amongst all the material in this book, we hope there are the sparks of a new flame for you, a new interest, a passion even. Be curious.

What to do now

Remember Shu-Ha-Ri? (p127) Where are you at? (We are assuming you have done an honest self-assessment of your capability. There is nothing so dangerous as the unconsciously incompetent.)

Shu: The student follows the rules of a given method precisely, without addition or alteration. Follow tradition. Apply known solutions.

Ha: The student learns theory and principle of the technique. Become free from tradition. Think for yourself, apply theories to create new solutions.

Ri: The student creates own approaches and adapts technique to circumstance. Transcend tradition. Create new theories.

And remember our four-level model for where an organisation is at? (p218) Where is your organisation?

- ☐ In **explore** mode, trying things, developing capability and experience, bi-modal.

- ☐ A mandate to **incubate** that new way, growing how it looks in our organisation.

- ☐ **Adopting** it widely, incrementally, feeding back.

- ☐ Starting to **transform** the operating model of the organisation and its suppliers and customers.

Map your current position[173]:

Me / Organisation	Shu	Ha	Ri
Explore	Great! Go learn. Dive in. Try stuff.	Share, teach others. Initiate experiments.	Coach, help set strategy. Mentor others.
Incubate	Have a view of how work is done but not how it should be changed. make sure your opinion is heard.	Think about better ways of working. Share your ideas. Help hypothesise and test.	Lead the thinking about new ways. Influence design. Create hypotheses. Track progress.
Adopt	Study hard. Start with learning the new ways for your org, and theory later. Stay positive about change, all is not clear to you yet.	Drive the adoption. Teach, test, listen, improve.\n\nSupport each other, this stuff is hard.	Track progress, monitor the climate, measure success. Determine strategy and approach. Coordinate improvement.
Transform	Watch in awe.	Share with others, help spread good ideas (and alert to bad ones). Be careful outside your own domains.	Collaborate with others from other domains, form guilds, merge ideas, confer on progress.

---

[173] This great idea came from Andreas Drechsler.

What to learn next

One of the great things about new ways is that so many new avenues of learning open to you. If you are the curious kind, then this is exciting. If you are comfortable in the old ways, then it might be intimidating, or overwhelming. Take it at your own pace, and seize the opportunity to add a little intellectual spice to life.

Look for what is interesting to you: build on your strengths, don't try and plug your "weaknesses". Although we all should have a basic understanding of as much as we can, be happy to be "T-shaped" with one strong ability or "comb-shaped" with multiple strengths, and a general knowledge of everything else. Just don't be "I-shaped': so focused on your strengths that you know nothing of anything else.

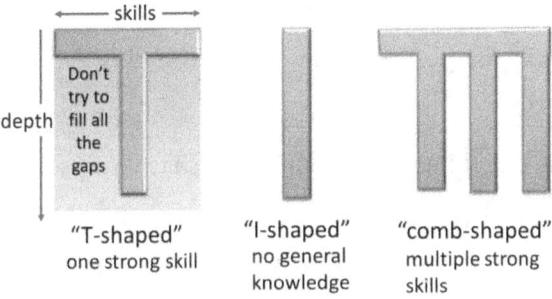

"T-shaped"
one strong skill

"I-shaped"
no general
knowledge

"comb-shaped"
multiple strong
skills

There are many paths to explore:

 ➤ New ways of doing your job

 ➤ Cool technologies

 ➤ Agile theory, Agile at scale, "enterprise" Agile

 ➤ Design thinking

 ➤ Service management

 ➤ Product management

 ➤ Lean theory (and Theory of Constraints)

 ➤ Complex systems theory, antifragile, resilience

 ➤ Organisational structure and behaviours

 ➤ Organisational change, culture change

 ➤ Communications, marketing, celebration

> ➢ Leadership: servant, transformational, open

> ➢ Work psychology, safety, human error, flourishing

> ➢ Wholeness, Integral theory, humanistics, ethics

Use the personal development model on page 177 to ensure you take a balanced approach to learning your chosen topic, across attitudes, behaviours, knowledge, and relationships.

A personal action plan

What will you do when you finish this book? Answer these questions for yourself and set a reminder to review them.

1. What is the most exciting idea in this book?

2. What will you do first, right away, in response to what you have read?

3. What is one thing you will do for or share with somebody else as soon as possible?

4. Where can your team start with an experiment? How will you float the idea?

5. How will you immediately change how you manage people? How can you practice and reinforce that?

6. What will you share with your boss?

7. What will you learn next? Aim to be done in 90 days.

8. How do these ideas impact your career? How will you adjust where you are headed?

9. What is your next move at work to take advantage of these new ways?

10. Where do you want to be with understanding and doing these new ways a year from now?

Where to start

"But there is so much! Where do we even begin?"

Think global, act local. Apply the grand principles of New Ways of Working, but start where you are, with small steps. Fix the pain. Understand what is possible and start there.

It doesn't matter what you work on first so long as it makes work better. Do what you can. The results will improve morale which generates more improvement spontaneously.

Work with those who want to, worker and manager. Change how work is managed as well as how it is done.

When experiments succeed, do more. When they don't, learn. Probe to find out what is welcomed or ignored, and avoid what provokes resistance.

Managers provide air cover to allow experiments to happen.

"What if we don't have a clear vision?"

If you don't know where you are going, anywhere will do. JFDI. You'll learn until a vision becomes clear.

"But what can we actually _do_ first?"

Do something to inspire: promote a book or arrange a talk or run a game. Then run a Lean Coffee for 2 or even 3 hours. It's easy to facilitate and the group themselves make it happen. Make it open to anyone who feels inspired, and wants to talk about what next. The ones who come are the right people. Customise it slightly to have 5 columns: ToDo, Discussing, Done, Insights, Actions. Everybody writes down any insights they have, and the facilitator(s) writes down any agreed action items with an owner. When setting up the Lean Coffee have a clear theme: based on what we have learned so far, what can we improve in how we work?

Brief the Lean Coffee attendees first: the actions we identify should lead to more specific workshops for smaller groups, to make improvements to work, to conduct experiments. Small steps, minimum blast radius. The objectives of the actions we choose are:
- to prove it works
- to create more headroom for more improvement

- to make work faster, higher quality, and easier

Let the people doing the work design the work. Nobody above line managers needs to get involved, except to provide direction: goals and policies.

Then set up the Improvement Machine in this book (p226), and repeat.

Hacking the organisation

"This is all well and good, but our organisation is conservative, and management are old-school command-and-control. How can we ever move beyond a few experiments?"

Mrs Beaton's rabbit stew recipe famously started with "First catch your rabbit." Easy to say and hard to do. All the "recipes" for cultural change say "You need executive support". But what if you don't have it and can't see that changing? What if you care enough about your organisation to try to fix it anyway?

Here we bring all the ideas of this book together to provide a model for how you might succeed without that all-important executive mandate.

Do what you can without permission, which will be some or all of these:

- an Experiment Programme (p241).

- an Improvement Machine (p226) as part of continual improvement.

- a working group (235).

- teams working in new ways, buffered (p166) by their manager.

Where three or more like-minded managers are fostering innovation, join them up in triads for mutual support. Now you are growing tribes of three innovating teams, and building a pile of proof-points.

Sooner or later:

- some executive will find out "what you are up to" and it will come to a head: either leadership recognise better, or you go work somewhere else.

- there will be a crisis, and a desperation for new ways of working, which you will have well advanced and ready.

- a tipping point is reached where everybody starts working in new ways by default and senior management can't do much about it.

Once the executives buy in, willingly or not, they will learn the need for new ways of managing and governing. The organisation will move to Open Leadership. Bam.

In terms of our earlier growth model (p234), you have only now grown out of Explore mode. You can bring those interested tribes together to begin truly incubating an agreed new way of working for all of your organisation.

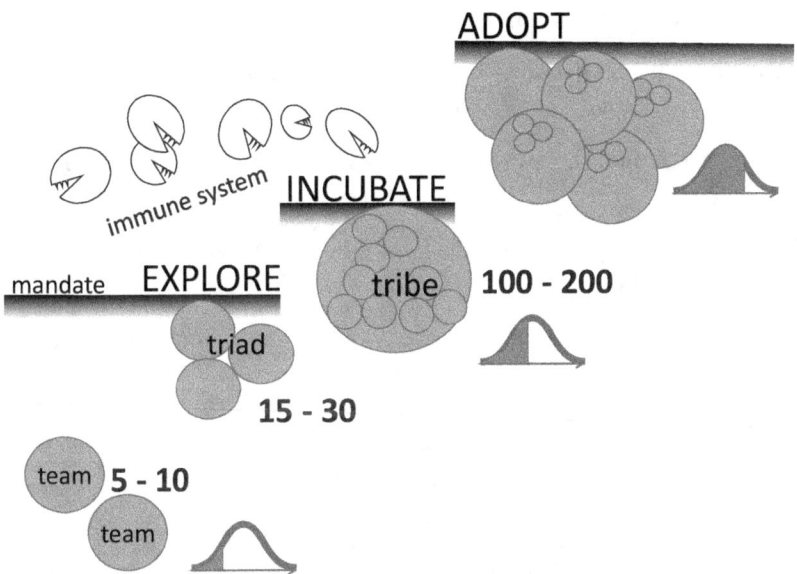

Everybody wants the magic answer, the one formula for success, the silver bullet. You had to read right to the end of this book to get anything: what you just read is as close as we get to The Answer.

Be brave

We end this book with two personal messages for you. The first is: be brave. Conventional command and control is the easy way, drawing on granted power and authority of the organisation. It takes real courage to exhibit these behaviours:

Be a servant, a gardener. Work to enrich, nourish, help, support, and grow your staff. Make their lives better, and feel better for it.

Be loyal. Trust people so they will trust you. Protect your team.

Grow successors. Hire people to do your job, mentor and coach them. Your intention should always be to move on to better things, not occupy a seat and fight off contenders.

Be vulnerable. Let people know when you are uncertain or worried. Ask for help. Work together to find solutions.

Be a truth teller. Be gentle, but speak up, call it out, address the unspoken.

Be authentic. Be your real self, don't fake it. Be transparent: what you see is what you get.

Most of all, it takes courage to love people: to tell them you love them, to show it in your work.

Have fun

And the second parting message is: have fun.

Life is not a dress rehearsal. You only get one. Act like today is your last, because so far it is[174]. So why spend it doing something that is unsatisfying and makes you unhappy. It's on you.

Make your work better every day. If you can't succeed in making your work fulfilling, do something else. If you can't get managers to see new ways, go work for managers who will. The world is enjoying unprecedented prosperity: most of us no longer exist solely to survive. We can begin to pay attention to self-actualisation and fulfilment.

Do it. We did.

---

[174] This is a variation on an old saying. We got this one from *Bloom County*, by the great Berkeley Breathed

Review 4

Come to www.agilemanagers.club for answers, discussion, and more questions.

Revision

1. What's wrong with changing how we work in big transformational steps?

2. How can you keep a balance in your own personal development?

3. How can you make people think and work in new ways?

4. How do you bring senior management along? Middle management?

5. We start in a mode of exploring new ways. What is the growth path from there?

6. Why is experimentation at the heart of how we work?

7. How does one group working in new ways start to transform the wider organisation?

8. What is a J-curve?

9. How can we get out of the way? Who needs to get out of the way? Of what?

10. Why is changing how we manage so key to new ways of working?

11. How soon can we be finished?

12. How might we hack the organisation?

Contemplation

13. How challenging is self-organisation for your ways of managing?

14. Where are the champions of new ways in your organisation? Where are the success stories?

15. Where is your organisation on the Explore-Incubate-Adopt-Transform model? All models are wrong - does it even apply?

16. What are the matariki? How can you get consensus on that?

17. Where is your organisation at? Could you hack it?

18. How does your current work provide you with satisfaction? Joy?

19. What does this book mean for your career?

Action

20. What crazy goals can you set?

21. Who is going to go after bureaucracy, to try to lighten controls?

22. Where can/do you keep an improvement backlog?

23. How can your management team grow their capability in new ways of managing?

24. What's a low-blast-radius experiment to see how ready the organisation is for new ways?

25. Did you do that personal action plan?

Appendices

Kaizen

In Japanese, *kaizen* means "change to be better," which refers to any improvement whether changing once or continuously. In the modern management context, kaizen is used to refer to continuous improvement measures.

Kaizen is about *culture* of continual improvement. It involves a general philosophy, methods (including the well-known PDCA and 5 Whys), a taxonomy (20 Keys), and specific rituals (e.g. kaizen burst, kaizen blitz, *joshin kanri* daily team management, *asaichi* morning market for rejects, quality circles...).

Improvement Kata

The four-step Improvement Kata is a simple pattern to coach in order to make it part of the organisational culture, the way we do things around here. We want this pattern to be adopted reflexively every time people in our organisation think about a way forward with anything.

A kata is a pattern and exercise that one repeats over and over until it is mastered as a reflex skill, until we develop "muscle memory", it is processed below your conscious mind. The Improvement Kata is a specific example of a kata which originated at Toyota.

Think about every change this way:

1. Where do you want to go, what are your matariki?

2. Where are you now?

3. What is your SMART goal? (Specific, Measurable, Achievable, Relevant, Timebound)

4. What steps can we take? (1) planning (2) implementing (3) checking (4) adjusting to the goal?

   Repeat step 4 until we reach the target goal.

Then repeat the entire cycle.

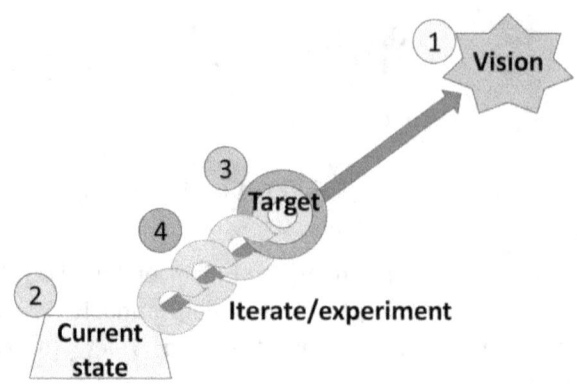

This sounds deceptively simple but needs to be repeated until it becomes an unthinking pattern of behaviour.

As part of the Improvement Kata we set our aspirational vision. One often uses the language of navigational stars, points of reference for sailors when navigating. As already discussed, we at Teal Unicorn use the term matariki for navigational goals.

PDCA

The Plan-Do-Check-Act Cycle (PDCA) is also known as the Deming Cycle or Shewhart Cycle. We prefer to call it Plan-Do-Check-<u>Adjust</u>, because that makes more intuitive sense explaining the underlying principle. As we work in small increments, we plan what we're going to do, do the work, then check what the result was and how well it worked, and adjust the way we approach accordingly, before another iteration.

There are other variations such as Check-Plan-Act, but this is the best known.

OODA

The Observe-Orient-Decide-Act cycle has military origins. It is designed for a commander in the field to use their current observed environment, plus the policy and objectives they have been given, plus their resources at hand and capabilities, to decide autonomously without referring back to higher command, and then to take rapid action.

Complex systems theory

Understanding of complex systems behaviour has come a long way in the last few decades, and we can now apply powerful new ideas to understanding our work, including the following:

Cynefin[175]

Cynefin is a generalised model for dealing with situations, in any context anywhere. It describes five states we are in when dealing with a situation[176]:

simple (the original word, which we still like) or **obvious** (the currently used term): we know how to respond

complicated: knowable, but requires expertise to respond.

complex: unknown, requiring the development of new knowledge and expertise to respond.

chaotic: unknowable, beyond our ability to learn.

disordered: we think we are in one state when in fact we are in another, we don't know what we are doing.

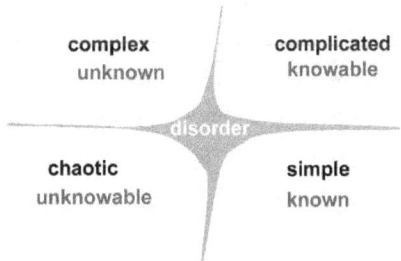

There is far more to Cynefin than this. It is a profound thinking system that continues to evolve[177]. The latest version is Liminal Cynefin which describes the transitional states between each state.

---

[175] https://cognitive-edge.com

[176] This is our oversimplified summation, which David Snowden, Cynefin's originator, may disapprove of.

[177] The latest (April 2019) is here https://cognitive-edge.com/blog/cynefin-st-davids-day-2019-5-of-5/

Complex systems failure

Dr Richard Cook wrote a seminal paper decades ago[178] on *How Complex Systems Fail*, which we summarise as "All complex systems are broken all the time". Those running the system keep it functional, but from time to time the multiple defects of the system align and overwhelm them, and the system fails. As Cook says "It's not surprising that your system failed. What is surprising is that it ever worked at all." Every aircraft you ever flew in was broken, and the system around it. But it takes at least three faults to align for it to result in an unplanned landing.

Cook and others are now doing interesting work[179] around resilience and recovery, including challenging ideas about the conceptual systems in our heads versus the actual systems which are often invisible.

We talk elsewhere in this boo about all the ideas of failure which flow from complex system theory to impact how we think about management.

Wardley Maps

Wardley mapping[180] is a technique to visualise organisational situations and strategy by mapping the domain of a system.

The horizontal axis represents a timeline of growth: evolution or maturity, e.g. from new product to commodity, or from novel practice to best practice. The vertical axis represents value visibility to the customer, from internal to external, the layers of the system.

The components of the system are mapped, and interconnected by flow of value.

To create a map, it considers Sun Tzu's five factors: purpose, landscape, climate, doctrine, and leadership[181].

---

[178] Available from the MIT website
https://web.mit.edu/2.75/resources/random/How%20Complex%20Systems%20Fail.pdf

[179] *The Stella Report*, SNAFU Catchers http://stella.report

[180] By Simon Wardley. The only book is online here https://medium.com/wardleymaps

[181] Sun Tzu was a Chinese strategist around 500BC. His book *The Art Of War* is still used to guide strategy.

Human error

A particular aspect of the failure of complex systems deserves special attention: human error. Human error is not the cause of anything.

There is a large body of knowledge around Safety Culture, driven by medical, engineering, factory, and flying sectors. Dr Sidney Dekker wrote a series of works[182] that we summarise as "If somebody does something stupid in your system, you should thank them for exposing the weakness in your system". If you are not designing to prevent human error, that is a fault of your system not the operators. People will make mistakes. We must allow for that and prevent it.

There is yet another Japanese term, *poka yoke*, for any mechanism or constraint that helps prevent human error, that avoids an operator making a mistake. We design to prevent expected or past errors.

It is often claimed that automation reduces human error. Whilst this is true most of the time, automation also amplifies any human error that gets past it. So, arguably, automation doesn't reduce human error, it just makes it less frequent and more catastrophic.

Checklists

The checklist is a simple but highly effective tool for minimising human error[183]. A checklist is as the name suggests: a list to be checked off before or as we execute an activity. One way to think of a checklist is as the first stage in codifying the assurance that all steps have been done, which eventually ends in automation.

The magnitude of today's knowledge has exceeded our ability to deliver it safely, consistently and correctly. A simple checklist can bring about striking improvements in almost any field (think aircraft pilots).

Checklists are an essential tool to minimise errors and maximise efficiency when the heat is on and you need to act: have the checklist ready when you need it.

---

[182] *Field Guide to Human Error;* and the videos *Safety Differently* and *Just Culture*
[183] The definitive book is *The Checklist Manifesto*, Atul Gawande

Pilots understand the importance of a cool head and correct action in a tricky situation. They understand that a cool head is kept when the thinking is done in advance. They also understand that situations are caused in the first place through basic procedural errors when we are in normal situations, and checklists are just as important to prevent them.

Checklists don't insult our intelligence: they don't tell us *how* to do something. They are not a script or work instruction. They just remind us that it should be done, and sometimes they also remind us in what order.

When pre-thinking, we should visualise - and plan for - failure more than success. So, we have one checklist that describes the normal successful actions, then we have several more checklists for each of the negative scenarios we can anticipate (e.g. in a pre-mortem, p155). In critical situations, we should spend more time planning how to deal with what could go wrong than how to do it right. (NASA plan an *emergency* spacewalk for more than 24 hours: nobody rushes out the hatch like in the movies).

Finally, checklists are a learning tool. When a review captures that an error was made, we fix the checklist. And when a situation arises that we had never foreseen, we create a checklist for how to deal with it next time. (See Standard+Case, p278).

Case management

Case Management is a body of knowledge[184], a discipline well-known in industry sectors such as health, social work, law and policing.

Whenever we are in a complex situation, we only know what we can observe from where we are. We can determine the actions open to us, and choose one. We don't know until we do. When we act, we move to a new state, and learn new information from what we observe from there. That information may invalidate planning we did at the previous state Sometimes it changes what we understand the goal to be. When we start, we don't know where we will end or when. This is true whether we are extinguishing a fire, healing a patient, investigating a crime, or in fact resolving any situation in a complex world.

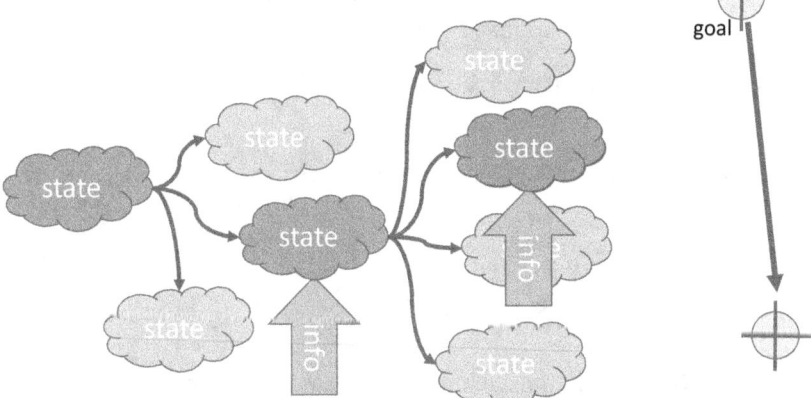

If you look carefully, you will see that Case Management is another lens on the same reality as Agile, or as the Improvement Kata, or any other approach that understands complex systems. These lenses are all based on our four behaviours: iterate, increment, experiment, explore.

Case Management is the main approach used by knowledge workers (p33), and it depends on the abilities of those knowledge workers. There is a fundamental difference from the process-centric approach of much conventional management designed for industrial and clerical workers. Process improvement often starts from the premise of external experts improving the way work is done. Case Management starts from the

---

[184] We didn't yet find a well-defined body of work, more of a loose affiliation of thinking. We liked *How Knowledge Workers Get Things Done*, ed. L Fisher.

premise that knowledge workers know what they are doing better than anyone else and need to be allowed to do it.

Case Management allows knowledge workers to manage the case professionally and dynamically as it unfolds. It is managers' role to inform the case workers of the organisation's objectives and policies, so that they can make their own decisions; and to provide the case workers with sufficient resources to be successful. This aligns nicely with Drucker's principle[185] of "Management by Objectives", and is of course an example of being a servant manager (p102).

Forrester[186] see three categories of Case Management:

- service requests (human communications): e.g. loans, claims, underwriting, benefits, new customers.

- incident management (event-driven): e.g. healthcare, complaints, disputes, exceptions.

- investigative (transparency): e.g. due diligence, compliance, fraud detection, audit.

These are driven by customer experience, cost control, and risk mitigation.

Standard+Case

Standard+Case is an approach to categorising and resolving any sort of transactional work, developed by the author in 2010[187].

You can only industrialise that which you can standardise, i.e. make known: described, predictable, and repeatable. Only some of the world can be standardised. The world refuses to be standardised: there is other incoming stuff that you haven't seen before - that you don't already have a defined response for - that has to be handled as a case. In any response to situations, some of the world will always be unfamiliar due to change, or unpredictable due to complexity.

[185] The Practice of Management, P Drucker

[186] *Dynamic Case Management – an Old Idea Catches Fire*, C Le Clair and C Moore, Forrester 2009

[187] To learn more about Standard+Case, go to our resource website http://www.basicsm.com/standard-case, or read the book *Plus! The Standard+Case Approach,* available at all good Amazons.

For standard situations, you define standard processes with instructions and templates. Many of your processes make the implicit assumption that the whole world can be standardised and treats non-standard situations as an exception condition. You should treat these non-standard conditions as normal, using Case Management (p277).

So, some of your activity is "Standard": known, familiar, defined; and the rest is "Case": unknown, unfamiliar, undefined. By combining these two approaches into Standard+Case, we get a complete model for how to respond to all situations, familiar and unfamiliar. The methods, people, skills, and metrics you use are quite different in each. Over time, you can document some repeating Cases as new Standard models.

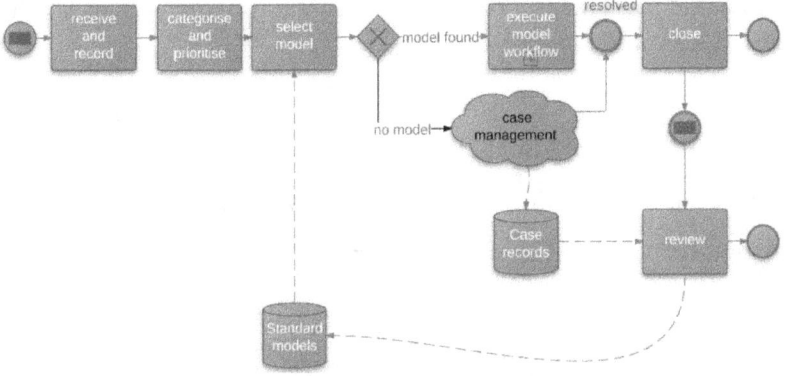

S+C addresses criticisms of process-centric approaches to managing responses that they don't deal with the undefined situations, and they don't allow customers and knowledge workers to be empowered to deal with them.

Standard and Case are yin and yang. Combined, they fully model the real world.

Viewing everything as a Standard model causes problems. For instance, let's take a long-running, complicated issue that has become an unresolved "cold case." Seen by a Standard model, it's reported as a statistical failure and makes you look bad. But if you separate it from Standard issues and track it as a Case, it gives you a more accurate depiction of reality. Cases can go cold: you don't always solve the unknown.

Lean

There is nothing new about Lean. It has been around since WW2, and its roots go back even further. But Lean thinking is still usually applied in narrow contexts such as manufacturing production lines. It needs to be more generally understood for all value flow.

This isn't the place to cover Lean – there are many books – but, at its core, Lean is about understanding what the customer sees as value, aligning your business to that, and removing everything else.

There are many tools to align with the customer view of value, including customer journey maps, persona maps, empathy maps, customer value propositions, and business model canvas.

Lean seeks to remove three factors from flow of work:

Inconsistency (lumpiness, surges, constraints)

Overburden (trying to do too much, trying to push too much in)

Waste (7 or 8 forms of unnecessary work)

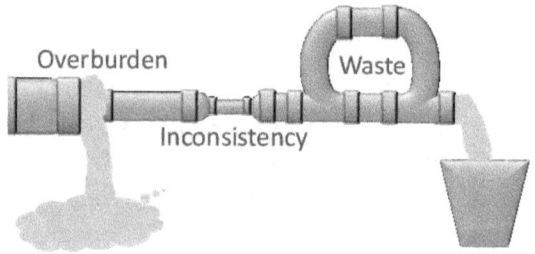

Lean is an extensive body of knowledge which brought us many of the concepts in this book. All managers should understand it.

Value Stream Mapping

Value stream mapping is a Lean tool that helps visualise the necessary steps from end to end in the flow of value to a customer. Like other business process maps, value stream maps help you better understand your organisation, but value streams take a much larger, more holistic view than conventional process mapping, looking at the value produced not internal activity. They analyse workflows to identify waste and inefficiencies.

Theory of Constraints

Dr. Eliyahu Goldratt formed the Theory of Constraints (ToC) and introduced it through the novel *The Goal*, which was his best-selling book of 1984. Since then, ToC has grown and developed to become an important tool in the world of management practices.

The Theory of Constraints has a scientific approach to improvement. It suggests that every complex system, including manufacturing processes, brings together many interconnected activities, one of which acts as a constraint for the entire system (i.e. the constraining operation is "the weakest link in the chain"). The top priority is always the current constraint.

The basic ToC logic is this:

1. Find the main constraint (bottleneck) of the system. Look for work piling up in inventory before it.

2. Improve the constraint (ToC has its own arcane terminology for this).

3. Once you get rid of a constraint, the bottleneck moves somewhere else.

4. Repeat.

It is theoretically possible to get rid of all the constraints in a flow. Once we have done that, the input to the flow is then the constraint. This is the way we like it: we manage demand.

Conventional management is prone to tell *everybody* to optimise when flow is too slow, but this is wasteful. Targeting the effort on the constraint is the most efficient way to improve flow.

Understanding how constraints affect flow allows us to minimise effort on improvement if the context is narrow enough that the flow is a linear stream. (The ToC community have evolved a wide range of tools which apply in broader contexts than just a linear stream, but this limitation holds true for the core ToC method).

DevOps

DevOps is a specifically IT-related method of improving flow of software delivery, but its thinking around Culture, Automation, Flow, Feedback, and Sharing[188] are becoming recognised as more generally applicable. Teal Unicorn works in DevOps within IT departments, but we avoid the term in other contexts because it sounds so technical.

In the general context, DevOps can be thought of as Agile with a stronger emphasis on end-to-end flow and system thinking, especially complex systems and human error.[189] DevOps has five primary concerns:

Culture

All change is about people: changing the behaviours, attitudes, and eventually their beliefs.

Automation

In order to achieve velocity through quality, we must go faster and better. We soon hit human limits: we need technology to do both.

Flow

We only deliver faster when we consider the whole value stream from end to end, not localised optima.

Feedback

Observation and learning provide value only when we have fast tight feedback loops to get the information to those who need it to improve.

Sharing

By creating flow of information and resources across the organisation, we bridge across siloes and get everybody on the same boat, collaborating. We share ownership and responsibility.

---

[188] Usually expressed as CALMS: culture, automation, Lean, measurement, and sharing, but we like CAFFS

[189] *The DevOps Handbook*, Kim, Humble, Debois, Willis

Agile

Agile is of course at the heart of this book: it's in the name. "Capital-A Agile" is a philosophy of work, so let's discuss the work aspects here from a small-a agile manager's point of view. This isn't a general book about working the Agile way - there are many of those[190] - so we will restrict ourselves to a brief overview of the method.

We summarise the Agile way of working as four principles:

Iterate: work in small cycles of time, repeating a work pattern.

Increment: build small pieces to work to grow the whole.

Experiment: test your design assumptions and hypotheses by doing.

Explore: find your way through the uncertainty and ambiguity of the real world, where you can't exactly predict the path or the destination.

We use a model that leans heavily on Eric Ries' Lean Startup[191] approach (pun intended).

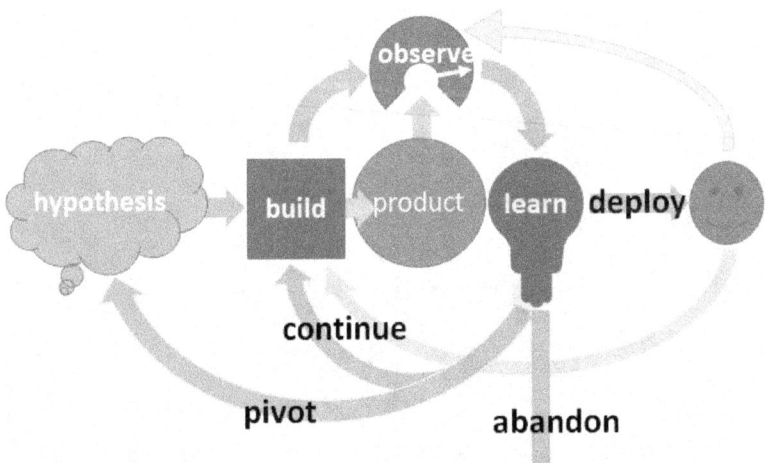

---

[190] For example:
Team of Teams, McChrystal
Lean Enterprise, Humble, Molesky, O'Reilly
Why Agile Works, De La Maza, Benz
[191] http://theleanstartup.com

Work starts with a **hypothesis** of what it is we think we want to build. Note that it is only a hypothesis, an unproven speculation: we don't know where it ends when we begin, we don't know what we are going to build or what it will take to get there.

Then we build a small increment of product which we then **Observe** and **Learn** from. This leads to one of four decisions.

We may **Continue** to build another increment and iteratively grow the product. Or we decide that we have enough of a product increment that we can **Deploy** (release, deliver) it to the consumers/users of the product which creates another powerful feedback loop to help us observe and learn. Or occasionally we decide that we need to completely **Abandon** the hypothesis, the product or improvement is a terrible idea. But at least with an Agile approach we do this as early as possible with minimum cost. The fourth option is that we **Pivot**, a buzz-word which has entered common use. This means we reconsider the hypothesis and change the definition of what it is that we are building, we decide to build something different. Usually this is because the assumptions on which we based the original hypothesis have been shown to be wrong.

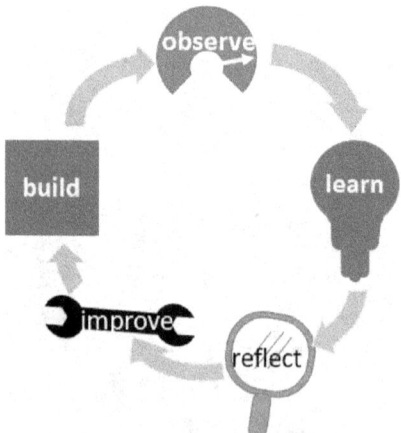

In Agile there are another couple of steps in each iteration of our work cycle not shown in the first diagram.

As well as Build, Observe, and Learn, we should also take time to **Reflect** on what we can learn from this iteration about the ways in which we are working, so that we can identify how we can **Improve**. These improvements become work for future iterations in the same way that work on the product is, and they should be prioritised along with product work, in the team's backlog.

The ideal Agile teams are small (average 5, less than 10), autonomous, self-organising, without a team leader. (They may have a line manager for HR purposes). They are stable long-lived standing teams aligned to a single product.

The product stakeholders decide the priority of the work, then the team decide how to get the work done. Ideally there is one representative stakeholder, the Product Owner.

The agile team has three primary concerns, leading to three primary roles[192]:

Value: Product Owner

Feasibility: Engineering

Usability: User experience (UX) design

A fourth role, alongside the team, is an Agile coach, or "scrum master". The name comes from a specific Agile technique called Scrum (p291), but it is a generalised term often used. The scrum master is there to assist the team. They:

- coach the team, including the Product Owner, in how to work in an Agile way.

- remove impediments to getting work done.

- communicate with other scrum masters.

- facilitate team meetings.

- measure progress and velocity.

- explain the team to outsiders.

- run interference with outsiders trying to give the team work or change how they work.

---

[192] *Inspired: How to Create Products Customers Love*, M. Cagan, SVPG Press, 2008

The Agile Manifesto

Agile is rooted in a document called the Agile Manifesto[193] which describes values and principles from a software development perspective. There are four value axioms and twelve underlying principles.

The four axioms could be generalised away from their software context by amending them slightly to say:

We value

> ➤ people over process
>
> ➤ results over bureaucracy
>
> ➤ customer collaboration over formal contracts
>
> ➤ responding to change over following a plan

The right-hand things don't go away, it's just that we need to get our values appropriate so that we value the left-hand items *more*.

The twelve principles can likewise be generalised to:

1. Our highest priority is to satisfy the customer through early and continuous delivery of value. [At Teal Unicorn, we respectfully disagree with how this is worded. Our highest priority is people. Our focus is our customer.]

2. Welcome changing requirements, even late in development. Why? See (1) above. Agile processes harness change for the customer's advantage.

3. Deliver results frequently, from a couple of days to a couple of months, with a preference to the shorter timescale.

4. Builders and their customers must work together daily throughout development of a product.

5. Build outcomes around motivated individuals. Give them the environment and support they need, and trust them to get the job done.

---

[193] The Agile Manifesto is © 2001, the authors listed at https://agilemanifesto.org/

6. The most efficient and effective method of conveying information to and within a team is face-to-face conversation.

7. Product improvement delivered and working is the primary measure of progress. No work output has any value until it is used.

8. Agile processes promote sustainable development. The sponsors, developers, and users should be able to maintain a constant pace indefinitely.

9. Continuous attention to excellence and good design enhances agility.

10. Simplicity - the art of maximizing the amount of work not done - is essential.

11. The best architectures, requirements, and designs emerge from self-organising teams.

12. At regular intervals, the team reflects on how to become more effective, then tunes and adjusts its behaviour accordingly.

That's all there is to the Agile Manifesto (this is our modified version: the original is even briefer). The Manifesto has semi-formal status, in that it is recognised as the parent statement for the Agile philosophy. There is no other definition of Agile with any widely accepted status. All Agile thinking and writing can be considered to derive from this one document.

Backlogs

A backlog is simply a list of work to be done, stored on anything from paper to sophisticated software tools. A backlog is prioritised by the product owner to sort the work in the order in which they want it to be done. The work in the backlog is estimated by the team doing the work, and the amount of work that is pulled from the backlog in some interval is known as the velocity of the team.

The product owner, the team, and other stakeholders will all collaborate to constantly refine the information in the backlog. Work that is low priority can be vaguely defined and lumped into coarse granularity, whereas work that is high-priority to be done soon is clearly defined and broken down into fine granularity. We don't over-invest in defining work that may change or never happen.

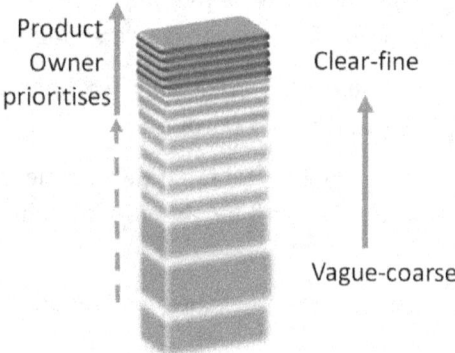

Product Owner prioritises

Clear-fine

Vague-coarse

Note that a work "ticket" tool is a backlog tool, so long as the queues of work are before the start of the value stream. If the queues are part-way through a value stream, that's inventory. It may provide a necessary buffer, or it may be inventory waste.

User story

The method of describing units of work in a backlog in the software world is known as a user story. This mechanism can be more widely used than just its IT origins. A user story defines a role, an action that the role wants to be able to perform, and the value that that action delivers: "As a [role] I need [outcome] so that [value]". ("User" is IT-speak for the consumer of a product or service.)

The user story may then break down that description into a series of tasks, and/or a list of defined completion criteria (a *definition of done*: we agree a common definition of done for all work, but we can also explicitly define done for a single story).

Agile models

As soon as a model becomes a certification industry, arguably it has lost the spirit of Agile, an open, evolving, uncodified community consensus. All models are wrong, and all models are useful. Caveat emptor - adopt and adapt with understanding and care.

Modern Agile

Modern Agile[194] is a movement to "refresh" Agile thinking, as the Agile Manifesto is nearly two decades old now.

It has only four principles:

Make people awesome. The enthusiastic American wording may not work everywhere, but the concept is good: help and free everybody, both internal to our organisation and external customers and suppliers.

Make safety a prerequisite. This speaks to protecting the wellbeing of the people involved in the value stream; and the integrity of the value stream.

Experiment and learn rapidly. Encourage experimentation by making it safe to fail, so that we may learn quickly.

Deliver value continuously. Break the work down into smaller pieces so that it flows, so that we deliver something sooner.

The Heart of Agile

Another recent body of thought is Dr. Alistair Cockburn's Heart of Agile[195] which distils Agile into four "imperatives":

Collaborate closely with others to generate and develop better starting ideas. Communicate often to smooth transitions.

Deliver small probes initially to learn how the world really works. Expand deliveries as you learn to predict and influence outcomes.

---

[194] http://modernagile.org/

[195] © 2018 Heart of Agile https://heartofagile.com

Reflect periodically, along the way. Think about what you've learned in your collaboration and from your deliveries.

Improve the direction of your ideas, their technical implementation, and your internal processes.

Agile Fluency

The Agile Fluency™ model[196] is a recently developed way to understand how Agile evolves in an organisation, and what is required to be "fluent" at various levels. It is useful for understanding the context of Agile, from team level to organisation.

Here is how we re-redrew Agile Fluency for a client:

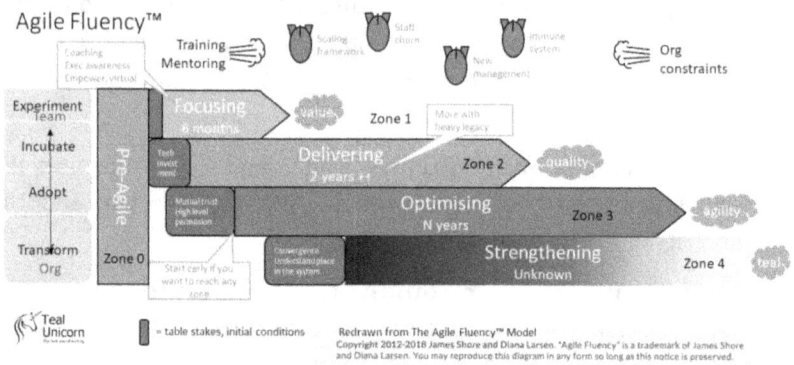

Maturity models are tempting for managers. Don't fall to the temptation of measuring teams by any model such as Agile Fluency (it's not designed to model maturity: the authors coach that any level is appropriate depending on the context of the work). You will only distort behaviour. Models such as this should only be used to guide strategy and improvement.

AgileSHIFT

AgileSHIFT® is a proprietary framework from the organisation that owns ITIL®, PRINCE2® and other "old fashioned" frameworks, as well as RESILIA®, PRINCE2 Agile®, and other forward-looking ones[197]. It

---

[196] Agile Fluency is a trademark of Diana Larsen and James Shore
https://www.agilefluency.org

[197] ITIL, PRINCE2, RESILIA, PRINCE2 Agile, and AgileSHIFT are all registered Trade Marks of AXELOS Limited. All rights reserved.

provides a full model of principles, practices, roles, tools etc, and method of delivery. AgileSHIFT is brand new, so we shall see what the uptake is. Books and certification are available.

Scrum

Scrum is a minimalist method for managing work based on a regular cycle and a small number of rituals and tools. It fits well with the Agile approach. Often Agile and Scrum are conflated, but Agile is a philosophy and Scrum is a particular pattern of working, and they arose separately (Scrum came first). Like Agile, Scrum works just fine in non-IT contexts, although you sometimes have to translate the software-specific language to something more general.

Scrum is regarded as too formalised for many Agile theorists, who accept Scrum only as "trainer wheels" for a team to begin learning to be agile.

It is a useful method, applicable in any context where a self-organising team draws work from a backlog. It involves three roles, four artefacts, and five meetings, and a simple set of rules connecting them. The basic construct is the sprint (a word that has become widely used), a cycle of 1-4 weeks of decide-build-release.

Like many simple definitions, it is quite "Zen", meaning the more you think about it the deeper and more extensive the implications. As a result, many books have been written about Scrum even though the original guide[198] is so small it looks like the brochure.

---

[198] See *The Scrum Guide*, Ken Schwaber and Jeff Sutherland, downloadable from the internet

Kanban

Kanban is a way of managing flow of work visually. The word means sign-board. The most popular approach is a kanban board: paper notes on a wall, or software equivalents, arranged into rows and columns to track the flow of work. But any visual representation and control of work is kanban, such as putting cards into boxes, tags on pallets, parts into trays, or milk bottles on the doorstep.

Strictly speaking it's not kanban unless the mechanism also limits the work in progress (WIP), and functions as a *pull* system, only allowing work in when capacity comes free for it.

There is an extensive body of knowledge around kanban – there is much more to it than most people think.[199] A common misconception is that Kanban is only a visualisation tool, used in Agile, but it is a standalone way of working that predates Agile and is sufficient in itself (or it is a useful tool to help with Agile iterations if that's how you want to regard it).

(This is our kanban board at Teal Unicorn. Lots of colour and fun.)

---

[199] Our favourite book is *Making Work Visible*, Dominica DeGrandis

Design Thinking

Design Thinking is a design methodology that provides a solution-based approach to solving problems. It's extremely useful in tackling complex problems that are ill-defined or unknown, by understanding the human needs involved, by re-framing the problem in human-centric ways, by creating many ideas in brainstorming sessions, and by adopting a hands-on approach in prototyping and testing.

There can be anywhere from three to seven stages in Design Thinking methodologies. The five-stage Design Thinking model from the Hasso-Plattner Institute of Design at Stanford (d.school) are Empathise, Define (the problem), Ideate, Prototype, and Test. [200]

Having generated a hypothesis, Design Thinking provides the input to our Agile cycle.

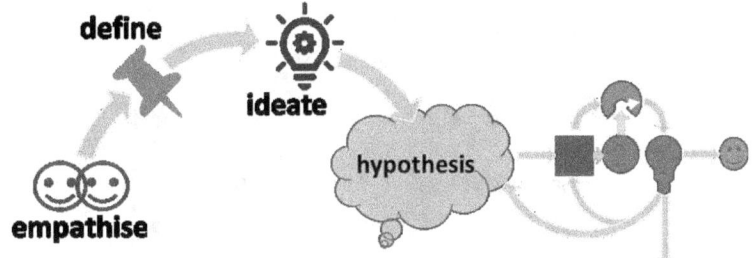

[200] *5 Stages in the Design Thinking Process*, R Dam and T Siang, Interactive Design Foundation https://www.interaction-design.org/literature/article/5-stages-in-the-design-thinking-process

Service / Product Management

The ideas of Service Management and Product Management are decades old, but they are still a novelty to many organisations.

We regard them as different lenses on the same reality (service/product, tomayto/tomahto). They have grown up independently as separate bodies of knowledge and they see the world in slightly different ways.

At times we do distinguish between product and service to talk about the product as something which is created by one value stream, and the service which delivers the product in a broader value stream encompassing the support and lifecycle of the product (Also see "Value-T", p145). Other philosophers would not agree with this model and would see it the other way around. Angels dancing on heads of pins.

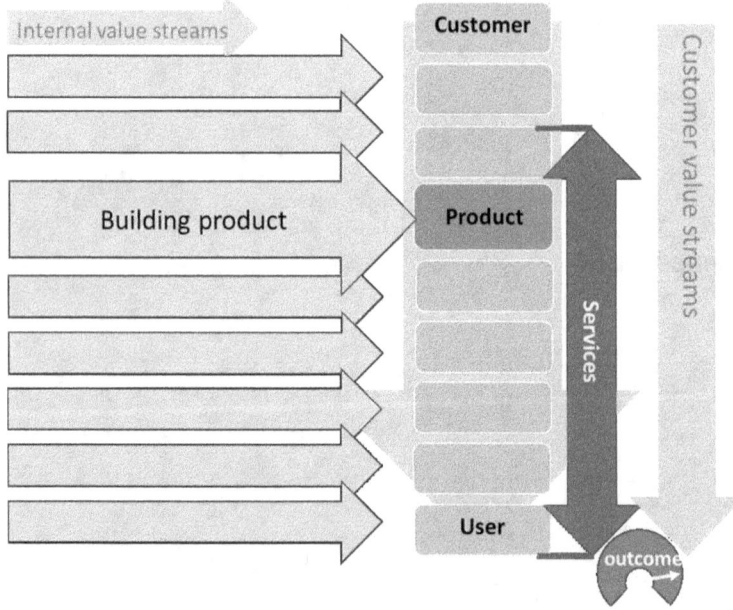

For pragmatic purposes, let's reduce a very long discussion to one thing we want you to know: these are two very large bodies of knowledge out there which provide us with considerable guidance for how we should plan, design, build, deploy, run, and retire our product and services. Adopt and adapt them to suit your organisational purposes as with all the other ideas in this book.

There have been several Service Management frameworks developed over the years. Most have a strong IT focus (ITIL, COBIT, ISM, eSCM...), but some more general ones include USMBOK™ [201] and now VeriSM™ (see below). See also Rob England's concise introductory book *Basic Service Management*, which depicts Service Management like this:

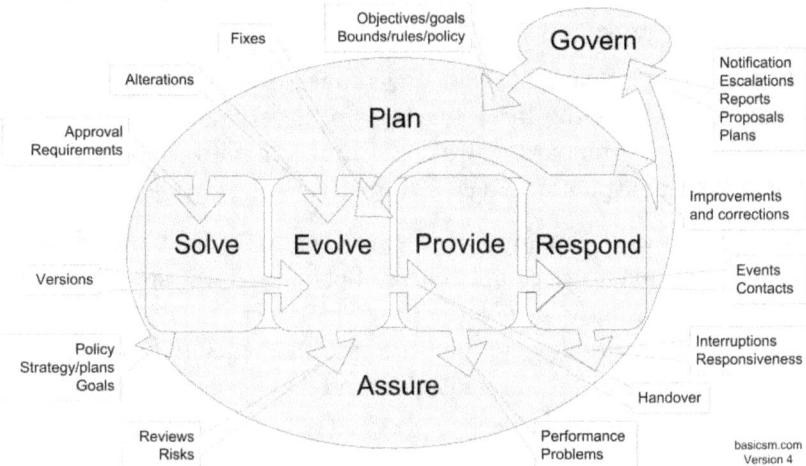

This is a conventional view of Service Management which doesn't reflect its recent (and overdue) embrace of agility. Many in that community are still stuck in this thinking.

Product Management is a body of knowledge[202] about a similar lifecycle of "product" rather than "service". The philosophers argue endlessly about the distinction, but to us it is moot. Product Management and Service Management seem to be barely different lenses on the same reality, differing only in terminology. It is very tribal. Don't @ me.

---

[201] https://www.usmbok.com/

[202] *The Principles of Product Development Flow*, by Don Reinertsen, is considered a definitive work. We find it heavy going.

Policy governance framework

If you set people free, empowering them to make their own decisions and define their own work as knowledge professionals, you need good policy for their sake and yours. If you give them a field to work on, they need to know where the boundaries of the field are.

Direct is Teal Unicorn's policy ("governance artefact") framework. The name comes from the three functions of governance defined by the ISO/IEC 38500 standard[203], which are direct, monitor, and evaluate. It also plays on the pun of "direct" as both a verb and an adjective.

Years ago, we looked for a framework which could be used in an organisation to ensure completeness of policy and we came up empty-handed, so we have developed this framework[204]. It embraces the *hoshin kanri* methodology to ensure that the policy flows adequately through the layers of the organisation, and that feedback is passed back to improve policy.

At the Organisational level, the vision and mission statements shape the organisation-wide governance artefacts defining general policy, applicable everywhere. These artefacts are in three groups:

Principles which are encoded in policy documents

Strategy which is defined in plans

Charter which is described in structures

The Organisational layer informs the Functional layer, where policy, plan, and structure artefacts are created specific to the various domains of the organisation, such as Sales, IT, Personnel, Finance, and so on. These artefacts should be local elaborations of the Organisational governance, referencing it directly, and not contradicting it.

The Contextual layer provides even more localised governance artefacts to collect, elaborate, and clarify Organisational and Functional

---

[203] ISO/IEC 38500 *standard for corporate governance of information technology*. The "of Information Technology" is misleading: it is a useful standard for all corporate governance.

[204] With the assistance of Alison Holt https://longitude174.com/ who chaired the original ISO/IEC 38500 committee.

governance in specific contexts, such as hiring employees, claiming expenses, dealing with suppliers, or using the internet.

This picture is an IT-related example. Similar pictures can be drawn for other domains of the organisation, with different Functional and Contextual objects.

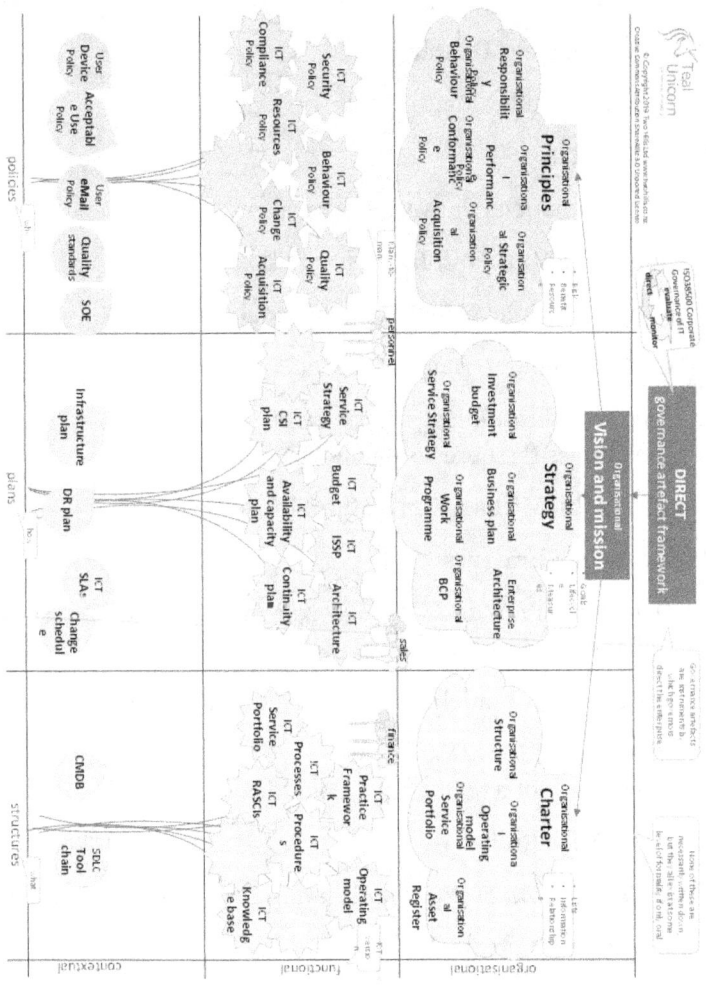

For a full-size colour version of this graphic, go to http://www.basicsm.com/direct

Reading

...on new ways of managing.

Loosely in descending recommended order for a manager to read them.

Most of us don't read any more, so visit **www.agilemanagers.club** for video and other online resources.

The Age of Agile, Steve Denning

Team of Teams, Stanley McChrystal

Slack, Tom DeMarco

High Output Management, Andrew Grove

How Complex Systems Fail, Dr Richard Cook

    A brief paper available as downloadable PDF.

Turn the Ship Around, L David Marquet

Reinventing Organizations, Frederic Laloux
    Don't miss the Foreword by Ken Wilber

Why Agile Works, Michael De La Maza, David Benz

The Lean Startup, Eric Ries

Spirit: Transformation and Development in Organisations, Harrison Owen, available for download at www.openspaceworld.com

Inviting Leadership, Daniel Mezick and Mark Sheffield

Cynefin framework, Dave Snowden
    A website not a book http://cognitive-edge.com/

Toyota Kata, Mike Rother

The Field Guide to Understanding 'Human Error', Sidney Dekker

Start With Why, Simon Sinek

Tribes, Seth Godin

The Culture Game, Daniel Mezick

The Fifth Discipline, Peter Senge

Making Work Visible, Dominica Degrandis

The Checklist Manifesto, Atul Gawande

How Knowledge Workers Get Things Done, ed. Layna Fischer

Thinking, Fast and Slow, Daniel Kahneman

Lean Enterprise, Humble, Molesky, O'Reilly

Out of the Crisis, J. Edwards Deming

The New Economics, J. Edwards Deming

The Future of Management, Gary Hamel

The Five Dysfunctions of a Team, Patrick Lencioni

Organize for Complexity, Niels Pflaeging

The Goal, Eli Goldratt

Antifragile, Nicholas Taleb

Open Space Technology: A User's Guide, Harrison Owen

Mastering the Unpredictable, Keith Swenson

Joy, Inc., Richard Sheridan

The Leaders Guide to Storytelling, Steve Denning

First Break All the Rules, Marcus Buckingham and Curt Coffman

Game On! Change is Constant, Karen Ferris

Dialogue, William Isaac

The High-Velocity Edge, Dr Steven Spear

Product Development Flow, Don Reinertsen

Freedom from Command and Control, John Seddon

The Systems Bible, John Gall

Plus! The Standard+Case approach, Rob England

About the authors

Rob England B.Sc., CITP is an independent management consultant, trainer, and commentator based in Wellington, New Zealand. Rob is an internationally-recognised thought leader in DevOps and IT Service Management (ITSM). He is a lead author of *VeriSM™*, and an acknowledged contributor to *The DevOps Handbook* and ITIL® 2011 *Service Strategy*. He is a published author of seven books and many articles. He is best known for his controversial blog and alter-ego, the IT Skeptic.

Twitter: @theitskeptic

Dr. Cherry Vu Ph.D. is an expert on organisational agility and training leaders; and an experienced consultant to government and business on organisational change, change management, and culture change. She has a broad background in law, culture, business, entrepreneurship, accounting, ethics, public management, and public policy. She has worked and studied in New Zealand, Germany, and Vietnam.

Twitter: @drcherryvu

Teal Unicorn is our brand as a team working together to provide Organisational <u>agile</u> Management consulting and training in Vietnam and New Zealand. In Vietnam, Cherry is the boss; in New Zealand, Rob is the boss (or at least he is under the illusion that he is). www.tealunicorn.com

Two Hills Ltd is our company, publisher of this book. Two Hills is a multinational corporation, which doubled in size two years ago. Rob is Managing Director and Cherry is CEO. Our World Headquarters Campus is in Porirua, NZ. www.twohills.co.nz

Join our mailing list: http://twohills.co.nz/subscribe

Index

Entries in **bold** are definitions. Entries in *italic* are quotations.

Parts of the index are a little tongue-in-cheek. Enjoy.

www.ingramcontent.com/pod-product-compliance
Lightning Source LLC
Chambersburg PA
CBHW071250220526
45468CB00001B/64